Edington

The Bishop's Legacy

GRAHAM LASLETT CBE

First published in the United Kingdom in 2010
by The Hobnob Press, PO Box 1838, East Knoyle, Salisbury, SP3 6FA
www.hobnobpress.co.uk

British Library Cataloguing in Publication Data
A catalogue record for this book is available from the British Library

ISBN 978-1-906978-03-7

Typeset in Scala 11/12.5pt. Typesetting and origination by John Chandler
Printed by Lightning Source

Contents

Introduction   vii

Day One   I
    Around the Exterior   4
    Inside at Last ~ Why the Church was Re-built   18
The Clock Strikes Twelve   26
    The South-West Corner   33
First Day - After Lunch   40
    From a Mason's Mark in the Porch   40
    Into the South Aisle   43
    Busy Times for Bishop William of Edyndon   46
    Moving to under the Tower   54
    Medieval Decoration   57
The Clock Strikes Two   59
    Into the Chancel   59
    The Architecture   64
The Clock Strikes Three   77
    The Master Mason   77
    More from the Chancel   84
    George Herbert and the Church Floor   85
The Clock Strikes Four   91
    Clergy Attire   91
    The Buckler Paintings   93
    Chancel Responsibility   93
    Cade's Rebellion   94
    The Murder of Bishop Ayscough   95
    The Chancel North Door   97
    Other Chancel Observations   100
    The Brissett Taylor Monument   102
    Francis Legatt Chantrey   105
    Easter Sepulchres and William Wey   106

Day Two   **109**
    Another Heavenly Guest – 1350s to 1550s   109
    The Effect of Protestantism   111
    Local Boy John Stafford   115
    The Influence of the Reformation on the Monasteries   121
The Clock Strikes Eleven   **126**
    The Dissolution   126
    Paul Bush   133
    Post-Dissolution – The Domestic Buildings   135
The Clock Strikes Noon   **137**
    Back to the Sanctuary   137
Second Day – After Lunch   **150**
    At Last out of the Chancel!   151
The Clock Strikes Two   **161**
    The South Transept Monument   161
    William of Edyndon's Will   173
    Encaustic Floor Tiles   175
    Banker Marks   177
    The Tower   179
The Clock Strikes Three   **181**
    The Cheney Monument – Cheney/ Paveley   181
    Margaret Erleigh   183
    More Confusion and whence the Cheney Escallops?   185
    The Rudder   187
    The Willoughby Connections   189
    The Bere Ferrers Connection   191
    The Head-Dresses   193
    The Final Lap   195
Bibliography   **209**
Index of Families and Persons   **211**
Index of Kings and Queens of England   **215**
Index of Places Worth a Visit   **216**

Introduction

You have signed up for a two day course which will effectively get the architecturally important stones of Edington Church 'to speak to you' on going around the building. Pre-eminent amongst the characters introduced will be the founder William of Edyndon, Bishop of Winchester and Chancellor of England (died 1366).

Your guide (assisted by two heavenly guests of the 14th and 16th centuries), Graham Laslett, retired from the Royal Navy in 1988 as a Captain after 38 years' service. He had been a nuclear trained mechanical engineer and always a keen yachtsman and artist.

Working from home in Edington thereafter as a member of The Lord Chancellor's Panel of Independent Inspectors conducting public inquiries, he has had time to become involved in the NADFAS* Church Recording there. A series of 40 plus articles on associated discoveries written for the local area magazine led to lecturing to the U3A, the National Trust, Marlborough Summer School, Historical Societies and many other groups. Pressure on him that the information he compiled should not be lost has resulted in this book.

The profit from it will help the Society of the Friends of Edington Priory Church.

The fondest hope is that you enjoy not just the reading of the book, but being prompted to visit Edington (seen in a new light), and also the numerous other related sites mentioned.

* National Association of Decorative and Fine Art Societies

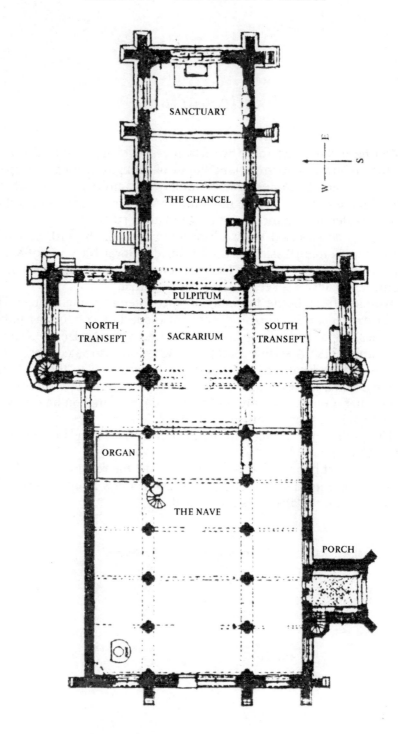

Day One

You are standing in the car park looking north, with the chalk escarpment of Salisbury Plain behind you. Great copper beeches obscure much of the flat panoramic view ahead, across what used to be called 'le cley'. But your attention is to the right on seemingly huge stone cubes; some six in a cruciform ground plan with another on top as the tower. All is lit by brilliant morning sun, emphasizing with sharp shadows the windows, the string-courses, the limb apex crosses and the crocketed pinnacles (oddly none on the tower). The flag of St George flutters aloft. Two ancient yews frame the eastern end, very possibly planted at the times of this construction and its predecessor. The clock chimes the hour, but is faceless. Eleven o'clock. I greet you. Welcome to Edington Priory Church – although this is probably a misnomer, for there was never a prior or an abbot here.

Before we start this lengthy tour I should tell you that what I say over the next two days will form the narrative of a book. (Supporting material is in italics.)

What you see was built in just nine years, 1352–61, with but one exception. That, I believe from my work on banker marks, is the second storey of the porch. Long since demolished from the 1350/60s construction are the monastery's domestic buildings adjoining the northwest side of the church and a vestry at the extreme southeast corner of the chancel.

There were various categories of masons involved in any project like this, and those who finish-dressed the blocks worked on the hewn stone at a 'banker' bench. They were called 'free-masons': that is, they worked the freed stone, and were allowed to mark their handiwork – hence 'banker marks'.

Not that this whole edifice was initially intended to serve as a monastery: in 1352 it was to be a collegiate place for priests to fulfil chantry functions, saying prayers and masses for specific persons amongst the dead, recent and long-gone. There was an earlier church here provided by the Abbess of Romsey, serving the communities of Edyndon manor and two others to the east, Tynhyde and Beynton. The rebuild also had to

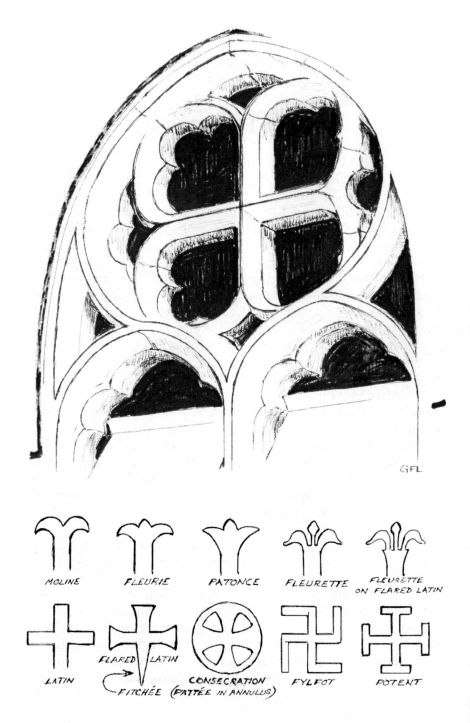

GFL

MOLINE   FLEURIE   PATONCE   FLEURETTE   FLEURETTE ON FLARED LATIN

LATIN   FLARED LATIN FITCHÉE   CONSECRATION (PATTÉE IN ANNULUS)   FYLFOT   POTENT

continue that parish function. By 1356 there were already twelve chantry chaplains, the leader of whom was Walter Scarlett, warden or *custos*. More on how we know this shortly.

It was mid-build in 1358 that the sponsor, Bishop William of Edington, decided that the building should become a house of an Augustinian Order called Bonhommes. Their original house, founded in 1283, was at Ashridge, then in Buckinghamshire; indeed, priests John of Aylesbury and John de Wakerley came from there to inaugurate the new house here, as rector and (ominously) corrector respectively.

Before we move closer there is more to note. Beyond, through the branches of those copper beeches, you can see the monastic fish ponds with two islands. To the right is a glimpse of the house named The Priory: what we see may well be a development of the east kitchen wing of a large Jacobean house, the Mansion House, once perhaps half the size of Longleat. More on this later.

Turning to the church, note what look like defensive battlements. From this side all you see is crenellated, but round the back it is plain parapet towards the former monastic domestic buildings. Was this an economy? Who was going to see? Construction took place during the Hundred Years War (from 1337), when crenellation was the fashion – but there was a catch: you needed a royal licence to employ it on a building. We know that in 1359 William of Edington, though Bishop of Winchester and Chancellor of England, fell foul of this ruling on the monastic buildings here. We can imagine him sweating somewhat at his normal abode in Southwark until the pardon of Edward III (1327–77) was rowed down the Thames to him from Westminster. Perhaps that meant all the domestic buildings had no crenellation. Incidentally William needed other pardons; one you will hear about might have cost him his head.

Note also the belfry windows. Unusually the stonework indicates these were originally glazed. But it is the tracery that is of most interest – curvilinear and in the form of the 'cross moline'. *Cross shapes are illustrated.* The presence of the cross moline here has been suggested as signifying Bishop William's gratitude to a benefactor; it was, not surprisingly, the charge in the arms of the Molineux family. Paveleys will be more significant than Molineux; their charge is given by many authors as a 'cross fleurie'.

The massive monastery garden wall is on the extreme right. A small child's tomb on its top is partly hidden by the yews and lime tree. Finally there are forty table-top tombs, all listed Grade II like the churchyard cross. The church is Grade I. *Listings by West Wiltshire District Council, 9 December 1987.*

Let us go through the extraordinary stile in this Victorian churchyard wall – presumably for pedestrians and dogs, so that the gates could be kept locked against stray cattle and horses reaching the yews or damaging the graves.

Around the Exterior

I know you are all dying to see inside, but while the sun shines shall we walk around the outside clockwise? It is most revealing. Here we are facing the porch, beside us the churchyard cross of unknown date. Its restoration commemorates the life of the Reverend Henry Cave-Browne-Cave, incumbent here 1880–90. The furnishings of the baptistery inside are another tribute to him. He was incumbent during most of the major church restoration, 1887–91, but fell out with the management of it almost from the outset – as we shall see.

From inscriptions here, note he was called vicar, but probably from the time of the Dissolution of the Monasteries in 1539 and certainly to the 1970s the incumbent was only officially a perpetual curate. This meant that until the 1880s he was beholden to the inheritors of the church estate here for support. For much of the 300 years from 1539 his housing would have been in the adjacent big house. Early in the nineteenth century this lack of a house meant that perpetual curates lived out of the village, including one at Warminster, another at Devizes. When the Watson Taylor family bought the estate in 1820 they built the incumbent what we now call the Old Vicarage, up on the B3098 road. I have found no one before Henry referred to as vicar, and guess that it was a courtesy first extended to him and enjoyed by his successors until official change in the 1970s, while Canon Ralph Dudley was the incumbent (1954–81).

You may well leave tomorrow feeling that little has been said about what actually happened here during the Reformation and through to that nineteenth-century restoration. The truth is that little is documented. The best I can do is provide the historical background and tell you as we go along how Charles E. Ponting, the restoration architect, described the state of the church when he started work in 1885.

Now that we are closer to the structure, compare the intricacy of the transept masonry with the relative austerity of everything to the west. For example, see the change of plinth design at the corner between transept and south aisle. Look up to see that pinnacles abound on chancel and transepts, but over the nave and aisles battlements alone suffice, except at the west end. Was this a conscious desire to reflect a split of function

GFL

between chantry to the east and parish church to the west? We will see the same inside with window mouldings. Some have suggested a more prosaic explanation: that the nave and aisles were the last part to be built, and money was running short.

Ignoring the porch till later, as we turn the southwest corner of the church we view one of the major problems Ponting encountered – the near collapse of this west face. The account of the work done printed in the *Wiltshire Times* of 3 October 1891 reports the underpinning of the foundations of the greater part of the nave, aisles and transepts, during which a running spring was found to be the particular problem with the west front. A photograph in an article by Canon J.E. Jackson (1805–91) published in 1882 shows severe erosion of the stone of the seven main mullions of the west window. The central 10ft of the jamb at the apex had dropped a few inches, with its three vertical supports buckled, leading to collapse below and shearing of the central main mullion about 3ft above the sill. When the wall was dismantled each stone was marked to ensure replacement in its former position. As elsewhere in the church no stone capable of fulfilling its purpose was discarded, and many had inserts applied in defective areas. However, an amount of new stone was clearly needed. The spring was ducted away and a pavement of surface Portland stone gutters was placed right round the church to deal with rainwater.

Incidentally, note the two heads either side of the doors; they are hood-mould label stops. In that early photograph they are much less weathered and appear to be crowned with short mitres, just like the one on the Winchester effigy of William (*see page 208*). An 1807 painting in Devizes Museum by J. Buckler certainly makes the southern one appear mitred. More research may show that the long hair under them was not totally out of fashion for certain bishops then!

I need to tell you about consecration crosses. These were placed over the places where the bishop(s) consecrating the church splashed holy water or oil on those walls basic to the cruciform structure, three to each of the four compass faces inside and out. At Edington the crosses were made from a disc of latten metal with four curved-cornered quadrants fretted out. The stonework was recessed so this metal annulus and cross could be flush with the wall. The metal was secured with pins (normally four) brazed on to the back and pushed into lead-filled holes drilled in the stone. Few locations retain metal, and in some places the easiest way to spot a cross position is by looking for the lead still in the holes. This is certainly true of the one on the mouldings above the double west doors. Can you spot the lead? It's not easy. That found, you can then just make out the recessing.

It is the cross location to the right of these doors to which I next draw your attention. It is central between two buttresses and central beneath the south aisle's west window. As we go round the church we shall see that a central position on the longest stretch of cruciform structure wall is the norm. But when we come to the cross on the left of the doors the window is closer to the symmetrically located inner buttress than was the case to the right of the doors. The cross is still central beneath the window, which indicates that this section of plain wall was shorter than the other side. This presumably means there was some protrusion from the west front equidistant to the left of this window at the time of the 1361 consecration. And yes, if you examine the stonework it is possible to see a discontinuity running vertically right up to the northern end of the crenellation above. This is higher than on the south side, and the window longer.

Come along to the north end of the west front and look southward along its profile. Do you see that the wall from the discontinuity to this near corner is not quite in line with the rest of the church's west face? Notice too that the plinth design is different, as is the string-course, and the stonework employs smaller stones. In 1886 Ponting published an article in the same journal as Jackson (perhaps drumming up interest to raise money for restoration) in which he writes that he traced foundations from under our feet 'for some distance northward in a line with the west front'; there is no mention of the offset. Thus what looks like a buttress now was, at some uncertain time, a wall of uncertain length, surfaced (on its east face particularly) with rough stones.

Ponting guessed that immediately against the discontinuity the church rebuild in the 1350s involved a protruding staircase turret to service the north aisle roof. He speculated that the turret disappeared when the domestic buildings were demolished, because access was not from inside the church but from those buildings. One would not see a doorway inside because lintel level is below an obscuring rounded structure in that corner. This is of seemingly later date, and Ponting only tells us he believes the structure to be hollow.

An alternative explanation has been postulated that the external projection westward at the discontinuity and the northwards buttress, projected forward, may have formed the corner of a building that already existed in 1351. This building's position might even have dictated where the west front was located.

By the way, the cross inside is central to that length of north aisle west wall – so it is not central beneath the window.

I think the explanations are not mutually exclusive. Low down to the left of the discontinuity there are a few ashlar courses of the same height as those to the right, as though re-used after dismantling a piece of 1350s build. One dry summer I remember seeing a distinct difference in the grass colour on a line westward from the discontinuity into the churchyard.

"Excuse me – what does ashlar mean?" Smooth finished and accurately square-cut stones.

How do we know there were any buildings here, apart from the original church, before the 1352 rebuild? At an auction at Sotheby's on 27 April 1807 a large part of the Marquess of Lansdowne's library manuscripts, many of them from Bowood House in this county, came up for sale. Parliament bought it, a first for such a purchase: £4925 was the figure, and the folios went to the British Museum. Among them was found to be the Edington Cartulary (EC), or at least a major part of it. *It is now British Library document Lansdowne MS.442.* A cartulary was a transcription of title deeds, etc. into a register, so as to preserve in a readily accessible form the justification of an Order's foundation and possessions. Its modern editor, Janet Stevenson, listed 674 documents; her work was published in 1987 by the Wiltshire Record Society. *I rely on her translation and spellings, sometimes giving alternatives.* We can surmise there were more documents here at the Dissolution of the Monasteries because of notes taken of an examination slightly before 1539 by the antiquary John Leland, after he became Keeper of Henry VIII's Libraries in 1530. In 1533 he was authorized to search monastic and collegiate libraries to establish their wealth and possessions. The exact date that he came to Edington is not known. Sir Harold Brakspear (1870–1934) in his presidential address to the Wiltshire Archaeological Society on 31 July 1934 stated Leland's notes include reference to a Latin book. Leland quotes the book as including 'Bishop William of Hedington laid the first stone of the house or monastery of Hedington on 3 July 1352'. Nowhere is that date recorded in what was purchased of the Edington Cartulary, and later evidence will arise that as a bishop he only came in 1361 and 1362.

Similarly Leland is claimed to have established that on his return from France in 1357 'Prince Edward called the Blak Prince had a great favor to the Bones Homes beyond seas. Whereupon cumming home he heartily besought Bishop Hedington to chaunge the ministers of his college into Bones Homes.' Certainly it is known that William was a member of the Prince's Council and his confessor. A leaflet by G.E. Chambers (for sale in the church) challenges this overseas connection to Orders of that name, and whether 'Bonhommes' was ever the name of an Order in England, either at Ashridge or Edington; yet he acknowledges that the royal confirmation of 16 July 1358 is positive that the church here was to be 'raised to the status of a monastery and a rector and brothers of the Order of St Augustine commonly called Boni Homines installed here' (EC.28). Referring to John of Aylesbury, EC.24 says he was a 'brother of the House of the Precious Blood of the Order of St Augustine'.

It is certain that Leland got the dedication of the church wrong, stating it to be St James the Apostle, St Katharine and All Saints, whereas from the earliest documents to the present it is clear that the first named has always been St Mary, the Blessed Virgin.

Other documents probably not seen by Leland, and not in the Edington Cartulary, give us other significant dates. A reference from Brakspear states that John of Aylesbury obtained the licence to become rector here from the Bishop of Lincoln in December 1357, was 'instituted to Edington by the deed of Robert Wyvil, Bishop of Salisbury, the 12th April, and was inducted on the 14th April, 1358'. Only the year of the consecration of the finished church was noted by Leland: 1361. We have long celebrated it on the second Sunday in July, but later I will give evidence for 23–27 July.

There are references in the Edington Cartulary to a messuage (a sizeable dwelling house, usually of stone) being procured, with 2 acres of land, to the west of the original church. EC.3, dated 12 March 1351, is the royal licence for the Abbess of Romsey to grant this to Bishop William; EC.12, dated 3 October 1351 is the charter of Bishop William for it to go to Walter Scarlett; and EC.16, dated 30 October 1351, is the public instrument under which Scarlett took office. Since we believe the rector's house was to the northeast of the church, a second messuage is implied by the latter document: 'the same day Walter took corporal possession of the prebendal church appropriated to the use of the Warden and priests of the chantry, entered the rectory house, and took possession of the goods therein'. A writ, dated 18 November 1351 (not in the Edington Cartulary), for an inquisition to ensure the king was not being done out of any income by these transactions, has been quoted as significant in that it uses the phrase 'a chantry to be founded', making Leland's foundation stone laying date of 3 July 1352 not unreasonable. However, EC.11 says 'which he has founded' as early as 8 July 1351.

EC.13 makes the implication of two messuages stronger. This is Pope Clement VI approving Bishop William's intentions for the ordinances of the chantry, as of 20 October 1351. It includes 'The Warden and chaplains are to eat together, but the Warden shall have a separate house.'

Until 1547, when income from cathedral or abbey estates was used to fund a priest to assist its administration, the finance was called a prebend and the clergyman a prebendary.

Since it may be relevant to what I want to show you next, bear with me if I quote from EC.23. This is a letter from Bishop Wyvil, dated 29 March 1358, which instructs the brethren to observe the ordinances set by Bishop William now that he has, 'in order to free the chaplains from the cares and obligations of the secular life, decided to raise the chantry to the status of a monastery'. This change meant that certain restrictions were applied:

> The Rector is to take care that women, except queens or mothers and sisters of the brethren, enter the monastery or its precincts only during processions therein. Mothers and sisters are to note that when the brethren wish to speak with them they must speak briefly and with the Rector's permission. A brother shall be allowed to speak to women if he celebrates mass in the nave of the church or hears confessions at the direction of the Rector. When a brother, with the Rector's permission, speaks with women of good reputation in the nave of the church or at the inner door of the monastic precincts, he shall speak briefly in the hearing of another brother assigned by the Rector for the purpose.

Onward round the corner. What do you see on the north aisle stonework? You are right; the consecration cross is central to the whole length through to the transept (ignoring the two 1964 buttresses introduced when outward movement was a problem). Yes, the windows are much shorter than those in the south aisle, because there was a roof covering a walkway. See the filled holes where the roof timbers were set in the aisle wall and the cross is low compared with elsewhere – to be clear of their line. Also there is no plinth here. Brakspear says this passageway 'has been stated to have been one of the alleys of a square cloister; but the weathering [weather-mould] of the roof does not return along the transept wall as it would have done in this case'. Also note that there is a plinth on this transept wall. He sees on the transept 'indications of the abutment of the parapet and outer wall of the passage, from which it is obvious this was the passage from the monastery and not part of a square cloister'.

Back here I hoped you would spot this irregularity in the stonework at the extreme western end. It looks like a blocked doorway in which a small window aperture had been left, subsequently also blocked up. If this doorway was the original way into the church for the chantry chaplains from their quarters to the west, it would not have been so appropriate when their mixing with the public in the nave was 'corrected' in 1358. Yes, all but one changed their status to become brethren. We believe that the double door at the other end of this wall was the way the brethren reached what became their closed chapel, the chancel. Does the double door date from 1358 and entail a mid-build alteration? Well, the passageway would have had no purpose without the doorway. But without the passageway the windows did not need to be so short – were they also altered? A conundrum. But back to this blocked doorway – could the aperture have been left for the brethren to communicate, as mentioned in Bishop Wyvil's letter (EC.23), 'at the inner door of the monastic precincts'? Or is this just the door to the stair turret of Ponting's speculation? He does not mention even seeing it, though someone clearly did in 1891 leaving their initials.

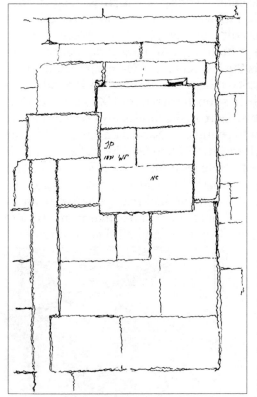

Let us go east along to that double doorway, prettily decorated with exquisitely carved rose motifs. No other doorway at Edington is so decorated. Perhaps this supports the 1358 date, for design was constantly evolving and the sponsor Bishop William appears, from other examples, to have always wanted the latest for Edington.

Ahead, can you see Brakspear's signs of abutment of the passageway wall? I can't. What I do see on this transept west wall are banker marks. That they have not weathered perhaps indicates that they were under some roof for much of their life. Is it significant that they extend out beyond where we would expect an aisle passageway roof to have sloped down? Maybe a north-going passageway was added after the initial build, and that horizontal cement line on the transept, at the passageway weather-mould height, was for its lead fillet. Certainly, when we turn the corner of the transept, we shall see a great confusion of such roof-line indications, of chiselled sections of string-courses and surfaces, and a corbel (*weight-bearing protrusion*) either side of the north window at about mid-height. Excavation of foundations would probably help us understand the history of monastic domestic building here.

Before we round the northwest corner of the transept with its roof access stair turret (currently access from inside the church), look up and note the rainwater heads; these are decorated with stone carvings (confined to the chancel and transepts). Called 'hunky-punks', they are of very high quality and excellent examples of the stonemason's art. As is normal, one that is discreetly placed is somewhat erotic; and here it is on this corner.

Looking at the north wall of the transept, the original stone surface is evidenced by the recess of the central consecration cross. That curious half door-jamb on the turret is a mystery until one notices the adjacent rough stone to the right of the cross. Surely it is another blocked access from former monastic domestic buildings. An indication that the latter existed here may be that this is the last section of plain parapet. Beneath are these four lovely shell-canopied niche seats of later date, around 1630–50. I always associate these with those on the east face of Montacute House, completed in 1601. There are two more in the Monastery Gardens behind the walls, where in the nineteenth century the Sackville arms could still be made out above a garden arch. It was 1629 when Sir Edward Lewys and his wife Anne Lady Beauchamp took a long lease on the Mansion House. Her father was Robert Sackville, second Earl of Dorset, of Knole in Kent. She kept the lease until her death in 1664, and had many Royalist relatives and friends of noble birth around here. Remember that from 1649 to 1660 there was no king – Oliver Cromwell and all that. Though only

a tenant, Anne seems to have lavished much on the property, including bringing the garden right up against the north wall of the church.

Moving on, look at the chancel's north wall. It appears remarkably un-weathered, and it is the same around the corner on the east wall. That is, we believe, because Anne had them scraped and re-dressed. To the right of the north wall's central window bay you can see the extent of stone face removal as there is a raised pad of untouched stone left behind the former securing point of a rainwater downpipe.

Several authors have said that only eleven consecration cross exterior sites remain. This must be the one they missed. Can you spot it? Yes, the lead is still in the bottom of the holes, despite the scraping having removed the recess for the metal. It is to the left, close to the string-course and above the top level of this strange decorated niche – near enough central to the wall length. I suspect that the niche's decoration bears no comparison with the quality we have seen because of Anne's over-zealous mason doing more than just scraping the adjacent wall – tragic. Brakspear thought the niche recess was built here for the display of a crucifix, and noted marks of fixings for the cross. This may have been the case after the 1450 sacking of the church (more of which anon), but when we look at the other side, inside the chancel, I shall conjecture a different original purpose. All I ask now is that you note this continuous length of plinth stone in the recess.

By the way, looking back westwards, that doorway in the north transept east wall does not appear on drawings of the external elevations of the church made in 1909. We know this set of steps down to a doorway beneath the chancel north wall into the crypt was put in place in 1964, when the latter was converted into additional vestry space. Transept access was also provided at that time, by unblocking a doorway. One of the 1909 drawings, an internal view looking east, shows the blocked doorway. There is at least one banker mark on stones in the opening. Irene Cave-Browne-Cave, who died in 1970, was Henry's youngest daughter, and she provided much of the finance for the crypt work. She has a floor slab memorial in the north aisle.

Round the corner and we have a closer view of the yews. In the great storm of 25 January 1990 a branch came off the further tree. It had to be cut off 14ft above the ground, and the annual rings showed it to be 275 years old. In 1924 the tree's girth at 3ft height was measured at 21ft.

Back to the walls. Recesses for the metal of the three consecration crosses on the chancel east wall are shallower because of the scraping, but not totally disappeared. And so round the southeast corner to what, at the outset, I said was the site of the original vestry. This corner buttress includes a slit window, the next westward a doorway, and the next a larger window with metal grill. Between the latter two buttresses there is a doorway into the chancel, rather plain on this side but (as Ponting says) 'richly moulded on the inside, and the label is carried up as an ogee canopy, with flanking pinnacles and crockets and dies into the string-course'. *Ogee – a curve of S-form.* He continues: 'this was evidently not originally an outside entrance to the chancel as at present, but opened into a long narrow chamber against the two eastern bays'. Notice that, just as with the passageway against the aisle wall, there is no plinth here. Ponting notes that the easternmost window is set higher than the others, 'four or five inches higher altogether, a break being made in the upper string forming the label'. He also points out the 'outer sills of the windows of these two bays are . . . kept higher – the splays being flatter to admit of it, and that the string-course which is carried all round the chancel and transepts elsewhere, becomes here a mere weather-mould'. Note that they are of different heights in the two bays, indicating that the width of roof served was less in the western one.

Here in the middle bay, I believe, was an enclosed passageway for processional assembly. The chancel door opened outwards against the western buttress. The eastern jamb of the door is heavily chamfered, which I think helped the crucifer to manoeuvre the processional cross into the chancel. I believe the slightly wider secure vestry/treasury/reliquary was abreast the eastern bay. Its door may well have had an open grill in it, so a through-draught kept the vestments aired. Surely the vestry and passageway outer walls would have had windows for light. See the slight rake on the weather-mould on the east side of the westernmost buttress. Is this an indication of how little slope there was on the lead roofs here?

I am sure Ponting is right when he says that 'The three buttresses have had their south faces rebuilt, and probably set back'. This would mean the remaining plinth sections around those faces are not in their original positions. I am less happy with his assertion that matching plinths never existed on the long-gone, buttress-joining outer walls of these buildings. Indeed, I shall suggest where one section was possibly re-used. Ponting continues: 'When I got thus far in my investigations, I looked for some indication of other openings in the chancel wall, and on critically examining the jointing, I found that there are two built-up squints or windows (with a mullion between) which once looked on to the sanctuary. The monument . . . effectively prevents an examination of these features on the inside'. He noted two further and larger blocked-up openings to the west. The offending monument was removed in 1901 and we can see Ponting was wrong. What he thought were squints are probably, like the larger ones, aumbries or lockable cupboards for valuables. That they were blocked up with mortar with oystershells in the joint led him to believe that happened 'at a very early period . . . I have never yet seen nor heard of these having been employed in post-

Reformation work'. In my pocket I have oystershells which were found between the effigy and the tomb slab when the monument in the south transept was dismantled in 1995.

Ponting also noted that the chancel wall under the easternmost window 'bears marks of fire'. It is this pinky-orange discoloration you see here. Inside the tomb I just mentioned were many pieces of rough stone, some with dressed surfaces and mouldings, a few this colour. Did they come from this fire? When I tried heating a natural stone piece I achieved the same colour. Is it possible that during that 1450 sacking the mob pushed a flaming object through that slit window or the ferraments of a broken vestry glazed window, and set vestments alight? *Ferraments – metal rod grids to brace leaded glass.* There are a few banker marks here, including one on the main burnt stone.

To digress . . . we know that when Mary ascended the throne in 1553 she tried to turn the clock back to Catholicism. The Bishop of Salisbury found it difficult to ensure that churches restored the required objects, many of which had been discarded or taken into private possession. Interestingly in 1556 the one deficiency at Edington was recorded in the Diocesan Register as vestments. Had the brethren been so poor as not to have replaced a fire-damaged outfit after 1450?

Moving west, the cross is central to the chancel western bay, in line with all that I have said before. The six side windows of the chancel and the four in the transepts are alike in dimensions and design – the start of mass-production? Rounding the south transept, note its cross is central to the window and not quite to the wall length between buttress and stair turret. Just beyond the cross is the graffiti of the earliest dated initials – 1639: ten years before Charles I lost his head, a hundred after the Bonhommes left. The stair turret has sundials at the top and inside access, so you cross the roof to enter the church tower. For those with stiff necks there is a scratch dial lower down.

And so nearly back to the porch, noting that it or a predecessor must have been there at the time of the consecration by the position of the aisle cross. There are additional lead-filled holes in the quadrants of the crosses – and here is a good example, three in an equilateral triangle. Might I suggest they were for a plain cover plate that was put over the cross during Holy Week, as altar and processional crosses are covered to this day from Good Friday to Easter Sunday.

The east wall of the three-storey porch, lobby, parvis room and loft retains several banker marks – this side is well protected against the prevalent winds – none, though, on the top storey. Despite the position of that aisle cross, authors have claimed the whole porch is not contemporary; and not just because the sophistication of its tierceron

star vaulting inside cannot be that early. The *Victoria County History*
(*VCH*) still claims the porch is a fifteenth-century addition. The earliest
publication found making such a claim is a church guide of 1924: 'of a
little later date – perhaps forty years (vide the diagonal buttresses); while
Mr Ponting considers that the upper stage . . . was probably added as late
as the 16th century'. That funny recess where this wall meets the aisle
window will be mentioned again; likewise the rough stone appearance
of the wall under it. *Tierceron – vaulting with some ribs of little structural,
more decorative, significance.*

I can remember an acknowledged expert on medieval architecture
lecturing here and adding the design of the first-floor parvis room window
to the reasons for not thinking the porch original. He was also doubtful
that the rectangular windows in the staircase turrets were original. I
was able to point to that banker mark on the second large stone up on
the right jamb of the porch window – a mark found all over the porch
and elsewhere in the church. Along with others, it is also on walls in my
home in Tinhead *(formerly Tynhyde/Tenhyde)*. Because it belongs to one
of very few masons who were not too particular in the size and orientation
of their mark, I have nicknamed him Pete the Slasher. The lecturer
pointed out that fathers
passed their mark down
to sons, but thirteen sons
would need to be here
for this porch not to be
original. Many of those
marks are on the stones
of the vaulting. Equally
there are marks on many
stones forming the jambs
of turret windows, and
no sign of disturbance
for   the   window
insertion. I believe the
architectural   features
generally thought of a
later date appear here
for the same reason I
put forward regarding
the processional double
doors in the north aisle
wall: Bishop   William
always wanted to have

the latest designs. But I also agree with Ponting, for I found no banker marks inside the loft above the parvis room – nor outside.

Incidentally, earlier I forgot to mention two observations of Canon Jackson made in 1882. To the southwest of the porch the nearest altar tomb is said to have been called the Dole Stone, still in use in his day, 'on which certain loaves are distributed'. He also tells us that the base of a former churchyard cross is located beneath the one now there. This is before the Cave-Browne-Cave restoration. We know there was a cross at Tinhead, and possibly it was moved over here at some stage.

Ken H. Rogers elaborated on the Dole Stone in the first edition of his church *History and Guide* (1980). He speculated that the tomb 'may possibly commemorate one William Tubb, a servant to Anne Lady Beauchamp, who founded a charity in 1640'. It looks older than the other listed tombs. The Tubb Charity still functions occasionally to help the village poor.

Inside at Last ~ Why the Church was Re-built

The suspense is over – the chance to see inside. The best seats from which to take in the beauty of this House of God, with the sun streaming in through so much plain glass, are at the back of the nave.

It is a huge building for such a small parish (there are about 620 residents) – so why here? I will put forward four possibilities.

First theory: Bishop William felt a great attachment to this place from his youth, particularly if it was a humble beginning, and wished (to quote from the 1924 publication) 'to show his gratitude to the Almighty for having raised him to so high a position in the land'.

Second theory: Historical knowledge was becoming more widely disseminated and an important battle site like Ethundune needed recognition. In 878 Alfred the Great's army had achieved a decisive victory over Guthrum, the Danish occupier of much of Wessex, somewhere near here. There was a religious significance to the event: Guthrum promised to become a Christian. He was perhaps the first Norseman to be baptised.

Third theory: The main Bath to Salisbury road ran through Tinhead and was experiencing increased traffic as a wool export route from north Wiltshire and Gloucestershire to the Solent ports. This was the half-way point between the two towns, and there was no major church on the route. Extra oxen were needed here to haul wagons up the escarpment. An eye to the main chance meant that it was worth building a sizeable church, buying the surrounding land and making a fortune as a town developed.

Fourth theory: The chantry concept arose because of the Black Death. It was particularly bad hereabouts from 1348 to 1350, with about a third of the population dying. There was a huge questioning of why God had allowed this to happen, and widespread social turmoil. Prominent people planning a number of regional church-building projects on a grand scale might demonstrate confidence that God would prevail and the pestilence pass. The need for chantries would clearly soar, and such buildings could serve to train priests, at the same time providing work for craftsmen and schooling for their apprentices – masons, carpenters and glaziers.

To deal with each in turn. Bishop William of Edington has a superb chantry chapel in the south arcade of Winchester Cathedral, his feet resting on two lions. It is in exactly the same position, relative to the crossing, as the Cheney memorial in our arcade here. The blue enamelled epitaph around the slab under his well-preserved alabaster effigy opens 'Edyndon natus – Wilhelmus' and ends with his date of passing, 8 October 1366. The inscription's author clearly believed he was born at Edington, but that is not to say he was! What do we know of this place up to the year 1300, which is probably the earliest he could have been born?

Ethandune became a royal manor under the Anglo-Saxons venerated through the chronicle of Bishop Asser, Alfred the Great's biographer, who detailed the defeat of the Danes here in 878. The manor was left by Alfred to his wife Ealhswith. Many Danes were assimilated into the population of the Anglo-Saxon kingdoms, but in 956 those in Northumbria had to be crushed after proclaiming a son of the King of the Norwegians as the head of state for their area. Following this a gathering of the kings along with administrators and bishops was arranged. Called a witan, it met in 958 at the Ethandune site (with obvious symbolism) to discuss commonality of law and administration across the kingdoms, royal grants of land, church matters, charters and taxation. This gathering was possibly told of King Edgar's intention to found a Benedictine nunnery at Romsey Abbey and subsequently endow it with this manor; this happened in 968. Incidentally, it may well have planned the final eviction of recalcitrant Danes from English soil – more on that shortly.

The grant to the abbess lists the boundary as from Milbourne Springs to the ford, then Lechmere, Cram-mere, Worseles-down, along Milbourne to Rodenditch, then another twelve names and so back to Milbourne Springs. Milbourne Stream, rising in Luccombe Bottom, is still the Edington parish boundary to the west. The only other boundary we perhaps recognize indicates clockwise listing. Wherewellesdoun is encountered as the fourteenth-century name of the slight hillock southwest of Housecroft Farm, alleged site of an oak under which the Whorwellsdown Hundred Court sometimes met. Wiltshire was divided into hundreds (100 hides) in about the year 600 (though some historians attribute this to Edgar, over three centuries later). The manors of Milbourne and Bratton to the west were in the Westbury Hundred but Edington, Tinhead, Baynton and West Coulston, making up the parish by the boundaries I just gave, were in Whorwellsdown Hundred – as to this day.

In the Domesday Book of 1086 the abbess was noted as holding 30 hides here, and one hide was with King William I. Tinhead probably derives its name from being sized at 10 of these 30 hides. ("Sorry – was a hide a measure of land area then, not a tithe of animal skins?" It was the land area deemed necessary to support one family, and therefore its size was variable, dependent on potential food yield.) Of the abbess's tenants one was the king's cook, who also held land in Westbury and Steeple Ashton. The tenant of the king's land here was a royal official, but also held land from the abbess elsewhere. Hence, entering the twelfth century, there was still plenty of connection in Edington to the top echelon of the realm's governance. The abbess would have been obliged to provide a church. Tinhead is first mentioned in surviving documents as a personal name in 1190 (Philip de Tunhede paying a forest fine).

A priest is first mentioned in surviving documents in 1225, and a church in 1241. Probably long before that time the abbess had established that the nominal rector of the original church should reside and attend her as a chaplain at Romsey – the Edington 'prebendary'. As such, he would have had to pay for a vicar to be at Edington to serve the needs of the parish. When a John de Romsey became the prebendary in 1241 he also had care of the chapel at North Bradley, about 5 miles west northwest of Edington (according to documents at the abbey). The list of incumbents in the north aisle gives names of prebendaries and vicars, starting in 1286 and 1297 respectively, and from what I have just said, and will tell you, its thoroughness could be improved.

That list shows a William de Romsey as vicar here from 1297 to 1317. Michael Marshman wrote, in the 1987 *Wiltshire Village Book*, of 'William of Edington', the then vicar, being required in 1314 'to abstain from further connexion with Edith, Harlot and four other women'. One can only reconcile these statements if the incumbent changed his name from 'de Romsey' to 'de Edyndon'. Such a change would not have been unheard of, particularly if there were other prominent folk using the same handle (and we shall see that there was at least one other clergyman styled William de Romsey at this time). Vicars were sent to parishes sometimes as young as eleven, so long as they could read, but if our future bishop was the William of the list of incumbents, and the dates are correct, he would need to have been born before 1286. We know exactly when Bishop William died, and it is difficult to believe he was then over eighty; or over sixty when a start was made on this church.

However, a sexual episode might not have been entirely out of character for our William. Later, as bishop, he was joint owner of the Southwark Stews, the main brothel in London. His protégé and successor as Bishop of Winchester, William of Wykeham, continued the

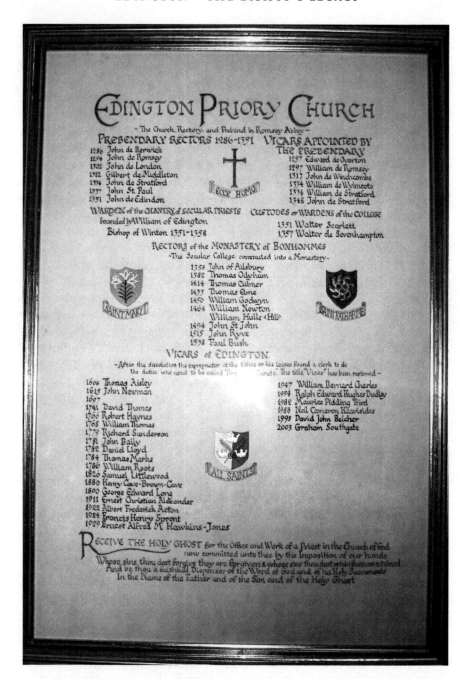

arrangement. Thus the new nave of Winchester Cathedral, which the one started and the other completed, has long been recognized as partly funded on the profits of prostitution. For that matter, so may what you are looking at today. Sir Arthur Bryant in his *The Age of Chivalry* (1963) wrote that 'such confusion of worldly and spiritual values ran through the Church's structure like a flaw'. Thus might not a teenage William serving here choose to change his name to 'de Edyndon', having realised the historical significance of the place, and achieved his manhood here? Let others later assume it was where you were born! Can heraldry assist this debate?

In *The Strife of the Roses in the West* (1890) W. Hamilton Rogers speculates that facts indicate that William was a Cheney, a prominent family hereabouts. This flies in the face of Canon Jackson, who wrote in 1882 that 'of the coats of arms variously attributed to him not one in any way resembles those of Cheneys in Wiltshire'. William, according to Jackson, had three, and of these the one from his 'secretum' or private seal on documents in the archives in Winchester is that by which his foundation at Edington is identified as early as the last quarter of the fourteenth century. Jackson quotes the Bedford description as 'Lozengy a cross engrailed five mullets pierced'. *The Revd. W K R Bedford had in 1858 listed all coats of arms of senior clergy down the ages.*

Edmund Kite wrote in the *Wiltshire Archaeological Magazine* in 1860 of it being here: 'In the chancel were other brassless slabs one of which (doubtless also the memorial of a rector) retained a single shield bearing the arms of the monastery: Or, on a cross engrailed gules five cinquefoils of the field'. In heraldry, Or (O) is gold and gules is red.

Lozengy means a diamond-shaped armorial bearing. Shield-shaped arms were generally only for men who might carry one in battle. The lozenge was, therefore, most commonly the shape of the arms of a female. That William's was this shape may of course refer to the common ellipsoidal shape of such seals. Clerics did go on military enterprises and their arms appear on both shapes. The mullet was the depiction of a rowel wheel from a spur (usually with five points). Perhaps because William was a clergyman, mullets have been changed to cinquefoils in most illustrations of William's arms, including those modern ones we see in the church today.

Canon Jackson mentions the rumour (perhaps recalling Kite) that before the Watson Taylor family made a crypt under the chancel there was 'a large blue stone with sockets of a figure and shields at the corners of which only one was left, bearing on a cross five cinquefoils in a semee, or circle of mullets'. 'Seme' normally describes a speckled multi-repetition of a badge all over the field of a shield, but here I visualise a circle of stars. It is of no matter, for he says 'It was removed to the west end of the church, but is not now visible.' Jackson also appears to have seen or been told about 'a stone in the floor, near the south door, bearing the arms of the See of Winchester encircled by stars; and on one of the returns of the mouldings of the porch his coat of arms, on a cross five cinquefoils, within a garter'. The significance of the garter will arise again. I have found no evidence of these, and presumably neither did Ponting because he does not mention them. The latter, of course, may have been painted on pre- or post-Reformation whitewash removed at the Victorian restoration. Jackson also states that glass in the east window of North Bradley church had been said to include 'the arms, a cross charged with five roses, for the coat of Edington Monastery; the same as appears in stone on Bishop Edingdon's work in Winchester Cathedral'. William's chantry chapel there has no armorial bearings; however, there is a stone boss on the nave string-course opposite it, carved with a cross engrailed five cinquefoils.

More pertinent is Buckland church, east of Faringdon, formerly in Berkshire, now Oxfordshire. William of Edyndon bought the advowson of Buckland church from Sir Thomas Bessels in 1353 (EC.519). He quickly transferred it to the warden at Edington (EC.521). The Bishop of Salisbury then manipulated this to provide funds to increase the number of chantry chaplains from six to nine (EC.525). Anyway, in that church are five almost certainly fourteenth-century depictions of shields of an engrailed cross (red on gold) with five cinquefoils on the cross. There are four shields as roof bosses in the eastern bay of the chancel and one in the glass of a big window strangely placed in the south wall of the twelfth-century nave.

"Excuse me – what was an advowson?" The right to present a nominee to a vacant clerical position. The clergy at Edyndon would have received money from a parish granted an advowson, in exchange for that parish to be able to nominate someone to come here.

The other two armorial bearings Jackson noted were 'Three bars wavy' from a gatehouse of his palace at Esher and manuscripts, and 'Azure [blue] two lioncels, passant O., in a bordure A.[argent – silver]'. This again comes from documents. Remember that in his Winchester chantry William has his feet on two lions.

I believe the cross engrailed and five mullets indicate that William of Edington is more likely to have been a descendant of families with no Edington connection. The engrailed cross, gules on O, is shown in Joseph Foster's *Dictionary of Heraldic Feudal Coats of Arms* (1992) to be the bearing of Sir Eustace de Hache, borne at the battle of Falkirk in 1298 and at the siege of Carlaverock in 1300. In the reign of Edward III (1327–77) Henry Peverell bore a shield including five gold mullets pierced in the centre red. Other later Peverells also bore engrailed crosses, but blue on gold (evidenced by Foster's 'Shield One of the Heraldic Atcheivement of the 15th Duke of Norfolk'). So I leave this theory with the question: was it really place of birth that inspired William's rebuilding here?

It was while trying to find out more about Sir Eustace de Hache (the latter thought to refer to Hatch in Somerset), that the three bars wavy (apparently used by Bishop William) took on significance. Eustace died in 1306 without male issue, but his daughter Juliane, born in about 1263, married into a family named Hardreshull, who owned the manor of Hartshill in Warwickshire. By 1303 the overlordship had passed to Baron Ralph Basset of Sapcote. His coat of arms was three bars wavy, sable (black) on argent. The black on silver was replaced red on gold (the Hache colours) by the time of Sir William Basset of Tehidy, Cornwall (1347–84). On this evidence surely one can make a case for Bishop William having come from a marriage of a 'de Hache' and a 'Peverell' (not local names by the Edington Cartulary). The only reference in the Edington Cartulary to a Peverell is a Sir Henry acting as a witness in Romsey in 1351 (EC.90).

The name 'de Hache' will arise again.

A postscript to page 8. A recent note by a Carcassonne family in the Visitor's Book read '. . . what we are calling Cathare were actually the Bonhommes. Cathare – it's the name the inquisition have choosed to indicate them'. Investigation shows the Black Prince was perhaps so moved by their virtual annihilation in the thirteenth century, and hoping for their support, that he took holy orders at Prouille nunnery in 1356. His revenge was horrendous when they subsequently attacked his army. In the confessional, might Bishop William have made his penance to name Ashridge after them? More research needed?

The Clock Strikes Twelve

We have taken a long time over the first theory, but can be more concise on the second. The battle of Ethandune (878) was a major turning point in British history. Its victor, the twenty-nine-year-old Alfred, had the wisdom to capitalize on the event and lay the foundations of the English nation. He had the chivalry, three weeks after Guthrum the Old's surrender, to invite the loser and thirty of his surviving warriors to Athelney, his stronghold in the Somerset marshes. At nearby Aller he personally stood sponsor for the Christian baptism of Guthrum, which honoured him with the Anglo-Saxon name Athelstan. The party lasted twelve days.

This was not all that it might sound. The baptized was anointed on the forehead with oil, which took time to be absorbed into the skin. That none should be lost, the forehead was swathed in a white band called a chrisom, which remained in situ for at least eight days until the ceremony of chrisom-loosing. The baptized kept his chrisom for life. This practice is the origin of the white christening robe. That there is an Edington near Wedmore (site of Guthrum's chrisom-loosing) probably commemorates these events.

The result of Alfred's chivalry was a treaty. England was split north of the Thames along the line of Watling Street; Guthrum's lands were to the east. Alfred went on to rationalize the disparate law codes of the various kingdoms he pulled together: his justice system defined the relationship between serf and lord, while protecting the underdog against exploitation and abuse. Equally important was his administrative skill in enforcing its operation, with ruthless punishment for those who got it wrong.

Edgar (who, remember, gave Edington to the Abbess of Romsey in 968) completed the founding of this nation when he saw the last troublesome Danes out of the northeast in 973. Edgar, king of the lesser realm since 959, was enthroned in 973 at Bath, the first true King of England. That year he took homage from the Kings of Scotland, Cumbria and the Isle of Man and from three Welsh chiefs. All this stemmed from the battle of Ethandune.

Back to Alfred – aged fifty, he died in October 899, only twenty-one years after Ethandune. Yet such was his confidence that there would be no uprising, he travelled abroad to Rome to be feted by the pope (he had been there before when he was four). Guthrum died in 890, and had a Christian burial at Hadleigh in Suffolk. He had kept his word, and even minted coins with the name Athelstan on them. It was this enduring conversion of a pagan which many here, in France and in Rome saw as Alfred's greatest triumph. In the last ten years of Alfred's reign, apart from seizing London in 896, he concentrated on literacy and learning, personally translating much from Latin into the local language and commissioning the collation of history. His translations include Pope Gregory's *Pastoral Care*. Such was the impression on his subjects that he almost attained a messiah status, seen to represent deep Christian belief and principles. Legend spread that the Almighty had intervened at the battle of Ethandune. By the middle of the eleventh century argument raged whether the miraculous help given to Alfred was through the agency of St Cuthbert or St Neot.

Bishop William and his generation would have been aware of just how important that victory had been and realised that, nearly half a millennium later, they could do with something of the same ilk. With the fluctuating fortunes of the Hundred Years War, could the building of a memorial church at this battle site inspire the nation to greater effort, with hope that the Hand of God might be seen again in any triumph? Was this Bishop William's intent? Might it help his master, Edward III, become another Alfred (the only recipient of the title 'Great' in our history)? Might his subjects embrace more closely the Christian faith? If so, why no mention in the Edington Cartulary?

One last thought – how significant might it be to all the foregoing that Alfred the Great was buried in Winchester Cathedral? Our William became custodian of that grave on his appointment as bishop in December 1345, having been closely associated with that place for the previous ten years as Master of the Hospital of St Cross.

Moving on to the third theory. That there was an important route through Tinhead as early as 878 is perhaps evidenced by the battle. It is a fact that Saxon and later battles often took place close to such routes. Guthrum's camp was at Chippenham. Alfred is thought to have assembled his army on the eve of the battle at Headley Wood, 2 miles southeast of Warminster. If scouting parties (Guthrum's based probably in Iron-Age Bratton Fort) located one another and the main armies marched to conflict along a recognized roadway, Tinhead is a likely meeting point. Chippenham lies to the northwest of the river Avon. Steeple Ashton to Tinhead is a watershed between the river Biss to the west and Semington brook to the east. Both flow northwards to join the river Avon, with Staverton the logical crossing point of the main river between these water confluences. But the approaches to a bridge there would be through flat marshy land. It was early May, and any rain might have slowed Guthrum. The advantage lay with whoever first reached the escarpment. Alfred's march would have been over the high chalk and quick-draining Salisbury Plain. Accounts of the battle speak of Alfred having time to prepare a shield-wall. Perhaps the Danes struggled uphill and Alfred's subsequent rout started downhill. There was apparently great slaughter in the pursuit back to Chippenham, where a siege lasted many days before surrender. The 'dune' of Ethandune points to a down or hill site, and there is evidence that fields directly above the site here were called Ethend in the late twelfth century (EC.373).

Staverton is also the most likely river crossing point between Bath and Salisbury for laden wagons, because of the steepness of hills at Bradford-on-Avon. That there was increased traffic on the road over that bridge and through Tinhead in Bishop William's time is speculation based on the vulnerability of ports to French attack from the start of the Hundred Years War. This speculation is based on the movement of sacks of wool – the English nation's main money- and alliance-earning export. The cost difference between long or short sea voyages had always been low compared with carriage cost overland. Suddenly now the risk of using the nearest port was so great that one paid for long road journeys to the Solent because it was being made secure. You can judge whether or not this created an investment opportunity here for William, but the war certainly helped his career.

Edward III's claim to the throne of France through his mother, Isabella, daughter of Philip IV, brought a swift response from the rival nephew claimant, Philip de Valois. In 1338 the French started raiding south coast ports, including Lymington and Portsmouth, and were seen in the Thames estuary. That year and the next Southampton was attacked several times, once sustaining massive fire damage when defenders were caught at mass. In 1339 Plymouth was attacked twice in a week. Ships were always the main target – to disrupt exports, on which the funding of aggressive action in France depended. Hastings, Winchelsea, Rye and Sandwich succumbed, and Folkestone and Dover fared little better. At sea two of our principal fighting ships and three others were taken, and quickly reinforced the French fleet.

The most valuable wool, produced in increasing quantities, was from the long-coated breeds on fine pasture in the Cotswolds and, to a lesser extent, in Lincolnshire. No short-coated wool from Devon and Cornwall could find a market. Wool export markets were chiefly the finest cloth-making areas of Europe, in Flanders and around Florence. The latter generally collected their requirements with their own ships.

In 1339 Edward III launched an unsuccessful land campaign, with the half-hearted support of Flemish allies, into northeast France. When he wanted to return to England for reinforcements in December he was so indebted to Dutch bankers that he had to leave his wife, Queen Philippa of Hainault, and their children against agreed return within four months. Back home, dissatisfaction with the war meant Edward could not meet this obligation.

Intelligence in early summer 1340 that a large assembly of ships, including huge Castilian vessels and Genoese galleys, was in the shallow Zwin estuary leading to Sluys, the port for Bruges on the Flemish coast, indicated a potentially serious threat to the trade with Flanders and, worse, a threat of invasion. Edward III led a fleet of some 260 ships (only thirty of which were in the king's ownership) to a superb victory over the 190 of the enemy, who were hampered by being moored to one another in lines. The Genoese rowed upwind to escape.

Edward tried again on land but lacked support, and was back in England by late November 1340, this time with family and a hero because of Sluys. Each time when he returned officials lost their jobs, having failed to find the finance the king needed. William of Edyndon was one who caught the monarch's eye as a replacement.

The coast now became relatively quiet, but vulnerable ports were largely abandoned, the harbours of the Solent better protected and trading ships escorted. Demand for wool grew, despite Edward constantly raising money by taxing it. Logic surely dictates that the route through Tinhead from the Cotswolds, skirting Salisbury, down to Southampton and other Solent ports gained in volume and importance? This was probably not just true of wool, for these ports became the main departure point for Edward's armies. Welsh archers (also renowned for their use of the long spear) along with bowman from Flintshire and Cheshire made up much of the fighting force, and may well have marched this route, which obviated the need to go into either Bath or Salisbury. This would have been particularly helpful because of the need for secrecy in 1345–46. Horses galore, all the baggage, tents, ovens, forges, and huge numbers of non-combatants (servants, carters, farriers, masons, cooks, armourers and so forth) had to be quietly assembled. Our William could perhaps see the need for a new town on this route.

Confident of naval supremacy in the Channel, Edward invaded the Cotentin peninsula at St-Vaast in July 1346 and pillaged his way to Paris. Short of supplies for a siege, he fell back followed by a growing French army, including Genoese mercenaries with crossbows. They caught up with him near his destination of Calais. The battle of Crécy on 26 August saved the day, but another alert was sounded by the discovery on the battlefield of documents indicating plans for an invasion of England. Just made a bishop, William was put in charge of south coast defence and coordinating and strengthening the 'Dad's Army' of the day. Was this how he earned his shield? Communication beacons were constructed and small garrisons were strategically placed. Success – no invasion.

William would have known all about these matters of concern in the 1340s, for he was Keeper of the Wardrobe from 1341. For a year before that he had been Collector of the Ninth, south of the Trent. These fractions were the taxation level (known as an 'aid') negotiated by the king with the representative bodies of those who possessed personal wealth that could be defined as 'moveable goods'. Those in possession of such goods were mainly the merchants of the chartered towns, flock-masters and wool-exporters. The wardrobe was part of the chamber, the private finance department of the royal household. William would have been responsible for the negotiations, thereby charged with ensuring availability of funds to fight the war. He clearly did well for he was quickly promoted to head of the exchequer in 1344, titled Treasurer of England, a post he held for twelve years. The exchequer was a national body and William's achievement was to bring the chamber under its control. Bryant says in *The Age of Chivalry* that 'he assured that concord between Crown and taxpayer, government and Parliament which for the rest of the present war was the basis of England's strength'.

That there is not much wrong with this third theory is proved by a town springing up on the route, though sadly for William's successors it was not Edington but Steeple Ashton. The latter was earlier named simply Aeystone (probably because it had a quarry), but by 1329 it was called Stupelaston according to the Edington Cartulary. The name 'Stupel' appears to have been added towards the end of the thirteenth century when a church with a steeple was built. It had nothing to do with the word 'staple', which is associated with the wool industry. But in the mid-fourteenth century Steeple Ashton became so prosperous a market town, based on cloth-making and trading, that in 1420 rebuilding of the church started. Progress must have been slow, for consecration did not happen until 1500 – when the church still did not have a chancel or side aisles. The wealthy clothiers, celebrated in high fashion figures on corbels in the church, suffered double strife early in the sixteenth century. Financial sponsors of the aisles, Robert Long (the north) and Walter Leucas (the south), had their houses burnt down in a major fire in 1503; and the woollen industry changed when cloth-making developed

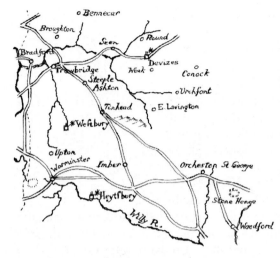

Copied from the 1784 Thomas Conder map

from a small-scale cottage industry to larger mill production, best powered by water. Edington came into its own at this stage, with several mills running on the springs out of the escarpment.

That the road through Tinhead was pretty major is only supported by one reference in the Edington Cartulary – a plea for financial help in 1394, based on the huge cost to the brethren's house of hospitality (EC.219). This perhaps mimicked a similar successful plea two years earlier by Trinitarian friars at their house at Easton on the other side of Pewsey – on a similar downland route connecting Salisbury with Cirencester. These downland routes flourished because valley routes were more likely to be impassable; a morass in winter and rutted in summer. Turnpike trusts reversed the situation over four centuries later.

The lack of road maps after Roman times until the mid-eighteenth century does not help us be definitive on routes. All I can tell you is that this 1784 Thomas Conder map of principal Wiltshire roads still shows no highway going north or south from Devizes. It is just a town on the west–east highway, Trowbridge/Frome to Marlborough. Seend is the only other name shown on that road. The only highway crossing it between Beckington (not named) and Devizes is the road we have been discussing, crossing the Avon at Staverton (not named) with only Steeple Ashton and Tinhead named. This is as on Kitchin's Map of 1769. North of the Avon, our road joins the highway from Chippenham to Bath at Bathford. South of Tinhead it splits into two highways, one southeast to Shrewton (not named), the other more southerly via Imber (named) to Chitterne (not named). This split corresponds with the two tracks from Tinhead today, unsurfaced Salisbury Hollow and tarmacked Long Hollow.

The diary of Jeffery Whittaker of Bratton tells us that the Salisbury coach to Bath passed through Tinhead in 1712. This is very early (probably owing to the popularity of fashionable Bath), for stagecoach schedules did not generally start until the proliferation of turnpike trusts in the 1750s. Such trusts were set up by local worthies for improvement of road maintenance, paid for by charging turnpike tolls. They tended to arise in connecting valley villages and, though the road through Tinhead was turnpiked in 1751, inevitably road connections without steep ascents and descents flourished. By 1754 the three coaching inns in Tinhead (the Paulet Arms or the Three Daggers, the King's Arms and The George) appeared to be

feeling the pinch, as greater expense was needed to advertise for custom. Three milestones remain in the parish, all on the south side of that road. Only the one up Salisbury Hollow above Coulston retains its inscription and the date 1753, the rest having been defaced during the Second World War to avoid being an aid to enemy paratroops.

Newspaper advertising shows that the coaches continued to run on the route until about 1777, though by then it was called the 'slow coach road' and may have changed its line to go via Trowbridge and Imber. The whole highway network changed dramatically over the next twenty years, as the present A36, through the Wylye valley, and A360, north–south road through Devizes, became more prominent.

Andrew and Dury's Map of 1773 depicts the forty-room Mansion House more elaborately than the standard large house symbol (typically used for Penleigh House, Westbury); perhaps the multiple gables to the frontage give a clue to its design. Two other points. The Salisbury Hollow road is omitted and an easterly alternative off the Stokes Hill road is shown, almost opposite Baynton House. On the 1773 and 1810 versions of this map the turnpike gate is still shown just north of the railway bridge.

Copied from Andrews and Dury's Map, 1773, with church symbol replaced by plan. The standard large house depiction was

"I always assumed the Steeple Ashton road went directly from that turnpike cottage to Tinhead until the railway necessitated a dog-leg towards the church – as to this day; but there it is in 1773." Indeed, and if you measure the distance between the milestone outside Ballards Farm and the next some 400 yards northwest of Ivy Mill (before it was recently moved some 10 yards southeast) you find you need the dog-leg for the mile.

Your mention of the railway reminds me that its station beside that road enhanced awareness of the village name, not only allowing widespread marketing of Edington daffodils, but by enabling hundreds of visitors to reach the leisure facilities in the Monastery Gardens. Besides the tea room and band concerts, pony and trap rides and boating on the lake, one could indulge the Victorian interest in Gothic Revival with a visit to the church. Church? Priory surely sounds more inviting!

But we are digressing. I suggest we go to the southwest corner. "But what about the fourth theory? " Not forgotten – I have a guest speaker for that.

The South-West Corner

The dominant features that catch the eye here were originally in the church over the hill to the south, at Imber. A framed account of their transfer hangs above the knight effigy in the niche wall canopy (also brought from Imber): 'When the village of Imber became part of a battle training area its existence as a separate parish ceased and the church of St Giles was dismantled. The two fourteenth-century stone tombs with figures of Knights, probably of the Rous family, the fragments of ancient glass and the Royal Coat of Arms were brought here in 1952. The Royal Arms bear the date of 1639, and are over-painted on Stuart Arms of an earlier date.' James I was the first Stuart king (1603–25) and Charles I followed (1625–49).

It would be unusual for such knight monuments to contain the body of the commemorated person; thus they are not strictly tombs. These two are very similar to many others throughout the country. Of the nine in the Temple Church, London, some have crossed legs like these, but it may not mean they are Knights Templar or crusaders.

I am no expert, but have read that by about 1280 the wearing of a close-fitting metal round cap above the ears for head protection was introduced. Called a cervelliere, it was worn by knights in battle, generally under a great helm, that metal bucket-like cylindrical head-covering with horizontal eye slots (commonly a feature in decoration of

coats of arms). Apparently not all knights liked the restricted visibility
of the great helm, and the cervelliere was developed as a lighter total
head protector. Our effigies depict some of this development. Both wear
an open-faced balaclava-like garment covering the chin. Most probably
this was of wool fabric, but may have had a chain-mail lower edge like a
shoulder cape. Both feature the cervelliere cap extended down to cover
the ears, with a raised ridge and conical shaping fore and aft over the top
to deflect the blow from above. The niche figure has chain-mail hanging
loose from the cervelliere down to the shoulders (the aventail). By 1330
the great helm was unlikely to have been seen on the battlefield. From
that date the aventail became a set of hinged metal plates (the ventail)
and a little later a protruding protective mouthpiece was added to what
was now named a bascinet. The lifting visor hinged at the sides did not
come in until about 1370, and in the early fifteenth century other hinged
modifications around mouth and neck resulted in the armet. Therefore
to have a hinged visor on a cervelliere (as on the niche figure) may be
unusual. For this reason the niche effigy is likely to be the later of the
two. It is more finely detailed in the carving; compare the depiction of
the chain-mail. Note the split surcoat on both for ease of mounting and
riding the horse, and the straps at the heel for attaching spurs.

To depict someone wearing a bascinet or armet was to hide too much
of his features (like the fine moustache of our arcade effigy). From the
mid-1350s onwards many are depicted bare-headed or with impractical

or ceremonial headgear. Perhaps our niche figure falls into the latter category.

The double cushions under the head, the upper being on the diagonal, is a common feature of effigies, but not much before the start of the fourteenth century. The arcade effigy has an angel either side of the head, which may be a forerunner of the introduction of 'weepers' (usually kneeling tearful women in relief) when it became the fashion to decorate the plinth, around the 1340s. Feet resting on a lion is a knightly sign of virtue and strength. Most animals had some allegorical identity. The dog symbolized faithfulness, and supports the feet of most female effigies. You will recall that William of Edington's chantry has the lion feature, perhaps another reference to the bishop's military activities.

The effigy depiction of the hands is typical, in prayer on one and preparing to draw the sword on the other. Was the former an indication of dying peaceably rather than on the battlefield? That the arcade figure was a knight banneret rather than a mere knight bachelor may be evidenced by the possibility that a vertical shaft was located by the right arm. The shaft would have had a square flag hung on it, to mark that he led a company of his own troops into battle under it. Knights bachelor bore a tapered pennon, and would not be so proud of their role as to display it on a monument. See the hole in the plinth and the support at the elbow.

The shield of the arcade figure has, in relief, three lions rampant (body and tail vertical). The other has nothing in relief and any original painting of the arms has disappeared. Joseph Foster's heraldic dictionary lists mainly Gloucestershire-based Rous family knights with this coat of arms, through to the 1350s from the reign of Henry III (1216–72). The name is thought to derive from a family with red hair in the company of William the Conqueror. The Edington Cartulary has over fifty documents involving members of the family, mainly in transactions relating to Imber and Baynton.

The Edington Cartulary spelling of the family name varies to include Roos, Rows, Rufus and Ruffus. EC.373-4D tell us that Richard Ruffus was king's chamberlain at the end of the twelfth century, when he was allowed by the abbess to keep twenty-four oxen with hers on her 'hill pastures of Ethend'. A Walter Ruffus features in 1239. Another Richard, this time Rous, was involved in 1362 (EC.31) as patron of the chapel at Baynton, in settling an earlier dispute between the Edington prebendary Gilbert de Bruera and Sir John Rous, a previous patron. (Gilbert de Bruera does not appear in the incumbents list previously mentioned.) There are at least two generations of Rous family members named John in early fifteenth-century documents and another earlier in 1242. A Sir

Thomas is a document witness in 1281. EC.393 (c. 1435) ties much of this together: 'The Abbess gave the manor (Imber) to Richard Rufus, the King's Chamberlain . . . Richard granted it to Richard, son of Roger Rufus, for a rent of 1lb of pepper at Michaelmas. The rent descended successively to Richard the chamberlain's kinsman and heir Richard Rows, Richard's son and heir John Rows, and John's son and heir William Rows . . .'

Rufus and William will ring bells in your memory. King William II (1087–1100), second son of William the Conqueror, was nicknamed Rufus because of his red hair. He died in the New Forest when shot by a fellow hunter while pursuing a deer he had wounded, his death attributed to breaking off the arrow while trying to pull it out. Is it merely coincidence that Imber church is dedicated to St Giles? The saint's legend goes that in 710 King Wamba chased a hind into a thicket, fired at it and on investigation found that Abbot Giles had been fatally wounded while protecting the deer.

Three more points. Reference in the Edington Cartulary to anywhere in the parish is always to Edyndon, prefixed by 'above' or 'below' depending on whether the site is on the escarpment or out into 'le cley', with just the one exception quoted above – 'Ethend'. Is this specific to a particular field complex, recognizing that the battle was fought there? Secondly, is the use of pepper as a currency in the abbess's dealings the origin of the term 'peppercorn rent'? No. The statutes of Ethelred (978–1016) exacted a toll on pepper import, and by the twelfth century 1lb of pepper was not cheap. Under the watchful eye of the Guild of Pepperers, one of the City of London's oldest guilds (c. 1180), it had a stability about it that eluded money quotation. Battlefield history is littered with bearers of the name Roos, up to the title of lord, but it is so common that there is little hope of identifying whether any were of our local Rous family.

There is a photograph by the niche recess of these effigies in their location in St Giles's Church, Imber, orientated much as they are here, as though in a family remembrance corner. The diocese now recognizes this as the parish of Edington and Imber, and we mark that with the chapel of St Giles, which is in the north aisle against the west side of the organ. Two other artefacts from Imber are incorporated there. Its altar has an ancient oak frame with baluster legs and gadrooned frieze. It may be as early as fifteenth century but probably has a later top. The other is the wooden eagle lectern, which came from its temporary home of forty-two years at St Michael and All Angels, Winterbourne Earls, in 1993. It is inscribed with the name of the incumbent who died in

1872 after twenty-four years at Imber. On it is a Bible 'given in grateful memory of the 60th anniversary of the sacrifice made by the community of Imber who gave up their homes on 17th December 1942 for their country'. Items presented in memory of members of the Williams family, formerly of Imber, are the altar rail and a small carved figure of St Giles above the altar. Gladwyn Muriel Williams (1910–86) gave a large bequest to Edington which has greatly helped with care of Imber items and Edington church itself. Incidentally, the covered Imber font is in the church of St Michael the Archangel, Brixton Deverill. Sadly, of course, the fine fifteenth-century wall paintings could not be removed, but their presence may well have influenced the recent decision to upgrade the listing of the part-late thirteenth-century church to Grade I.

Apart from the First and Second World War Edington and Imber war memorials (in the southeast corner of the south transept), we have other testament to the role Edington then played. Canadian troops stationed in the locality gave a bible inscribed 'A gift from A Battery, R.C.H.A. in memory of their visit to Edington Parish January–March 1915'. That gleaming brass plaque on the south wall of this aisle adds the Horse Artillery brigade staff to the commemoration of that occasion.

But it is lunchtime, and we will take a break. Lunch is served in the parish hall up the footpath from the grass triangle above here. That sturdy stone building was constructed to serve the congregation while the 1887–91 restoration took place, and afterwards as the Sunday school venue.

A word on the stone. The churchwarden, Gilbert Green, was a geologist when, in 1998, a car had a collision with the left-hand churchyard gate-post that you will go through. A stonemason dismantled it and found two slabs inside giving the names of the mason and mason's boy who had built the wall, with the date 6 July 1891. Additional ground had been incorporated on this south side from that previously enclosed by a dilapidated fence. The geologist wrote of the walling: 'the materials used are the same as the Parish Hall . . . namely Bath freestone for the copings, quoins, etc. and yellow-brown shelly Forest Marble limestone for the bulk of the walls. The Forest Marble overlies the Bath stone in the quarries at Westwood and Limpley Stoke which are the nearest source to Edington . . . Somewhat surprisingly, Forest Marble does not appear to have been used in the medieval buildings.'

A footnote adds that subsequently large blocks of Forest marble were dug up near the monastic ponds, and he now concludes they may have been used in the foundations of the monastic buildings. I remember he went to the quarries and thought the structure and graining in the church's stone meant Westwood was the more likely source. Westwood is this side, rather than the Bath side of the river Avon. Thus cartage did not entail crossing a major bridge over that river, only one over the tributary – the Biss. Today with tarmac roads and speedy vehicles, we forget how important was topography then.

Enjoy your lunch. Our guest speaker will meet you in the porch when you return, and take you eventually to the chancel, where I shall rejoin you.

First Day – After Lunch

From a Mason's Mark in the Porch

Why be ye laughing at my attire? The skull cap covering my ears and secured under the chin, belted tabard, thick stockinged arms and legs with soft leather pointed slip-on shoes – that's what we wore, as you can see from fourteenth-century drawings.

It's good to be back again. The last time was when the Society of the Friends of the Priory Church asked me to talk to members during the music festival in 1990-something on a late August Saturday, after their AGM. I brought them greetings from the equivalent heavenly society of which I am a founder member, having worked here from 1350 as a mason.

My problem is I've heard so much over the six and a half centuries that I can't be sure what's really true, but it'll be as good as Graham's given you!

How did I get involved? Well, I was working with Pete (that's Pete the Slasher as we called him, with his crude mason's mark – it's all over the porch here and inside, even up the tower) on the usual parish church extension over in Gloucestershire, adding a north aisle, when the Black Death struck. Most people think it only came the once, but it recurred several times that century. It came ashore first, they do say, in Melcombe (you call it Weymouth now). That was in June 1348. Some places it wiped out so many that there weren't enough left to bury the dead. Wise villages wouldn't let survivors in. Some just left the bodies where they lay and started again in nearby fields. Spread like wildfire it did, from Dorset and another ship in Bristol.

Well, the parish we was at had promises for the money to pay us, but we could see that'd all gone to rats (there's a joke – it was the rats as spread the disease I heard afterwards). The priest died on the Tuesday and everybody who had confession from him on the previous Sunday caught it. Over half were dead by Thursday. So we left smartish for

Gloucester, where they'd been making the abbey more like a cathedral ever since Edward II had been buried there in 1328. It was becoming a place of pilgrimage and the abbot had loads of money coming in. It was like a school for masons because of all the work going on.

Pete had previously done some of the chiselling away of near half the thickness of the round Norman columns and started facing them with the new-fangled vertical shafting right up to the ceiling. When we got there they were already talking about that huge Crécy window for the east end, commemorating the recent battle. The weight of it was going to have to go on the plinths of a pair of columns, so the quire splays out towards the window – most odd. At any rate that was William de Ramsey's design. I was with him at Lichfield Cathedral in about 1337 and since then he'd become the king's chief mason, and from 1344 was much preoccupied with buildings at Windsor.

Also in 1344 William of Edyndon became Treasurer of England. The previous year the king had declared his intent to re-establish interest in King Arthur's mythical Knights of the Round Table with gatherings of three hundred knights (double the legendary number) for which he required a round building like a chapter house to seat them at Windsor, his birthplace. Work started in February 1344, but stopped in November. Three years later his intent was scaled down to an all new Order of Chivalry, involving the King, the Prince of Wales and just twenty-four knights. The focus was on the Blessed Virgin Mary and St George, and a celebration of English nationhood.

In 2006 a Channel Four Time Team found traces of the incomplete 200ft diameter building with stone seating for 300. It is interesting to note that in the thirteenth century Henry III had also attempted to revive the legend, having a round wooden table built for an inaugural gathering. Can our William's hand be seen in this injection of financial reality whilst retaining the promotion of nationhood (in line with the second theory I outlined), particularly as the table was moved to the Great Hall at Winchester in 1348? It was then unpainted. Recent study shows it did, before hanging, have legs and is made of 121 pieces of oak worked in the period 1250–90. The painting, as on it today, dates from the time of Henry VIII (1509–47); that it shows only the king and twenty-four knights may reflect Henry then having no male heir.

The word was that Edward told Bishop William in late 1347 that the Order was to be named the Blue Garter, and that he should prepare the Order's constitution and coordinate building works ready for early Windsor inauguration. Our William sent his protégé, William of Wykeham, there to oversee work. We were told nine knights wore the insignia for the first time at a joust in front of the king at Eltham in January 1348. At the nineteenth such event at Windsor, in mid-1348, after the churching of the queen for her seventh son, the constitution was adopted. *By tradition new knights are announced on St George's Day; the gathering of knights is in June. William of Edyndon became its first prelate, and Bishops of Winchester have continued in that position ever since.*

It is believed that, through the Windsor building programme, Bishop William developed a close personal relationship with the master mason there, William de Ramsey and his successor. Documentary evidence survives of William's continued deep involvement even after the alterations to the chapel of St Edward and St George were complete and the need was instead for domestic buildings for the canons of the Order. In 1353 he is cited as the employer who agreed a contract with the carpenters led by John de Glemsford.

Masons were in great demand in the years before the Black Death with, seemingly, every cathedral having embellishments (like the great spire for Salisbury) and with demands for many to go to France to build and repair castles. Press-gangs for the latter were out on the roads. William decreed that masons working at Windsor on garter buildings should wear red clothing, and woe betide anyone who pressed them to go elsewhere.

Well, things had slowed at Gloucester by January 1349 and people were scared of contact with new arrivals. We survived through that year on labouring jobs, mainly on the land. The sheep round there didn't get the pestilence, so someone had to tend those whose owners had died. Who paid was the problem. We heard that by the end of the year over a third of the country's masons had died. Not wanting to get press-ganged, we made our way south the next July in a guarded wool convoy, with wool bales hiding our tools on a pack horse. This was the only way to move wool safely because of all the brigands on the road. We'd had a tip-off that Bishop William was planning to go ahead with a chantry church for his dead parents at Edyndon. It was said he'd been making a bob or two for his skill in finding money to finance the war, and from a bit on the side. For example, in November 1347 he was caught for misappropriating part of the annual rent due to the king from a Gilbert de Benham – 15s 4½d, *equivalent to at least £1000 today*. That was an offence punishable by death, but sure enough the royal pardon, like several before and after, got rowed down the Thames from Westminster. If we got caught who better to get us off, we thought.

The sixth day we made it to a hostel in Tenhyde. You only travelled in daylight; it wasn't safe even in a group at night. Next day, when we walked across the fields to the site there were some men demolishing most of a former stone church – much smaller than this, it must have been. I guess its tiny chancel didn't reach to where the nave altar is now. Can't remember how far west it went, but Ponting tells me he found the base of a round Norman column under the present west wall. Actually we can see part of it in a minute, because he left it exposed in gravel chippings (behind the south arcade effigy plinth). Perhaps the master mason put the west front on a column base for the same reason as that Crécy window at Gloucester I was telling you about.

'Was it a complete circle, or could it have been the end of the arcade as now?' I don't know, but whichever it was surely means a south aisle on the previous church. Since aisle addition to churches was an early fourteenth-century fashion, could this south door date from when the aisle was fairly recently added? Look at the architrave's wavy profiles and the 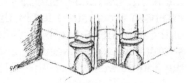 stopped keel moulding at the bottom. Mouldings like this, and those in the west window of the south aisle, were introduced in the mid-1330s in major abbeys and cathedrals, and later in remote parish churches like this one – unless, perchance, William or someone of that ilk was involved and sending drawings. I don't see them anywhere else in the rebuilt church. Was William the sponsor of that earlier aisle? Certainly he was doing great building works elsewhere from the early 1330s, as I'll tell you in a minute.

Into the South Aisle

Let's go inside and look back at the doorway. The jamb is finished in much the same way as doors elsewhere in the church, but the surrounding wall stonework is very different. There are no ashlar courses, but a jumble of odd-sized pieces – as there are outside, immediately to the east of the porch. There are no banker marks, not that there are many on the aisle walls. All this endorses my memory that the porch was built round this doorway at the outset to accommodate the master mason. His porch design was to cause a bit of a problem for him when he received the aisle and clerestory window design sent down by Bishop William. They were wider than he expected – hence that recess in the east wall of the porch.

Now, go and see the two possible items from before the rebuild: the column base and the aisle west window. "If we're right about the door, that means a very wide aisle for a smaller church?" That's true. Perhaps the master mason moved the base and relocated the window; I really don't recall. As for the window, maybe those here before us dismantled and stored it; or perhaps it came from what you call a reclamation yard! It has bull-nose and other mouldings unlike any others in the church;

Graham tells me that its surviving glass is thought by an expert to pre-date any other glass in the church. He pointed to the higher standard of painting of the leopard's head here than over there in the north aisle.

Alas, what has happened to the stoup inside the south doorway? It's been vandalized. Don't you use them now? The basin contained holy water in which you dipped your chrisom or finger and wetted your forehead with the sign of the cross, so as to remember your baptism and the promises made. Such an entrance was the only way in for the laity, except in processions led by the clergy. Notice also the holes either side of the door in the jamb just above the stoup level. They were there for a strong-back to add security against attempted break-ins. Look across at the double west doors: the holes have edges reinforced with iron bands.

Let's go along the aisle so that you can sit facing the Cheney monument.

Cheney monument watercolour by John Buckler, 1826

When the previous church was built it would have been the practice to have two doors opposite one another half-way along the length of the nave. Most likely an aisle door would have been in the same relative position. So whether the Norman column base was the end of the arcade is probably pertinent to the length of the original nave. I think I can

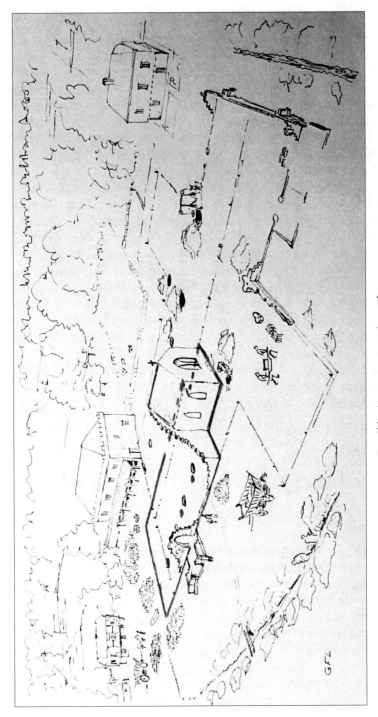

Possible site appearance in early 1351

remember the chancel, with its small opening off that old nave, being left to serve as a chapel for the first year or so of the rebuild. It must have been about opposite where the choir stalls are now.

A clerk of works took us on here, but there was no site master mason then. There was a stone building over there beyond the northwest corner against which we built our timber lodge lean-to. We cleaned up and dressed a lot of the dismantled stone before winter. Thatched the exposed walls, we did, to stop the frost getting in, and plaited plenty of brambles to dissuade children climbing up. Then most of us went home to our families for a while. This was November 1350.

I went back to near Winchester for the first time in several years, and heard say the bishop wasn't as astute as some of those villagers I mentioned. Three months before the plague reached Hampshire, William sent out warning orders dated 24 October 1348 to all the clergy in his diocese, just a month before he went across to Calais.

Calais capitulated after a siege of eleven months on 1 August 1347. It remained an easily defensible foothold in northern France until 1558. A ball there to celebrate the capture was the alleged occasion when the blue garter slipped from the leg of the king's cousin Joan, the Fair Maid of Kent, Countess of Salisbury, giving Edward the idea of the name for his new Order. He put it on his own leg and remarked 'Shame to him who thinks ill of it' – 'Honi Soit qui Mal y Pense'. This is seen on the Charles I coat of arms in the south aisle. The king returned to England in October 1347, having concluded a truce with Philip VI until June. A year later his cousin Joan was the subject of a great scandal.

Busy Times for Bishop William of Edyndon

In that 24 October directive Bishop William wrote:

> A voice of Rama has been heard; much weeping and crying has sounded throughout the virtuous countries of the known world. Nations, deprived of their children in the abyss of an unheard of plague, refuse to be consoled, because it is terrible to hear cities, towns, castles and villages, adorned with noble and handsome buildings and wont up to the present to rejoice in so illustrious people . . . [Notice how his interest in buildings is included here.] . . . All these have been stripped of their population by the calamity of the said pestilence, more cruel than any two-edged sword . . . fruitful country places without the tillers, thus carried off, are deserts and abandoned to barrenness . . . this cruel plague, as we have heard,

has already begun singularly to afflict the various coasts of the realm of England. We are struck by the greatest fear lest, which God forbid, the fell disease ravage any part of our city and diocese.

'Rama' has nothing to do with the Indian prince venerated in Hindu, Buddhist and Islamic religions. Jeremiah 31.15: 'A voice was heard in Rama, lamentation and bitter weeping.' St Matthew 2.18: 'In Rama was there a voice heard, lamentation, and weeping and great mourning.' They refer to Ramah on the pilgrimage route between the port of Jaffa and Jerusalem. There is thought to be the tomb of Rachel, matriarch of two tribes of northern Israel, the descendants of her grandsons Ephraim and Manassah. She is associated with weeping because these tribes were carried away into captivity in 799 BC.

After a homily along the lines of who are we to question the divine counsels that judge and punish our sins, the bishop recommended that his clergy should exhort their flocks to attend a sacrament of penance on Sundays, Wednesdays and Fridays, at which they would recite the seven penitential and fifteen gradual psalms. They were also to take part, barefoot and heads bowed, in processions around market-places or through churchyards on Fridays, reciting the Greater Litany. Suggesting that people should congregate like this wasn't a good idea.

The Greater Litany is believed to have been the Lord's Prayer and Hail Mary; people would have recited them in Latin. It is known that the psalter was highly esteemed in the fourteenth century: in about 1343 it was the first religious text translated into vernacular English (by Richard Rolle, an ex-Oxford academic turned hermit who died during the Black Death). French was the courtly language, that of law and of Parliament. William was to change this before he died in 1366.

Some weeks later, back at his palace at Esher, Bishop William urged further penitence, but all to no avail: almost half the diocesan clergy died, the worst months being February and March 1349. However, by early 1350 things were more or less back to normal, and going home in November involved no difficulties, just the sadness of finding out how many acquaintances were gone.

A reminder of the use of those twenty-two psalms may be found in the scratchings on the archway of the Cheney monument by the brasses slab. Graham tells me that an article in the Monument Society magazine of summer 1989 referred to them as a chequered pattern of twenty squares in a double row, the author believing the slab was used to stack dues on as they were paid. There's a similar pattern on a thirteenth-century grave slab at St John's Church, Yeovil. In fact both graffiti are eleven rectangles side by side; that at Yeovil has all of them divided in half, and ours may have been like that originally, before youths 'enhanced' it. If the pattern was used to check the saying of the psalms by the chantry priest, the parallel scored lines beneath the slab moulding may record the number of repetitions. What think you? *There's also a similar graffiti pattern on the west wall of the north aisle that seems to be a straight ten accountancy aid, and there are similar vertical lines on the west end of the south transept monument.*

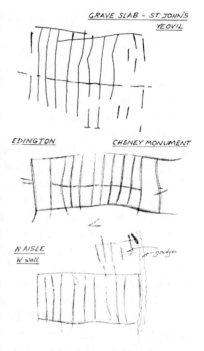

In late February 1351 we'd cleared the brambles and thatching, and the clerk of works called the fifteen of us together on the grass, behind where the nave altar is now – to meet the master mason appointed by Bishop William. He told us the intended purpose of the church and that the celebrant chantry priests would start to arrive during the year. He explained he would peg out the site to a basic design sketched for the bishop by de Ramsey before he died on 3 June 1349. John Sponlee had taken over technical supervision at Windsor from de Ramsey and was going to send down drawings of architectural details. Priority was a secure room for the master mason and his tools, so Pete and a team started building the porch. *This build sequence is supported by marks from all thirteen masons in the porch being on stones in the church itself, several in early build locations.*

Digging started in the pasture here to the east of the old chancel for the foundations of the tower pillars. The wet greensand created a few problems; we had to get down to solid chalk. It still wasn't half as bad as building one of the Bristol churches, a mate told us. There they had to go down 47ft before they found anything solid enough. This being an isolated site we forgot lodge rules and all mucked in with the digging. We also excavated a big east/west conduit to collect all the springs coming out of the hill and lead the water round the ends of the site. I gather you had a few problems with that choking up by the nineteenth century – standing in water in the nave when it rained.

So by the end of the building season in 1351 the only new building was the porch, but all the foundations were in and the ground was drying out. Of course, all the planning was accompanied by formal documentation. I'd like to read the charter that confirms the deal done by Bishop William to get the abbess to give up the Edyndon prebendary in exchange for another prebendary and an expensive property purchase in Romsey. It's dated 8 July 1351. The Black Death caught up with the nunnery, it seems, for William had to deal with three abbesses – Joan Icthe (1333–49), Joan Gervays (1349–52) and Isabella Cammoys (1352– 96).

Charter of Joan, Abbess, and the convent of Romsey, reciting that William, Bishop of Winchester, in consideration of the impoverishment of the convent caused by the effects of plague, with the consent of Winchester Chapter, appropriated to their use for ever the prebend of St Lawrence in the church of Romes' (which until now John de Nubbeleye has held); and in exchange for the advowson of the prebendal church of Edyndon with the chapel of Bradeleye annexed (which belongs to the church of their convent of Romes'), and for a messuage and 2 acres of land in Edyndon (given to them by the Bishop and now taken to endow the perpetual chantry of chaplains which he has founded to celebrate in the prebendal church), the Bishop gave them [the nuns] tenements, messuages, lands, rents, and meadows formerly in the possession of John le Rede and others in Romeseye near their convent and therefore useful to them, which he had acquired at great cost and with royal licence. [EC.11]

Phew. It's all one sentence, but you get the drift.

It's worth reading the rest of the document to illustrate the way future commemorative masses (called 'obits') were set up for remuneration. Perhaps an obit was read at the Cheney monument for a number of quarters, except when the appointed weekday fell on a major festival or saint's day – hence the variable number of scratchings in the lines beneath the slab. This is all conjecture, obviously.

To read on:

Since the insufficiency of the income of the house prevents the Abbess and convent from making a temporal return to the Bishop, they now grant that he shall be remembered for ever in their prayers and offices and that yearly on the feast of St James the Apostle one of the chaplains of the convent shall, in the presence of the Abbess and convent, sing mass for his well-being during his life, and that after his death the Abbess and convent shall sing the office of the dead before vespers each year on his anniversary, and on the morrow, in the presence of all who are able to attend, have a requiem mass celebrated for his soul, for that of King Edward after he dies, for those of his ancestor kings of England, and for all the faithful departed. In order to encourage the nuns to attend the said office and masses, on days when mass for the living and the dead is celebrated, and on the said anniversary, the Abbess shall distribute among the nuns present and to those who have a reasonable excuse for not attending, 10 marks from the profits of the lands given to them by the Bishop. From the same profits, which are more than sufficient for all these purposes, the Abbess shall pay to each chaplain celebrating in her convent and presented by the holder of the prebendal church of Edyndon 13 shillings and 4 pence yearly as a stipend (which, according to the custom of the convent, has been paid hitherto by the holder of the said prebendal church), and livery of victuals sufficient for one nun, so that the holder of the said church may be discharged from the payment of the stipend. If the Abbess and convent fail to fulfil those premises they promise to pay 100 shillings to the Bishop and 40 shillings in aid of the Holy Land.

It is interesting that the feast of St James was selected; perhaps Leland's surmise about the early church dedication was correct.

Romsey is the place where Bishop William makes an obit for himself. Could that be his true birthplace? We speculated earlier that he might have been of Peverell descent – and remember that a branch of that family is documented in Hampshire.

William's 24 October 1348 letter also raised the matter of sex: 'Still, it is much to be feared that man's sensuality which, propagated by the tendency of the old sin of Adam, from youth inclines to all evil, has now fallen into deeper malice and justly provoked the Divine wrath by a multitude of sins to this chastisement.' And what do you make of Bishop William wishing a female Order to make the remembrance? Was he fond of the ladies? Did he instruct the carving of a lovely girl's face here to symbolise the Romsey connection? We will see what may be a representation of that abbey's patron saint, St Ethelfleda, in a moment: a beautiful face is on the string-course on the corner of the west wall of the south transept. Certainly her feast day, 23 October, would have been celebrated in this church, for the abbess retained much around Edyndon, even after Bishop William's brother John started procuring large amounts of land here.

Recounting the legend of this obscure saint must have had the choirboys sniggering. In one version she was brought to the attention of the king and queen and invited to stay at court. When the queen became suspicious of her

St Ethelfleda?

habit of sleep-walking at night she followed her, and suffered a nervous illness when she discovered that Ethelfleda enjoyed nude bathing (for ascetic religious reasons, of course). This episode gave the abbess the opportunity to ingratiate herself with royalty, by affecting a cure on the queen through her intercessions. It's a slim reason for becoming a saint. Another version of her story says that Ethelfleda was the daughter of King Edgar, founder of the Romsey convent. She joined the convent as a nun, became famed for reciting psalms while submerged in icy water, and went on to be the abbess in 999.

EC.89 shows there was a chapel of St Ethelfleda in Edyndon in 1358, possibly on high ground adjacent to the church (by Ralph's Seat?). The Wiltshire VCH states that in 1413 the reeve gave two geese to a brother to celebrate mass in her chapel on 23 October. Call in the archaeologists!

Remember I said Bishop William was in Calais in November 1348? Was the king there? If so, did William travel abroad to discuss the economic chaos in the West Country? Did he warn that those previously paying for martial obligations were going to be less able to contribute, starved as they were of labour and income? Did he see that inflation was inevitable because of the scarcity of produce? Did he recommend the royal ordinance that came the next year, instructing that labourers should neither demand nor receive more pay for piece-work than they had earned before the plague? Did he suggest further truces with the French, because the Black Death meant neither side could spare any effort to wage war?

If the king wasn't in Calais, then was this visit another of those special assignments that he tended to give the diplomatic and efficient Bishop William? Was it to deal discreetly with a scandal at court that involved the king's cousin, Joan? The Archbishop of Canterbury, John de Stratford, had died on 23 August 1348, making Bishop William the obvious choice to achieve some harmony between the parties. The Earl of Salisbury had just found out that his seven-year marriage to her, arranged by Edward III in 1341, was bigamous. Aged twelve, she had secretly married Sir Thomas Holland of Broughton in 1340. Almost immediately Sir Thomas had gone off on crusade. After his return to join the 1346 invasion of France, he had made his fortune by capturing and ransoming the Count d'Eu, Constable of France, at Caen. Made a founder garter knight, like Salisbury, in 1349 Sir Thomas was successful in asking Pope Clement VI at Avignon to confirm his marriage – and Joan's second marriage was annulled. Rumour had it that the king's son, Edward of Woodstock, later called the Black Prince, saw the possibility of both marriages being annulled. Bishop William was already his counsellor and confessor, something the king had decreed. Headstrong after making his mark at Crécy aged just sixteen, the prince had to wait eleven years before he married Joan, his second cousin, three months after Holland died. Their son was Richard II.

Joan and Edward III had the same grandfather. She was the daughter of Edmund of Woodstock, 1st Earl of Kent, son of Edward I. Her father was executed on 13 March 1330 for plotting against Roger Mortimer and Edward III's mother, Isabella, who virtually ruled in the name of her son, then aged seventeen; Joan was just two. Part of the reason for relating all this is that her badge was a white hart. This will be relevant later.

Of perhaps more interest to the Edyndon story – while in Calais did Bishop William canvas for donations for his building enterprise amid the euphoria of victory, and from pockets lined with loot and ransoms? You bet! Among those knights to join the elite of the garter was Sir Walter Paveley, whose relative Sir John Paveley was Lord of the Westbury Hundred. (Sir John was later to ask Bishop William to act as guardian to his young daughters.) Their arms featured a cross of some sorts, and word was that the tracery in the church tower here was a quid pro quo. *Another to be a replacement garter knight in Edward III's reign was Baron Bassett of Drayton whose coat of arms was three bars wavy – which should ring bells.*

It probably did Bishop William's career no harm that John Offord died in May 1349 before he was enthroned as Archbishop of Canterbury; similarly that the great scholar Thomas Bradwardine died on 26 August 1349, before Simon Islip provided continuity until 1366, when Bishop William was offered the position. Was the Black Death why Islip's enthronement was not at Canterbury? On 20 December 1349 he was consecrated at Old St Paul's by the Bishop of London, and on 25 March 1350 received his pallium (archbishop's cloak) from the hands of our William at Esher Palace.

Completing this saga, some believe it was William de Edyndon who in October 1361 married the Prince of Wales to Joan in St George's Chapel, Windsor. Holland, who had four children by Joan, became popular with Edward III, who made him 2nd Earl of Kent shortly before his passing on 28 December 1360, respecting his wife's lineage. The king was appalled when his son quickly announced his engagement to the earl's widow. Archbishop Islip had recently fallen out with the prince, and warned that any children by such a union would be illegitimate while the Earl of Salisbury was alive. As they were cousins the marriage required a papal dispensation. Islip might not have had much heart for negotiating the latter. The prince had nominated as Bishop of Lichfield and Coventry a blind and paralytic old man, Robert de Stretton, whom Islip refused to consecrate. The prince appealed to the pope, who ordered that Robert be instituted. Bishop William's involvement is quite feasible, therefore.

We all knew that William was frenetically busy in the wake of the Black Death, with financial affairs of state and diocesan clergy appointments, but he clearly found time to talk to the king about including remembrance of the Kings of England in his chantry plans for Edyndon. We can expect he stressed the importance of regional projects at this time, to demonstrate the confidence of the nation's leaders in the future. The help of chantry activity in grieving, the lifting of the spirits when recalling great past triumphs like Ethandune, and the focus on the debt to monarchy down the centuries may all have featured in the case-making. Perhaps he was silent on private hopes of pilgrimage – and money, as at Gloucester.

Remembrance of the royal family was included in the chantry college proposals sent to the papal palace at Avignon for the pope's confirmation. These were set out in letters from William and from Robert Wyvil, Bishop of Salisbury, dated 20 and 28 October 1351 respectively. Obviously they took several days to reach their destination, but delay may have been contrived because relations between the papacy and England had recently not been trouble-free. The reply was not dispatched until 22 April 1354, with the excuse that Clement VI had died shortly after agreeing on 17 November 1352. Incidentally, Clement was thought corrupt and a notorious womaniser, whose partners disappeared without trace. Accusations against him by 1350 fuelled anti-papacy sentiment throughout Christendom.

Nowhere were there more accusations than in Britain. The strength of feeling and the increased status of Britain in Europe after Crécy make it surprising that another two centuries elapsed before the eventual break with the papacy over the pope's refusal of a divorce for Henry VIII. It wasn't just the uncertainty in decision-making and papal hypocrisy: Bryant argues that money was a major factor. By 1330 clergy appointments, for the higher posts, were nominated by the king and just endorsed by the pope. The nominees bound Church and the nation's administration to mutual advantage, as they were drawn from the best educated, as with William de Edyndon and his protégé. The quid pro quo was that the pope had a freer hand in the appointment of lesser clerics. Arguing for the universality of the Church, successive popes sought to introduce as many foreigners as possible because it suited them financially. The king resented the resulting drain of money overseas, particularly as he suspected that, as the Pope was in Avignon rather than Rome, some found its way to help his enemies. There was also the suspicion of spying. To keep more money available for the English war effort, a political excuse was found: a grievance among the laity. May McKisack writes in The Fourteenth Century *that in 1343 Edward III 'voiced the resentment of his people in a strong letter'. The pope was told that when foreigners took* up livings they 'did not know the faces of their flock and could not speak their language'.

Retaliation from Avignon may have been behind the strange events surrounding William de Edyndon's appointment as Bishop of Winchester in late 1345. When the previous bishop, Adam Orleton, died on 17 July, within days the monks of St Swithin, Winchester, received a papal licence to elect a successor, and quickly fired off the name of one of their number, Nicholas Devenish. They should have known that nomination was the prerogative of the Crown. By royal writ dated 27 July the licence was revoked, and the prior and another monk were ordered to appear in Chancery on 5 August. After some delay William became bishop by papal provision at the request of Edward III on 9 December. This did not endear William to the monks. Finally papal appointments were formally restricted, with Parliament passing the Statute of Provisors and Statute of Praemunire in 1351 and 1353 respectively.

I can tell you, William didn't wait for the papal reply to his 20 October 1351 letter for 'founding the said chantry to pray for the souls of himself, his father Roger, his mother Amice, his brother John, the Royal Family of England and the Bishops of Salisbury and Winchester'. Obviously we took it that the chancel would serve as the chantry for the royal family, because the master mason, as you'll see in a minute, made the hood mould stops to each side window male and female. I'm not too sure if a monk and a nun in a north bay should count as family! This being in the see of Salisbury, the north transept, as the senior side, became the chantry for its bishops, tying in with the order in which they are mentioned in the letter. Thus William, as a Bishop of Winchester, would be remembered there in the south transept, along with his predecessors and successors.

Moving to under the Tower

It's time to stand up and turn around. There are the remains of two original-build piscinas in the south aisle wall behind you. A piscina is a bowl with a drain, almost invariably on the epistle side of an altar. (The south is called the epistle side and the north the gospel side, relating to the ends of the altar from which those readings are presented to the congregation.) It was used to dispose of residual consecrated wine, water and crumbs at the end of the Eucharist. If you examine the eastern one you'll see that the protruding base stone with the drain hole is still there. On the other, the hole is in the remaining part of the bowl, and the drain runs down through the stone beneath at an angle towards you. The profile of the missing exterior part is quite clear; indeed, someone seems to have emphasized it with a crayon or charcoal. When we reach the north transept you'll see that the external part of the piscina there was chiselled away, but has been replaced.

These piscinas confirm my memory of where chantry chapels were constructed for William's father and mother – his father had the easterly one. His brother John was still alive when all this work was going on, so nothing was incorporated for him at that stage. But I believe the two indentations in the south wall – there further west – are at the right height to have been for keying into the wall the top of screening, similar to the Cheney monument. The further west indentation was, I imagine, for the screening around John's later chantry chapel, abutting that of his mother.

We have an invaluable commentary on the life and times of Bishop William from the work of Dom.S.F. Hockey, of Quarr Abbey, Isle of Wight. Rather as Janet Stevenson did with the Edington Cartulary, Hockey enables us to read easily the Bishop's Register of William of Edyndon (RWE). This is a record of the letters sent out by the bishop in the twenty-one years between his enthronement and his death at his Bishops Waltham palace (some 9 miles southeast of Winchester). Hardly a day passes without some document.

The register shows that Bishop William made full use of the anti-papacy changes before and during the wastage from the Black Death to further his relations and protégés. In 1351 (RWE.Pg.ix) he appoints the son of his brother John, another John de Edyndon (having succeeded him as master of the Hospital of St Cross at Winchester from 1346, when aged sixteen, and warden of Domus Dei, Portsmouth, from 1348), as one of the two archdeacons in his see, that of Surrey. Another relative, Thomas Edyndon, was made a Canon of Salisbury and Chichester when aged seventeen. A William Wolf of Edyndon received rapid advancement. There is no Wolf family in the Edington Cartulary, so the name probably stems from William's sponsorship: 'Wolv' was an abbreviation for Wolvesey Castle, Winchester – the bishop's treasury. Canon Jackson observed in 1882: 'It was the case that established surnames were sometimes capriciously relinquished in favour of names descriptive of residence, as conveying a notion of greater importance.' Remember that we think this might have applied to Bishop William himself: intriguingly, a 1358 (Latin) document refers to William of 'Edington . . . whence he derived his birth'.

The Bishop's Register tells us that nephew John held the Archdeaconry of Surrey for forty years. Such a post was not totally absentee, unlike many of the lesser posts. William held (and then passed on) many of the latter as sources of income. Corroborating the Portsmouth appointment of John (but with an earlier date of 1346) is the Hampshire VCH, which references consequent laity unrest there. The pope became involved and is noted as not having previously been aware of John's youth or that he already held the St Cross post, a canonry and prebend in Lincoln diocese, a canonry of Salisbury and the valuable rectorship of Cheriton (another post that his uncle relinquished to him). Respecting the code we have referred to, perhaps reluctantly, the pope backed William and confirmed the appointment.

EC.141 of 20 February 1361 is absolutely specific that nephew John had become a knight by that date: 'Charter of John de Edyndon, Knight, granting in frankalmoign, with warranty, at the request of his uncle William, Bishop of Winchester, and for the souls of his father John de Edyndon, his ancestors, and all the faithful departed, to John (of Aylesbury), Rector of Edyndon, and the convent there all his lands and tenements with all reversions, services, and rents of his tenants in Edyndon, Bratton, Mulbourne, Coterugg, and Tynhyde.' Frankalmoign – a form of tenure of land offered by the owner to religious houses on condition of remembrance in prayer.

Could a person be a knight and an archdeacon at the same time? We know that non-ordained people were appointed to ecclesiastical positions during the shortages caused by the plague, and perhaps a royal edict of 1353 applied to them. Our William as Treasurer of England, in need of funds for any resumed war as much as the king of men-of-arms, may have been behind this. It says that all men worth £15 a year were 'ordered to accept knighthood and its military responsibilities or be fined in default' (Bryant). That rather devalued the title – take one or pay up. Cash or honours!

Thus John the elder and his son could have become knights without having previously seen war service. A Sir John de Edyndon also appears in litigation and land-deals recorded in the Hampshire] VCH from after 1353. One, in 1383, involves a suit against Ralph and Joan Cheyne for the recovery of the manor of Baddesley (near the Beaulieu river). They are questionably commemorated in our south arcade Cheney monument. More of this anon.

The Wiltshire VCH adds to the conundrum around the John de Edyndon name. It states that the 1351 transitional Edyndon prebend of that name was not necessarily a relative of Bishop William! Remember that the post was deleted when Walter Scarlett was made warden. Canon Ralph Dudley looked into this with the diocesan registrar and the county archivist of Hampshire in 1966, and they found that William's presentation to the Bishop of Salisbury for the interim prebend (dated 28 May 1351) couched the nomination as 'Master John of Edyndon, clerk to yourself'. Surely it would have said more if he had been a nephew.

Here in the south aisle, there are also signs of stonework repair where a wall may have protruded as the back to Amice's altar, and possibly where a communion rail was fixed into the aisle wall. I really can't remember such details, but do you see what I mean? Now let us look for the remains of decoration.

Medieval Decoration

Take a further step back down the aisle and look at this capital on the column west of the Cheney monument. See the well-defined remnants of painted decoration? One column west has some under-colour. This side of the south door there is some text painted on the wall – but that's not from my time. *An 1882 article in* The Antiquary *says they are 'from the Proverbs, of the supposed date of Edward VI' (1547–53).*

Right, let's go up the steps on which Amice's altar may have sat, into the south transept, and decide whether the face is that of a sleep-walker. Now across the crossing; stop here between the two north tower pillars. Look over to the north wall of the north transept. Above that blocked-up doorway, do you get the impression of a painted figure, perhaps kneeling? Go closer and any pigment becomes just a dirty mess on the stone, but can you see a possible nimbus above the head?

But for these few pieces of salvaged decoration, the state of the interior now is as it was when the glaziers finished in about 1363. Around most windows in the church you can see the filled square holes, about 5in across, which were where scaffolding was supported by timbers pushed into the stonework for the glaziers: these holes were called 'putlogs'. Once the scaffolding came down and we'd filled the holes the whole surface was covered in layers of limewash, and plaster in places, to get

it smooth enough for decoration in colourful painted patterns and pictures, of which those few areas are the only ones left today. Oh yes, you're right to point to that north transept piscina; there's some under-colour there. Pete stayed, but I didn't stick around to see that decoration work complete or the monastic buildings finished.

Canon Jackson tells us that in his day (the 1880s) traces of colour could be seen in the north aisle consecration cross quadrants, alternately red and blue. But perhaps more significantly the niche and piscina in the north transept were said by Ponting to be still 'covered with the rich colouring and gilding; and the lily painted on the splayed sides, with the predominance of blue in this decoration, indicates that the altar which stood here was dedicated to the Blessed Virgin Mary'. What we must remember is that both these gentlemen were looking at the church before restoration, walls covered from the Reformation onwards in centuries of whitewash on top of the medieval paint. This was removed in the 1887–91 restoration, and with it went the majority of the painting underneath. An article in a 1968 Edington parish magazine noted that a recent attempt to preserve the remains of a lily painted in the niche had been unsuccessful. If you look carefully there is still some colour in the side capitals and boss in its vaulted canopy.

The Blessed Virgin Mary is the symbol of the Diocese of Salisbury and the niche decoration, if original, would perhaps support the theory that this transept was the chantry for its bishops. However, the construction of lady chapels at this time and earlier was quite common in cathedrals, usually behind or south of the chancel, so one cannot rule out that William wanted one here. A beautiful example is in Ely, built 1322–49 (off the north transept). Perhaps ours fulfilled the two functions from the outset.

So if the south transept was a chantry, why doesn't it have a piscina in the east wall? One might expect it to be in the south wall, but I can't remember one there, nor imagine it was obliterated with that war memorial. Indeed Jackson and Ponting describe the church in sufficient detail for us to say that there was no wall piscina here. Of course William, like his brother, was still alive, so perhaps the use of free-standing pillar piscinas was eventually envisaged. They are to be found in fourteenth-century churches and look like a slender mini-font. Certainly the raised level against the east wall in both transepts points to altars having been in both.

Ponting clearly thought that Winchester's bishops were remembered in the south transept, for in replacing the Jacobean plaster ceiling he included tributes to William. That Bishops of Winchester have been the prelates of the Order of the Garter from his time makes one wonder how long the altar in this south transept has been dedicated to the order's saint, St George? In 1934 Brakspear wrote, presumably by mistake, 'The transepts, in spite of their length, only had one altar in each as is shown by the piscinas which remain.'

The Clock Strikes Two

Into the Chancel

L et's go up the steps through the pulpitum screen to look at the greater embellishment in the chancel, which involved so much carving work on the niches.

In 1886 Ponting referred to medieval colour on the niches on the east wall of the chancel. Of the inner ones flanking the window, he wrote: 'Both bear evidence of rich gilding and colouring beneath the whitewash, and the spirit shewn in their handicraft by the respective workmen is very instructive; for while Bishop Edington's artist gilded every part, even where hidden from view behind the canopies; the churchwardens' whitewasher only smeared over the

Chancel watercolour by John Buckler, 1826

parts which can be seen from below – or perhaps the latter was more sparing of his whitewash than the former of his gold. The niche on the north is richer in some points of detail than the south . . . I would suggest the probability that the figures of the two principal saints occupied these niches and that of Our Lady, the richer one on the north.'

The niche against the north side of the east window involved added decoration, such as the added embellishment of floriated carving where the niche meets the string-course. It was for the senior of the figures – the Blessed Virgin Mary. St Katharine was in the corresponding niche on the other side. I seem to remember that the king and queen and the four evangelists were also carved.

As a server I was taught that this seniority relates to the church's cruciform shape, with the cross laid down so that Christ's right hand is to the north. For example, in lighting candles it is alternately epistle then gospel from farthest from the altar; the reverse in extinguishing. Thus I would expect Edward III to be in the north corner chancel niche and Queen Philippa in the south. You can check in other churches.

I believe the hood-mould stop figures above are saints whom William particularly wished to be displayed. It explains the bishop on the gospel side and the king on the south, if the saints are St Thomas Becket (murdered in the north transept of Canterbury Cathedral in 1170) and St Edward the Confessor (King 1042–66); the former was held in the higher esteem. The latter – the only royal saint – has to be included in this royal family chantry! Both were carved with beards in our day. Other bishops we generally represented as clean shaven, as I expect you saw outside the west doors.

A clue to William's thinking on this is in those letters sent to the pope (EC.13): 'The Warden and chaplains are to say the office of the dead together every day after the midday meal and before vespers, and also the usual hours according to the Sarum Use. They shall also sing choral masses daily: on Mondays for the founder and his kin, on Tuesdays for the founder during his life and after death a mass of St Thomas, the Archbishop of Canterbury, on Wednesdays a mass of St Katharine, on Thursdays of the Holy Spirit, on Fridays of the Holy Cross, and on Saturdays of the Blessed Virgin Mary. One mass for the dead shall be said daily, and in commemoration of the dead they shall remember the founder and his kin, then Adam, Bishop of Winchester, and Gilbert de Middleton, Archdeacon of Northampton and official at the court of Canterbury.' It is somewhat surprising that the Abbess of Romsey does not receive a mention, perhaps reflecting she did little by way of patronage for William when young.

We also know that Edward III always made a point of visiting the shrine of St Thomas in Canterbury Cathedral as he returned from the continent through the Kent ports. St Edward the Confessor was the patron saint of England until 1348, when he was replaced by St George. When in London Edward III had his namesake's tomb to hand in Westminster Abbey. He ordered that his own effigy and that of his faithful queen (who died in 1369, eight years before him) had to be placed as close as possible to that tomb, which had been moved in the twelfth century and again in the thirteenth to ever more prominent positions. The Black Prince similarly asked for and had a position at Canterbury beside St Thomas Becket, until Henry VIII had the saint removed.

I didn't carve any of the statues, just most of the niches, including the allegorical figures under them. All the ones I did had different canopy vaulting designs. That was the detail William dictated. *Jackson writes that they are 'of very elaborate design and delicate construction, the slender proportions of their tabernacle work (the smaller shafts of which are only 7/8 in square) being suggestive of wood rather than stone'.* Reflecting the intensity of his interest was William's demand in 1352 that the building of the carved stalls for the royal chapel of St Stephen's, Westminster, should be halted for the carpenters to erect mock-up panels of the reredos – the decorative screen behind the altar. *According to* Building in England *down to 1540 by L.Z. Salzman, this was to 'demonstrate to the Treasurer and others of the King's Council the form and fashion'.*

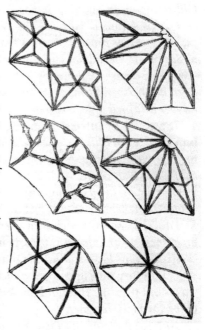

Anyway, William started long before that, many citing him adding the porch to All Saints' Church, Middleton Cheney, while rector there from 1322.

We have speculated about William's association with Edington in his early years and have proof in the Edington Cartulary that at least one family there knew he was at Middleton Cheney in 1329. EC.132 shows William receiving a legacy of a tenement with dovecot in Edyndon in that year from the estate of a Roger Enoc.

Graham tells me that experts see features in the All Saints' mouldings that are only slightly advanced with those of the inner doorway of the porch here. *Support for this comes in Dr J.R.L. Highfield's 1962 Friends' lecture on William, in which he said that William swapped his living of Dallington for that of Middleton Cheney, and Jackson added Cottingham before that. We do not know when William came under the patronage of Gilbert de Middleton, but it seems likely that these livings, all three in Northamptonshire, might have followed Gilbert becoming archdeacon there in 1316.*

According to that maligned incumbents board in the north aisle, Gilbert de Middleton was Edyndon prebendary rector from 1312 to 1334. If William was already under his patronage by 1314, then perhaps he was sent here by Gilbert as vicar, making it possible he was the guilty party in the 'harlot' episode mentioned earlier. The Wiltshire VCH record of that unseemly incident, under the section on Whorwellsdown Hundred, refers to the Register of Simon de Gandavo, Bishop of Salisbury, 1297–1315, and calls the culprit 'William, Vicar of Edington'. Because William made a bequest to Oxford later, did he spend time there in his teens or twenties? There is no record that he ever attained a degree.

It may be of interest to digress into the career of Gilbert. Highfield has him as a successful ecclesiastical lawyer in Lincoln, before moving in 1308 to the courts of the Archbishop of Canterbury. In 1309 he headed those courts as Dean of the Arches, where his services were retained by clergy from bishops down, in cases concerning pensions and appointments. As rewards he obtained prebendaries, not just at Edyndon but also at the cathedrals of Old St Paul's, London, Chichester, Hereford, Wells and Sarum, before his 1316 preferment to archdeacon. Clearly he could not have been all that attentive to every position. He also held the manor of Bradford-on-Avon from the Abbess of Shaftesbury and appointed a vicar there in 1312, Richard Kelveston. That was about the time Bradford-on-Avon's Great Barn was built, and some think Gilbert was its designer.

Any support for the idea that our William was here as vicar, before he went to Cottingham, has to be balanced with another record of Gilbert's activities. Remember that the board says a William de Romsey was vicar right up to 1317. Gilbert is recorded as exchanging the prebendary of Leighton Buzzard for that of Thame in 1316 (both were answerable to Lincoln), where he presented a William de Romseye as vicar in 1318. This could possibly be the just-relieved Edyndon vicar.

Before Gilbert died in 1330 he had held a high post at Oxford University, possibly chancellor. Following the pattern of William benefiting at Middleton's whim, perhaps this is when William attended Oxford, not taking a degree. This was common practice then. Clearly, Gilbert recommended William to his friend Adam Orleton, Bishop of Worcester, a powerful figure during the regime of Queen Isabella and Mortimer. Orleton's brother was principal of a college at Oxford. (Modern historians discount the assertion in Christopher

Marlowe's play Edward II that Orleton ordered the king's death. That regime ended on 29 November 1330 with the hanging of Mortimer at Tyburn and the imprisonment of Isabella at Castle Rising, Norfolk.)

William became clerk to the bishop's household in 1332 and, along with most of the 'familia', moved to Winchester when Orleton became bishop there in 1333. The pope regarded this as a very powerful diocese because it was the second richest in Christendom, surpassed only by the Archbishopric of Milan. This power may be reflected in the Bishop's Register finding that William when in post consecrated nine bishops, the first being the Archbishop of Dublin in February 1350 (R.W.E. Pg.x). This may explain William's refusal of the prime archbishopric of England in 1366: he is believed to have said 'though Canterbury is the higher rack, yet Winchester is the richer manger'. This was when William secured valuable posts, as did other familia members – first of all Master of the Hospital of St Cross and Rector of Cheriton, both in 1335. Five of the livings William held before he succeeded Orleton in 1345 were in that diocese and also in Hampshire.

At the Hospital of St Cross, in his ten years as master, William undertook major restoration, put in a clerestory, lead roof and new west window, and also improved the accommodation at huge personal cost. We have a reminder of it here in the chancel floor – 'Have Mynde', the hospital motto. Not that these floor stones date from my time, least that I recall.

Graham tells me that to this day William is not forgotten at St Cross by its thriving community of twenty-five elderly gentlemen in their delightful medieval sheltered housing (mostly post-William's time). Most wear black gowns with a silver cross potent badge (the de Blois foundation, 1136), some a magenta equivalent (the Cardinal Beaufort foundation, 1445) – designs that go back to the Knights Hospitallers. Some act as guides, and proudly point to the clerestory windows at the mention of William de Edyndon.

The ecclesiastical posts granted by Orleton continued as William devoted his time increasingly to royal service: a canonry of Lincoln in 1342, Salisbury in 1343 and Hereford in 1344. All had to be vacated when William became bishop in 1345. In 1344 he had acquired the Romsey Prebendary of Timbersbury and the rectory of their chapel at Immer. About then he added to the endowments of the chantry at Wappenham, Northamptonshire, which was perhaps the model for Edington. Gilbert de Middleton had set it up in 1324.

What else should I mention? Well, note the metal in three of the four visible consecration crosses. It looks like the original to me. *The fourth was filled in 2005 to mark fifty years of Edington Music Festival, founded by Ralph Dudley and David Calcutt, the eminent lawyer who was knighted in 1991.* All four have pricket candle holders beneath them that also look original. *In fact the north wall pricket was skilfully reproduced by a blacksmith in Bratton to drawings I prepared in 2005.* Much else is a bit of a mess, but I'll leave Graham to tell you how that came about. Goodness me, just look at that sedilia – the three seats for celebrant, deacon and sub-deacon recessed into the epistle side wall behind the altar rail – and the broken and missing statues.

But I was asked to tell you about the consequences of the Black Death and about William's interest in architecture. I'll turn to the latter.

The Architecture

Ponting saw the touch of Bishop William in the remodelling of a quite superb church at Bishopstone, down in the Ebble valley southwest of Salisbury, then as now in that diocese. It is a church isolated from the village: the original houses were abandoned because of plague, though not the 1348 outbreak. The date of the alteration work is unknown. The north window of the north aisle with pear-shaped bowtell and fillet mouldings is reticulated, just like our chancel and transept windows. Otherwise the windows introduced were perhaps earlier than Edington, for they are wonderful examples of Late Decorated Gothic – all curvilinear tracery.

Was it through being a Salisbury canon that William found this church, and did he decide on a similar financial speculation to that at Edington because it was on the wool export route? The church is said to have been owned by the Bishops of Winchester until the mid-sixteenth century.

Probably within a few months of being instructed about Windsor, Bishop William was similarly tasked in 1348 with drawing up the statutes of another royal collegiate church, St Stephen's, Westminster. It is difficult to imagine he was anything other than very interested in the architectural aspects of turning the old St Stephen's chapel into a church, and in the design of the new smaller royal chapel that was required, and ordered in 1342. I already mentioned his involvement in the finishing touches of the latter in 1352 – remember the wooden mock-ups. In my lifetime people said that this chapel was one of the three architectural masterpieces of William de Ramsey. You will recall that he was the king's chief mason – who died in 1349.

The second was the lady chapel of Old St Paul's, which Ramsey finished in 1337, following the chapter house of perhaps 1332.

The third, Gloucester Cathedral's quire and south transept, which I've already mentioned, wasn't finished in his lifetime. He established a new respect for us masons. He was given a coat of arms (compasses flanked by ram's heads) and a seat at the king's table.

St Stephen's Church and the royal chapel were part of the growth of the Palace of Westminster, which was already dominated by the Great Hall of 1097. Long a major residence of the royal family, it now became the principal one. This was appropriate because London was growing to be the true capital of England, with concentration on all arms of government – administrative, financial, judicial and parliamentary. Before this the king held court wherever he was; the exchequer only moved from York in 1338.

In 1547 the former St Stephen's Chapel became the meeting place for the House of Commons. Panelling covered the original wall paintings that glorified royalty. They were exposed during refurbishing in 1800, and destroyed as inappropriate. The building was lost by fire in 1834, leaving just the crypt. Ramsey's royal chapel was also lost then; the Great Hall survives as Westminster Hall. Old St Paul's was gutted in the Great Fire of London in 1666. A limited idea of the architecture of both has been pieced together from drawings and rubble fragments, but Gloucester remains the best yardstick to judge how very contemporary Edington church was with the introduction of the features we have been noting.

In 1815 the antiquarian Thomas Rickman wrote An Attempt to Discriminate the Style of Architecture in England, *in which he identified the attributes of the new '1350s' style. He named it Perpendicular.*

First is squareness of form. You can see this in the church outline. The use of the segmental arch adds to this feel, particularly when set in the square framing of the west double doorway.

Second is the connection of earth to heaven in vertical lines of shafting and mullions from floor to ceiling, avoiding the effect of storeys in the building. There is not too much through-shafting at Edington, but when people first came in they must have gasped at the size of this tower opening into the chancel. The height and width had probably never before been seen in a parish church.

The third characteristic is the use of vertical mullions in window tracery to take load, so the apertures could be wider. The amount of light would have been breathtaking. Related to this was the use of other forms of arch in place of the lancet. Improvements in stained glass techniques enabled windows to better illustrate biblical stories.

Finally Rickman pointed to the growing sophistication of vaulting. This has already been mentioned in connection with the porch and the chancel niche canopies.

Change did not come in overnight; there was always gradual overlap. But here many think that William collated truly transitional steps at a very early stage of what was to be an enduring style, making this church such an important architectural treasure.

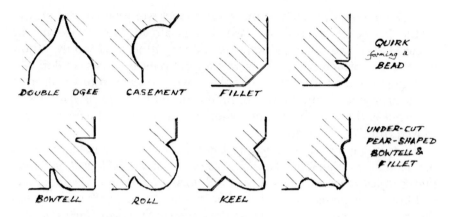

In *The Medieval Architect* *Dr John Harvey wrote that 'whoever may have been the mason-in-charge at the site, there can be no doubt that the architectural advice and probably drawings were coming from John Sponlee'* (who took over from de Ramsey at Windsor).

We have already discussed an expert's opinion on the mouldings of the inner doorway of the porch here. Other experts have compared them with those in the porch at Middleton Cheney and seen a progression of architectural features, going back before the Windsor and London influences on William. Perhaps the first to talk about this was Ponting in the 1880s: 'The form of the arch and the knee of the label, as well as the mouldings of the doorway, are corresponding features. Taking, then, this doorway [Middleton Cheney] as a specimen of Edington's early work – we have two orders of the wave-mould divided by a small but deep hollow or "casement". Then in the inner doorway at Edington, we have the same features advanced a stage. The inner sinking of the wave-mould is quirked . . . while the outer sinking remains as before and the casement slightly flattened.' That is comparing 1322 with probably 1335. He moves on: 'Taking next the doorway into the cloister [north aisle, east end] the early form of the filleted-roll, with the deep outside sinking, and the small rolls which soften the outline of the casement, are here combined with a wide flat casement, which indicates a much later feeling.' We have seen the church's history would suggest 1358.

I passed a lovely banner just now, showing William with a model of this church cradled in his arms (*see back cover*). I never saw any model, just templates coming down those stairs into the porch to go off to the quarry. The master mason always kept a duplicate set, so that when the shaped stone came back he could check it was right. These templates were stored in that parvis room where he worked and slept, guarding his precious two sets of iron compasses, one large and one small, and other tools.

No models have survived from the fourteenth century, though they were certainly in use on the continent in 1390. Similarly, whole building design drawings and ground plans from the fourteenth century (and possibly thirteenth) survive in Europe but not in England. There are only pieces of parchment here from around 1350–75 with moulding profiles on them. Salzman believes they must have existed: 'The mason's working copy would be unlikely to outlast the wear and tear of the workshops; the employer's copy, when he had one, would have no value once the work was completed and would only be kept by accident, or if on parchment, would very likely be rubbed off so that the parchment might be used again.' Old parchment was commonly used in book-binding. Authors like Harvey all refer to the tracing floors at York Minster and Wells Cathedral as still having on them the earliest remaining architect's drawings, prepared so that templates for profiled stones could be lifted from the scratched lines in the plaster on the floor. At Wells this tracing floor is immediately above the north porch, just as we think it was here. The evidence for the latter is an inscribed stone on the west wall. It has a banker mark, one of thirteen in the porch building. There is a central hole where one end of the compasses was placed, several concentric circles being made by the other end. The stone is at just the height the master would have found convenient for setting his compasses while kneeling on the floor. What all the thirteen radii correspond to is not known, but we can surmise they are those he frequently needed to repeat in tracings. Similar circles have been observed in fourteenth-century cloisters at the mainly Norman Norwich Cathedral and the French-built thirteenth-century Bellepais Abbey in north Cyprus, where the radii are thought to relate to three adjacent tracery details. Here one radius happens to correspond with that of the semicircular shafts on the nave columns, not that this can be claimed as its purpose.

Dressing the stone at the quarry, rather than on the banker here, was a bit of a novelty. The clerk of works told us it was because of the cost of cartage. It was pretty boggy whichever track you took to cross the river Biss, and the lighter the weight the cheaper it came. As I recall, most came through Trowbridge and West Ashton.

Besides, they charged the earth for cartage, labour being short. It was people like us who suffered when that royal ordinance of 1349 came out, limiting labourers' pay for piece-work to what they had earned before the plague. Because the ordinance was largely ignored, Parliament issued a stronger First Statute of Labourers based on piece-work rates in 1351. That was difficult to administer; the problem was that one block of stone might be larger than another, and there were always arguments about the average. But the bits in the statute about it being illegal to give to sturdy beggars and no one having the right to refuse offered work improved security. However, the next thing we knew there was a second

statute in 1352: this fixed a daily wage for each craftsman. We received 5*d* a day; in 1347 we had earned 4½*d* a day. Some who arrived on site told us of freemasons still only getting 4d a day. *In the thirty years after the first statute nearly 9000 cases of enforcement were tried in the courts. The employer almost always won!*

At any rate, during the early 1350s here each stone was marked. The clerk of works said it was to check each mason's output at the quarry, and to check that nothing fell off the cart on the way over. We all took turns at the quarry. There was still work to be done on the local banker, shortening marked stones to special requirements and all the carved items, for example. But, truth be told, we broke the lodge rules under which freemasons worked, and occasionally did the lower grade job of ligier (setter) – putting the stones in place. Privately we suspected that marking every stone meant the boss felt safer, because he could demonstrate compliance with that first statute.

Stones seem to have been marked in the centre by all masons, except one who, with a very italic 'F', marked his on the centre of the top horizontal edge. Having studied these marks at up to 13ft above the ground, many instances arise of blocks clearly having been cut to a shorter length so that the mark is no longer central. This occurs almost exclusively where the ashlar course comes up to a window jamb or corner. It seems the freemason at the quarry sent blocks to set heights and as long as possible from the hewn stone. The setter, needing a particular length, sent the closest one in stock to the local banker for shortening. Had hewn stone been brought to site and dressed to size on a local banker as the setter needed it, surely one would expect all central marks. Also supporting the case that marking was at the quarry, we find stones set with the banker mark upside down. It is doubtful that the freemason would have stood for that on site: he would have insisted on taking it back to the banker to do whatever was necessary to avoid the inversion.

In churches that have been examined, banker marks only appear every one in five to one in ten stones, sometimes less frequently. Inversions have not been seen. Less rigorous marking has been explained by the possibility that each freemason worked with just one setter, and the former only marked the last stone in a run of placements to show the clerk of works their output. That might be true if construction involved scaffolding, but not if constructing a wall meant a block at a time on each ashlar course to create a slope up to the full height, so that the wall was effectively a moving ladder.

Fourteenth-century illustrations of construction mostly show the moving ladder technique. A paucity of marks on the inside of the cruciform structure aisle walls has been mentioned. Had a change to scaffolding happened at Edington for these walls, we would expect to see many more putlogs than those already noted for the glaziers. We do not, so a possible explanation for the lack of marks might be a change of management monitoring. Was it a new clerk of works who had a different way of doing things? As we suggested before, was

money running short and was time saved on marking stones an economy? Or perhaps, as it was about 1356–7, the threat of enforcement of the statute had subsided. It is probably more likely that the salvaged stone from the original church needed using up, so little needed to come from the quarry.

I don't remember the clerk of works changing, nor do I remember his name being William of Wykeham. What's more, I don't remember Bishop William coming down to the laying of the foundation stone in 1352. A history of the church compiled in 1914 by the then vicar, the Reverend E.C. Alexander, was found in the parvis in the 1990s. It stated that William of Wykeham assisted in the rebuild here. Ponting in 1886 questioned whether he had been clerk of works: he probably knew that Bishop William had recommended Wykeham to the sovereign before the rebuild here, and he had been made surveyor of the works at Windsor and later supervisor of all the king's building projects. Wykeham might, of course, have been here if William was the sponsor of a south aisle in, say, 1335–40. The Bishop's Register shows that William did not come here between 1345 and 1361. This could be noted as a black mark against Leland's reliability regarding foundation stone-laying. A similar anomaly for a date in December 1351 will arise shortly.

A feature attributed to William de Ramsey is the design of our nave columns – the move to the octagon. It is in the base beneath a torus, with four semi-circular shafts up to the octagonal capital. He is identified with the increasing use of this over the hexagon, though the fact that the shafting bases in Gloucester south transept are hexagonal puts the stage at which he became involved into some doubt. Incidentally, it seems as though every stone in the colonnade construction here has a banker mark in contrast to the aisle walls, perhaps giving the lie to everything west of the crossing being economised upon for one reason or another – purpose or cash-flow.

The hexagon was much in favour in the wake of the Crusades (1098–1270) thanks to contact with Islam. Harvey writes: 'Within a few years of [Sir Geoffrey] Langley's embassy [in 1289] (to Constantinople, Trezibond, Anatolia, Erzerum and to the Mongol Court), diaper patterns appear in English art, notably Canterbury Cathedral, suggesting directly Saracenic inspiration in their geometry. Interlacing circles, forming hexagons, and the use of the hexagon as a plan form, continue through the first half of the 14th century and are accompanied by exotic motives such as those of the famous north porch at St Mary's, Redcliffe, Bristol.' Diaper means a pattern of diamonds, as in much of our window central leadwork, and reticulation describes it when it takes on a uniformity to appear like a net.

Among the graffiti on the walls of the church (particularly in the porch), there are several where the hexagon has been generated with compasses, but its use in design here is perhaps limited to window tracery. Look at the reticulation in the tracery of the identical transept and chancel side windows, and the central light in the transept west windows. Certainly our nave columns are among the earliest to survive of a design that was to endure in hundreds of parish churches for the next 200 years.

Pevsner wrote that 'this significant church is less an example of transition than of co-existence'. The designs of the windows to a degree bear this out.

The west window of the south aisle is pure Decorated Gothic. Remarkably it is exactly copied in the north equivalent, but with late 1350s mouldings – like the rest of the aisle and clerestory windows. The use of the segmental arch in the latter, to allow three bays to each window, is only possible by the vertical support. I suppose this means it counts as Perpendicular. Those intriguing west windows of the transepts have verticals in the very top, but they are hardly load-bearing to permit greater width. I'd call them transitional.

The east window of the chancel is again transitional. It comprises three bays between Perpendicular vertical mullions. To left and right the bays are pure Decorated pointed lancets. The load-bearing verticals are braced apart by a horizontal member, which imparts a feel of squareness to the whole. This bracing member is called a 'transom'; the regular trefoil decoration along its top surface is called 'brattishing'. This is the earliest surviving example in England of a brattished transom.

The west window of the nave is pure Perpendicular: nothing transitional about that. So what dates can we put on these two great windows? Well, as I told you the first chantry priests arrived in 1351 and we were under pressure to provide them with somewhere to say their offices that was larger than the temporarily retained chancel of the old church. The new chancel was the obvious place, and we made it more draught-free once the walls were up and roof on by putting sacking drapes in the windows and the crossing opening.

But of course the master mason said we couldn't do the moving ladder thing of one block at a time on each ashlar course against those novel tower columns without the risk of them moving. So we braced the easternmost ones against the western ones, and those in turn against the first nave columns westward as we went up in height. Likewise we partially built the east walls of the transepts against north/south movement. So I guess it was about 1353 when the master mason learned what design Bishop William had in mind for the east window, and we put it in place in probably 1354.

Of course we finished the transepts next, then the nave and aisles, and finally the tower. I think the drawing of the great west window arrived in about 1357, and it was erected within a year of that.

In his book The Perpendicular Style *Dr Harvey suggests the sequence for the introduction of the Perpendicular features into window tracery as Gloucester south transept, Winchester chancery chapel and Winchester west front and aisles perhaps 1350 or soon after, then Edington east window 1352 and the Edington ten chancel and transept windows 1353. Swapping the latter two dates would be more logical. At first sight it is surprising that Harvey sees anything Perpendicular in the latter design, unless he felt reticulation was also a feature of the new style. However, Ponting wrote: 'The reticulated windows of the chancel and transepts have the double ogee (or brace-mould) with a very flat casement, and an attenuated form of filleted roll forming a group of mouldings of decidedly Perpendicular character.' Certainly the design of these is said to be just like that of a window in the Aerary at Windsor – possibly a Ramsey design. (The Aerary was the muniment room and treasury of the dean and canons, at first-floor level over the Porch of Honour, and is believed to have been constructed in 1353–55.) Most experts seem to add ten years to Harvey's Winchester dates. Thus the whole picture of Edington's significance in relation to architectural change hangs together, and has to be down to Bishop William's interest and influence.*

Let us complete what Ponting has to say about Edington's windows: 'The east window has the same members [as the chancel and transept ten] with the addition of the quirk and sunk chamfer, to throw into relief the fillets of the inner order of the tracery which are features of Bishop Edington's work, both here and at Winchester. It also has the somewhat unusual arrangement of

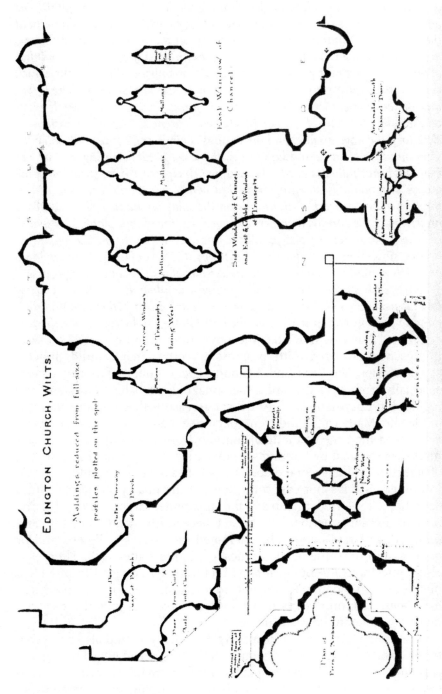

Ponting's compilation of Edington mouldings

two filleted rolls set at right angles, forming the inside edge of the jamb. The label and string-course are of the same late type, which prevails throughout the building. A similar kind of quirk occurs in the outside splay of the two narrow windows in the transepts, forming (with the line of the splay and that of the outside face) the peculiar angular outer member of the mullions, which occurs also in the great west window of Winchester. The casement here is flat, and the outer member of the jamb is the quirked wave-mould which exists on the inner doorway of the porch. The window mouldings of the aisles and clerestory, the nave arcade, and the various copings and cornices all show the same mixture of early and late forms, the latter predominating, but all are rich and beautifully designed. The leading principle in the construction of the groups of mouldings at Edington is that which is a special characteristic of the Perpendicular work – that all lie on the splay or chamfer plane, and the projection of the various members all touch the line of that plane. The splays, whether sunk or not, are also parallel to this line, so that the mouldings are, as it were, sunk from the surface represented by it. This applies not only to jamb and arch mouldings, but also to the undersides of cornices and string-courses.'

From such studies, Ponting adds the east window at Middleton Cheney and the west porch at Winchester to our William's credit. Others see William's hand in possibly earlier work than the latter in the presbytery at Winchester.

I hope that I've indicated the build time of nine years here was impressive compared with progress on other major build projects at Gloucester, Windsor and London. The number of masons here, especially from 1352 onwards, was amazing, probably because of the regular high payments and for the same reasons that we were attracted to the site. Many came and went, of course, and I guess Graham has a better idea than me of the total number from his study of the banker marks, as revealed by Ponting's cleaners. He tells me that his mapping of where individuals worked does support to a degree the build schedule I outlined. But it's not easy with those at the quarry swapping round back here. I've tried to explain the apparent disappearance of some masons for long periods. It doesn't necessarily mean they left and returned: as I said before, they demoted themselves to ligiers, and/or made a start on some of the domestic buildings after 1358. There was also a guesthouse to build, for the brethren were obliged to provide a night's accommodation for anyone on the road. Pete, for example, must have been back on the main task by 1360, for he is one of those who marked a stone in the final course.

That topping out was quite a party, I can tell you, and also a farewell for me. They rigged extra long ropes on the huge tread-wheel here in the crossing and erected a pulley gantry out from that last course so as to lower me over the southeast corner of the tower. Boy, was I scared when

they kept saying there wasn't any more rope and I'd have to climb out of the wicker basket and jump.

On remote sites like this, those assembled post-plague would have acted as a team. The clergy may well have lent a hand, if only in interregnum, sickness or leave of absence. There are plenty of documentary examples of monks and priests developing skills if there was a lack of labour to hire or a lack of funds for pay.

Anyway, all the priests and the hierarchy of masons were here, along with the villagers to cheer me on my way. I was particularly sad to leave the children. We'd played a lot with them, as did the chantry priests. Some of the graffiti in the porch was us teaching them, because we knew it would be covered over. Other bits were probably them playing when we weren't looking. That reminds me – I always loved that support carving beneath the northeast corner niche, thinking it symbolized the quote 'suffer the little children to come unto me', but I was told by the master mason that it was the aged Simeon recognizing in the child Jesus the future Messiah (St Luke 2.25).

The Clock Strikes Three

The Master Mason

It occurs to me that perhaps I haven't said enough about the master's important role in all this. He was responsible for the building being structurally sound. There were plenty of disasters where master masons got it wrong, almost always while trying to introduce something novel. Everyone's heard of Ely's tower in 1322. A certain secrecy surrounded their expertise: it wasn't the product of being taught formally, rather of having been afforded the opportunity to examine others' successful work and copy it. They all knew about proportions that were pleasing to the eye, usually those that could be generated with compasses. Important were side to height in the equilateral triangle (1:1.55), diagonal to the side of the square (1:1.414) and diagonal to the side of a regular pentagon (1:1.618) – the Golden Rule or Cut. They could assess the acceptable skill levels of all tradespeople and could judge the quality of materials. They knew the importance of dressing stone accurately to minimize the mortar between blocks for wall strength, and the importance of bond-stones through the wall where construction was, as here, inner and outer blocks (about 5in thick) with infill between. And, of course, they had to decide what to use as infill. Here I suppose he had to use the local chalk.

With Edington the feel is of a unified construction, in a rather chunky sense, which achieves an aura of simplicity and spaciousness. No flying buttresses here. The master perhaps set out with this conservative approach, fearing that structural safety margins would be eroded by the refinements that would inevitably come winging down from Bishop William. Notably he knew to expect bigger windows, to give more light than in churches of the past: the shining of faith in God over the gloom of the plague. We've seen how he might have been caught on the hop with the segmental arched wide windows for the aisles. Remember, one of them fouled the east side of the already finished porch. He came up with rather a neat solution, don't you think?

Then there was the shock of learning about that very wide west window. What to put underneath it? A return to the Norman rounded deep surround and a tympanum over a single doorway? No. The problem was solved when he realized that the impending consecration might involve two bishops: William (Latin name 'Winton') and Robert ('Sarum'). With a single doorway, who would have precedence? It was well known that the latter, Robert Wyvil, Bishop of Salisbury 1330–75, had as a young man been Queen Isabella's favourite clerk. The usurper Mortimer had made him a canon of Lichfield in 1327 and bishop very shortly before Edward III started on his long period of personal rule. He was lucky to keep his job, and was only confined by the Crown to his see for some years. The master's inspiration was two separate doors, so the bishops could enter at the same time. Having that pillar between the doors helped the loading on to the foundations.

The master also had to watch the career of his employer; death or a sudden loss of wealth could be disastrous. In 1355 the royal role in the very public outcome of a feud between Bishop Lisle of Ely and a cousin of the king, Blanche Wake, must have caused him concern. She appealed to Parliament when thugs acting for the bishop burned some of her properties. Initially the seizure of all the temporalities of the bishop was ordered. Subsequently the king issued a reprimand for slow seizure action against his chancellor and treasurer, respectively John Thoresby, Archbishop of York (1352–73), and our William: 'We are of the opinion that, had the matter concerned a great peer of the land, other than a Bishop, you would have acted differently.'

Edward III had vacillated throughout his reign: he favoured clergy for high posts of state and then threw them to the dogs. Would he do it again? What if William was forced to flee abroad, as happened to Bishop Lisle in 1356? It was a relief for the master when that year William was elevated to the post of Chancellor of England. *The nearest equivalent post today is prime minister.*

Also in 1355 came the third campaign of the Hundred Years War. Tuchman seems surprised at the matter-of-fact tone in which the Black Prince wrote to William that year. He is relating the breakout from Bordeaux: 'Harrying and wasting the country we burned Plaissance and other fine towns and all lands around.' Troops stormed and burned Mont Gascar, where he boasts many men, women and children, hitherto ignorant of war, were mistreated and slain. They plundered Carcassone for two days – 'and the whole third day we remained for burning of said city' (*see page 25*). Then in 1356 came the drive brutally northwards from Gascony, culminating in August with the great victory of Poitiers and the capture of the French king, John II.

Did William feel Poitiers was the end of the war? In his new position as chancellor he had sufficient prospect of wealth to start on his greatest architectural indulgence – the lengthening of the nave and the construction of a new west end to his cathedral. Besides hope of a generous benefaction from the Black Prince towards that project, William may have seen merit for the Edyndon project in getting even closer to him, a prince who any day could become king, on his return from such a triumph.

When he was in England the principal residence of the Black Prince was Berkhamsted Castle. His nearest monastery was the Augustinian at Ashridge, almost in its grounds. This had been founded in 1283 by Edmund, 2nd Earl of Cornwall (1249–1300), a cousin of the prince's great-grandfather, Edward I. Edmund's father, Richard (1209–72), the second son of King John, died the year before in the castle and the foundation may have been a long-planned tribute to him. Patronage of that foundation was to stay with the Earls of Cornwall.

In 1337 dukedoms were introduced, and among the first to be elevated were the Cornwalls. When issue from Edmund had died out, the new title was bestowed on Edward III's eldest son, Edward of Woodstock – who was aged just three. A second house had been founded at Ruthvin in Denbighshire (today's Ruthin) in 1310. It is not known when it closed. Was it William who suggested to the prince Edyndon's conversion from a chantry college to be an Augustinian foundation, perhaps recently called Boni Homines? He may have doubted that Edward III would ever come to see the royal chantry here, but a royal visit would enhance the chance of a township developing.

Incidentally, Highfield has Edmund founding the Bonhommes in 1325 – after he was dead! In 1268 Richard and Edmund brought a relic of the Holy Blood back from Germany; it was thought to have belonged to Emperor Charlemagne. One third went to Hailes Abbey (Richard's 1245 foundation near Cheltenham) and two-thirds were set aside for Ashridge (fifteen years later) and perhaps that second house. Could one third eventually have come to Edyndon? Remember John of Aylesbury's E.C. 24 title 'of the House of the Precious Blood'.

Did the master mason get wind that Bishop William had plans for great works at Winchester? Was he apprehensive of, or suffer, a decrease in finance in 1357? Could this explain the style difference between the west and east ends of Edington church? Or, if the nave arcades were already finished, was there a panic to complete the aisle walls? Perhaps this explains the economy of not marking every stone, making do with left-overs and a rougher finish on each block. Was it a huge relief to be told in 1358 that there was to be a change of function here, that

Walter Scarlett would go and a stop-gap warden would come, Walter de Sevenhampton, followed by a change to a rector and corrector from Ashridge? There would be implications for the builders if the chancel were to be made the brethren's chapel.

Incidentally, the incumbents list may be wrong in showing Sevenhampton here in 1357. He was the second warden for only one month, from induction on 5 March until his agreed resignation on 5 April 1358. Unlike the other chantry chaplains (probably twelve by then – EC. 352), Sevenhampton did not stay on as a Bonhommes brother. He was, however, a faithful official to William Winton, nominated as an executor to his will – which was made less than a month before the bishop died.

None of these questions can be answered now, but in the Middle Ages it rarely paid to get into a wrangle with a monk. They owned huge lands, grew much produce and kept thousands of sheep. The master would have kept his eye on the relationship between William and the monks of St Swithun's, the priory of the cathedral. Remember the fall-out over William becoming bishop.

William had done something to repair an unhappy start by winning back land between the cathedral and the High Street. This land had been given to the priory by Henry I (1100–35), but possessed subsequently by the mayor, bailiffs and citizens for a market. *In* The Black Death *Ziegler relates that in 1349 argument occurred between the monks, who insisted that burials were in consecrated ground, and the populace, who demanded that they be buried outside the city – to contain the plague. This culminated in an angry mob attacking a monk who was conducting a burial. William was outraged at this aggression by 'low-class strangers and degenerate sons of the church' against a man 'whom, by his habit and tonsure, they knew to be a monk'. The ringleaders were excommunicated but, ever the diplomat, the bishop granted most of the requests of the people by opening and consecrating new remote burial ground, by later demanding and achieving return of the market site in exchange for the added burial ground. The monks were delighted.*

However, William rarely went into the cathedral. What did the monks make of their bishop wanting to knock it about? He alienated them again in 1362 by quashing their election of a prior and installing an outsider, Hugh de Basyng, instead. *This is related by Dom. Hockey; his source is documents in the Bishop's Register. He goes so far as to say that he found an 'absence of any sign of cordiality between Bishop and monks' at any time, though he 'cannot exactly be considered an absentee prelate; he was generally present in his diocese, though acting usually through his officials' (RWE. Pg.viii).*

After William died the monks had the last laugh, putting it about that William of Wykeham, his successor, was the great architect bishop who embellished the cathedral! When Ponting visited the dean in 1884 he discussed whether Wykeham had perhaps been at Edington as clerk of works, and the dean replied that he thought Wykeham was there to show Bishop William how to build the church!

Remember our William went as treasurer to Calais for eighteen days in November 1348. He went again as chancellor in 1360 – 24 August to 6 November. By May military activity in France had ceased, and he went for the negotiation of the Treaty of Bretigny which was signed on 24 October. William was the first signatory for the British. Edward III was supposed to give up all claim to the throne of France (of course he was to renege on that), but the terms illustrate the wiliness of William. The treaty set an enormous ransom for the French king. A papal bull of Innocent VI had in April levied a tax on all clergy worldwide, but William, instead of paying the English contribution of a tenth over two years, had our bishops offer just 100,000 florins. The cunning was that they should not have had to pay even that much, because by an ingenious arrangement this sum was due to be paid into the English exchequer as part of the ransom. You may recall the story of what happened next: it is often recounted as the height of the age of chivalry. The French king was allowed home when the total was only part-paid, but returned of his own accord when the full sum could not be found. The truth might be that, bad as England had become by the 1370s, it was far worse in France!

Chancellor Edyndon was now effectively a national hero. It was lucky the west double doors had worked out so well, with a bishop's head on each side: in 1361 there was now no way the diocesan bishop could walk in ahead of the sponsor!

But was William Winton here at the dedication? Little doubt on that occasion but experts can give differing views, and sometimes documents appear to contradict one another. For example EC.17 is presented by Janet Stevenson as an account of an event that took place in the rectory house at Edington 'in the presence of William, Bishop of Winchester, Robert, Bishop of Salisbury' and others on 17 December 1351. It is a public instrument prepared by John de Beautre, 'clerk of Worcester Diocese and Notary Public'. However, from the letter headings Dom. Hockey finds that William was in Hertfordshire at this time. And who was the RWE registrar? Most of the time – John de Beautre: much of it was, to quote Dom. Hockey, 'as he frequently reminds us, written by his own hand' (RWE. Pg.ix). This event was of a trivial nature, concerning a corrupt incumbent of the Baynton chapel, so the letter headings are probably correct. It goes to show you cannot believe everything you read!

Another example of disagreement arises with Dr Highfield's view of Bishop William's enthusiasm for visitations, which is in conflict with that of Dom. Hockey. However, Highfield does say that 'it will only be possible to appraise Edington's work for the see of Winchester, when his unpublished Register is one day brought into the light'. Dom. Hockey, of course, has done that. Highfield says: 'Ceaselessly the Bishop rode about his diocese, accompanied by a train of servants, with his impedimenta rolling along in wagons behind him, as he went to hold ordinations or to visit a monastery or a church.' Dom. Hockey sums up his impressions from the Bishop's Register: there was 'full activity, with ordinations normally celebrated by the bishop himself, in spite of the disorganization and stress of the Black Death. But there is little sign of pastoral activity or of visitations. The essentials of the diocesan administration were carried out by the officials, the Commissary-General and the Sequestrator-General, but always it would seem, with the clear direction from the Bishop.' He says that the bishop 'resided almost continually at his manor of Southwark with only the Thames to separate him from Westminster, and a barge to convey him'. Again, 'we note that he did not go far from Southwark and the manors of his Bishopric – Farnham, Bitterne, Highclere, Marwell, Bishops Waltham and Bishops Sutton, then Downton in Wiltshire, Brightwell and Wargrave in Berkshire and Witney in Oxfordshire; he does not seem ever to have visited Taunton' (RWE. Pg.x). The ordinations, sixty-four in twenty years, happened mainly in his personal chapels, not out around the diocese; the last was the first tonsure of thirteen young men at Wolvesey Castle. Hardly 'ceaselessly roaming', but one trip he couldn't miss.

I wasn't here for the dedication or consecration (whatever you call it), because the master mason whom our William had appointed for the Winchester work asked me to go there as a sort of foreman. In a way it was an understudy position, because on the continent there had been subsequent outbreaks of the plague. William was being cautious and rightly so, for sure enough we had a pretty severe one in England in 1361. But that didn't stop him travelling here.

The Bishop's Register shows William leaving Southwark on 5 July 1361. He was at his Esher palace on 5–7 July, Wargrave near Henley on 18 July, Brightwell near Wallingford on 21 July, Buckland on 22 July, then Edington on 23–27 July.

Assuming William was here for the consecration, the earliest he could have arrived was 23 July, which couldn't possibly have been the second Sunday that month (the date it's celebrated these days). Any rate, they'd probably take at least a day to unpack. Where did John of Aylesbury and the master mason house the bishop's huge entourage? Was the guesthouse over at Tenhyde on the Bath to Salisbury road complete?

Highfield tells us that the bishop's will 'shows that he had at least 132 servants. Probably at least seventy or eighty of these went round . . . with him. He had a travelling "capella", or set of chapel fittings, which was carried on two horses. It usually filled two chests and contained all that was necessary to enable the bishop to carry out the full duties of his office'. Typical contents are listed and then 'Behind came two carts carrying baggage. Each cart was in the charge of a page and a boy. Then came the Bishop's Chancery Clerks, men like John Wormenhall, the Bishop's Official. The horses were in [the] charge of the Marshal, Robert Erheth. The travelling kitchen took up a great deal of room. There was a poultry department, a brewing staff to brew ale, a pantry and a buttery, a bakery and . . . a scullery. Each department had to be mobile and capable of being set up in whichever of the Episcopal manors the Bishop might happen to stay at.' The horses would have been particularly important for communication.

I think I've covered all the things that I've been asked to. There's just time to point out something of significance for us masons. See the base of that corbel support on the north side between the middle and east bays: it's a carving of a long-haired and bearded man pushing with his back and arm to hold up the weight above. That's a medieval allegorical depiction of a master mason. *There is a wonderful fourteenth-century example in Italy, in the rear porch of the Basilica of Santa Maria Maggiore in Bergamo, where two slender columns are supported on the back of lions. Each has a mason's head and shoulders braced with pained expression under the rib-cage of the lion. It's amazing how far this symbolism spread.*

So that's it from me. Thank you for listening. I've enjoyed it greatly. Over to Graham now!

More from the Chancel

I hope our guest covered the fourth theory – that this church may be the consequence of the Black Death. From timescales, though,

I find it difficult to imagine that William Winton did not start on the Edyndon idea until the August 1348 outbreak. His induction as bishop in December 1345 seems a much more reasonable commencement date for all the planning that would have been necessary before demolition of the former church could begin. But let us leave it there.

The colourful reredos, the painted screen behind the chancel altar, provides an opportunity for a résumé of what has been covered (*see back cover*). The brass plaque on the north side inside the communion rail tells us that the family of William Chapman, who died in 1934, gave it in his memory. Starting at the top, the three shields are the spiked wheel of St Katharine of Alexandria, lilies for the Blessed Virgin Mary, and a crown and three scrolls for All Saints. St Mary is not on the senior side – a mistake! Looking at the shields below from the extreme gospel side: first is that of the Archbishopric of Canterbury. It should be Azure (blue) an archiepiscopal cross in pale Or (gold) surmounted by a pall Proper (denotes a natural colour), charged with four crosses patee fitchee Sable (black). A pall is a Y-shaped bearing on a shield coming from that decoration on a pallium (a medieval archbishop's rectangular cloak). Next are two shields – that of William of Edyndon over that of his protégé, William of Wykeham. Moving inwards then are the royal arms, with a silver label – that bar across the top with projections down; that is the Black Prince. The central focus is in the form of a rood; Christ crucified with the Blessed Virgin Mary and St John on either side. This time St Mary is correctly positioned. Continuing southward she is holding the Christ child – the Diocese of Salisbury. Then the upper shield, with four scallops on lozenges, is that of the Cheney family. Beneath it is the cross fleurie of the Paveley family. The last, crossed keys and a sword, is Winchester Diocese. Notice the precedence: Salisbury nearer to the senior side.

George Herbert and the Church Floor

Now the interspersed statues. First there is Katharine, then Bishop William, then John of Aylesbury. Lastly, on the south end, is George Herbert, the poet priest, who was married here to Jane Danvers on 5 April 1629, two days after his thirty-sixth birthday. They almost certainly met during George's stay earlier that year at the home of Henry Danvers, 1st Earl Danby, who lived at Dauntsey, northeast of Chippenham. At the time George was suffering from consumption. She was a cousin of the earl, whose home was at Baynton. George's state of health certainly motivated action, and they spent the last three years of his life, 1630–

33, in the living at Bemerton, close to Wilton House, west of Salisbury. Wilton House is the home of the Earls of Pembroke.

George Herbert was born in Montgomery, Wales, and educated at Westminster School and Trinity College, Cambridge. His poetic ability led to his being university public orator from 1620 to 1628. He looked set for a career at court, with James I recognising his descent several generations before from early Earls of Pembroke. In 1624 he became the Member of Parliament for Montgomeryshire, but ill health and financial problems led to his seeking ordination that same year.

The death of James I in March 1625 and two other patrons was a blow to George. He resigned his seat in 1626, but the livings he acquired did not support him. The situation improved with help from those who recognised his talents and, for some reason, a royal grant of land in Worcestershire in 1627. At Bemerton George wrote fine sermons and more poetry until his death of tuberculosis on 1 March 1633.

One of George Herbert's poems is said to reflect on the pattern of flooring in the chancel and nave here. I doubt he remembered it from the day of his wedding; it is more likely that he noted it on visits at other times, while seeing his wife's relatives or perhaps when he met someone here who was an acquaintance of the Pembrokes, Anne Lady Beauchamp. (She who lived at the Mansion House and lost her second husband, Sir Edward Lewys, in 1630, within a year of coming here.) She was more than just an acquaintance of those at Wilton House: her brother Richard's widow, originally Lady Anne Clifford, was remarried to the Earl of Pembroke. The two Annes seem to have been close friends, according to a diary kept by the countess.

A further connection? Our Anne, née Sackville, had first married Edward Seymour, Lord Beauchamp of Hache, great-grandson of Edward the Lord Protector. Anne had a son by Seymour who died in infancy. Seymour died after nine years of marriage, and no children remained when their daughter died two months after her father. Two brothers of Anne's first husband were nearby. William Seymour lived at Amesbury, less than 10 miles from Bemerton; Francis died at Marlborough and is buried in Great Bedwyn church.

To digress for a moment. Remember a Sir Eustace de Hache who died without male issue? Early in the fourteenth century a member of the Beauchamp family made his seat at Hatch in Somerset. The association is marked with a 1st Lord Beauchamp of Hache (1299–1361), and the village became Hatch Beauchamp. However the use died out for over a century before it was revived in 1536 for Edward Seymour, made Viscount Beauchamp of Hache when his sister Jane married Henry VIII.

Yet more coincidence? Keeping her married name, Beauchamp,

Anne married into the Lewys family, of the Vane, Glamorganshire. About the only thing known about that family is that they were considerable landowners – in Montgomeryshire.

And so to the poem entitled 'The Church Floore':

> Mark you the floore? That square and speckled stone,
>   Which looks so firm and strong
>   Is Patience:
> And th'other black and grave, wherewith each one
>   Is chequer'd all along,
>   Humilitie:
> The gentle rising, which on either hand
>   Leads to the quire above,
>   Is Confidence:
> But the sweet cement, which in one sure band
>   Ties the whole frame, is Love
>   And Charitie.

The 1997 Edington Music Festival took George Herbert's poems as the basis of reflection throughout the week of services, with the one above on the Sunday. Some of these poems have been set to music by composers including Ralph Vaughan Williams, Lennox Berkeley and William Walton.

I will leave you to judge for yourselves whether George Herbert is reflecting on the floors here. However, I should tell you that what we see in the chancel today has had two great upheavals since his day. The only clue to its possible state in 1629 is a surviving watercolour painted in 1826 by J. Buckler before the first changes. It shows the floor with three steps, not the one of today, where the communion rail is now. There is no rail in the painting, but then there are no furnishings shown at all – no Lewys monument or consecration crosses. Instead of two steps as now just west of the south door the painting shows only one, meaning that the south door has two steps up into the doorway. Everywhere the floor slabs are shown as irregular rectangles around large memorial slabs, several of which appear to have been for brasses, shaped as though commemorating rectors or brethren (perhaps ten in number).

But we cannot be too confident about Buckler's accuracy. He shows what appears to be an intricate wide seven-bayed reredos behind an altar block that is half the width and also seven-bayed. They are drawn as though of stone. Careful examination of the stone behind the present painted wooden reredos shows no sign of disturbance of the surface caused by removal of a stone one. Buckler must have had his view of the sedilia and piscina on the south side obstructed by the Lewys monument, which stood in front of them. He uses artist's licence to recreate the sedilia, probably very fairly, but gets it wrong in not showing it integral with the piscina. There are errors with the decoration of the doorway in the west bay on the north side, which he may have been re-creating based on the south doorway. This was because the decoration was almost certainly already chiselled away, just as we see it today. The north doorway is shown by Buckler with one step up from the western section floor level, which we do not have today. More on that doorway anon. Buckler's use of artist's licence may go back, therefore, to an envisaged state before the Reformation. However, I doubt this is true of the flooring.

The first disturbance was caused when the Watson Taylor family put a crypt under the chancel before about 1830, with central access stairs down into it at the west end. It extends far enough east to be under the communion rail, and its construction entailed raising all but the sanctuary floor level. Thus the black and white marble floor in the sanctuary today could well have been there in 1629. Of the rest of the chancel flooring, as painted by Buckler and probably seen by Herbert, only the memorial slabs (presumed to be of brethren) remain in relocated positions, most in the floor of that crypt. It is equally likely that this was when the floor stones you are standing on were introduced. Just imagine how ridiculously short that north doorway would then have looked with the floor 1 ft 2in higher.

The second disruption was at the 1887–91 restoration, when Ponting felt he could support the roof of the crypt so that the chancel floor could return more closely to how it had been originally. He put the difference at the amount I just said. Thus fifty or so years after paying for the first upheaval, the Watson Taylor family paid to put it back to the way we see it today. It is unlikely that Ponting saw the Buckler painting, as I will explain later.

To quote the *Wiltshire Times* article of 3 October 1891 again: 'The floor of the chancel has been lowered, and new steps of Purbeck marble, fixed to the ascertained original levels and positions, and a new pavement of marble laid in the sanctuary. Entirely new paving and steps have been provided in the rest of the church – stone and concrete in the open spaces, and oak blocks under the seats.' This makes it sound as though the adjusted level floors in the chancel kept the same stone; that is, the stone laid probably in about 1830. Thus 'Have mynde' and the three nails of the cross you see here could have been carved in about 1830 or at the restoration. To me, those two words are a challenge to self-assessment as one approaches the chancel altar by way of a cross similarly inscribed on the level above. They may, of course, have been inscribed on stones of the previous irregular chancel floor that Buckler drew in 1826.

Similarly, though the *Wiltshire Times* article speaks of new paving in the nave and aisles; this may have copied an existing pattern of flooring somewhere else in the church, which George Herbert had seen.

By 'sanctuary' we can be pretty sure the article refers to the tower crossing and the westwards site for the then returned nave altar, where the black and white squared marble we see today was laid. Perhaps it was even mimicking the chancel black and white marble area. A pre-restoration sketch, possibly of the 1850s, indicates that flooring in the tower crossing and right down the nave was irregular rectangular slabs then, much like Buckler's chancel and Cheney monument (*see pages 59 and 44*).

Unfortunately the use of the word 'sanctuary' in the *Wiltshire Times* article has been taken by some authors to refer to the east end of the chancel. Certainly nowadays we reserve the name uniquely for that area and call the area around the nave altar the 'sacrarium'. This was the usage of Canon Ralph Dudley (his floor slab memorial is your side of the communion rail), particularly after my wife and I gave a reserve sacrament aumbry to be installed in the north wall. Given in 1967 when we temporarily left, it was prised out of the wall in 1989 and damaged beyond repair. The filled silver pyx was taken. 'Have mynde' meant nothing to the culprit.

"Speaking of which, are you sure that the nails are not the three daggers of the Paulet family arms?" It is possible, and if they were inscribed at the same time as the family's first arrival they could pre-date the visits of Herbert.

But back to the one he almost certainly did see – the sanctuary's black and white triangular-patterned marble floor. You can see the outline where the Lewys monument was removed in 1901. See also the indications that the monument had metal railings round it set in the floor – with possibly a round socket for the gatepost. Those railings were not added at the restoration. I am confident that this floor was laid at the same time that the Lewys monument was erected, probably within a year or two of 1630. Perhaps George travelled over for its dedication: there is an inscription on the monument that some think could be from his pen. We will look at it anon.

The Clock Strikes Four

Enough about the floors – all triggered by the George Herbert statue. Incidentally, that was a replacement carving for one of St Margaret of Antioch that was stolen in 1970. Why she should have featured in the reredos is a mystery. The designers were Randoll Blacking and Christopher Webb; the former was church architect at the time and the latter a friend of his who designed the figures – a fine draughtsman and designer of stained glass windows. Christopher's son John was asked to design the replacement and it was made by the same firm in Oxford, who remembered well the original work.

Clergy Attire

Let us turn our attention to the statue to the left. The attire of John of Aylesbury is based on that directed for the brethren in 1358. Had this changed from what they wore as chantry priests? We know about this from EC.13, dated 22 April 1354: 'The warden shall provide a clerk to serve mass and wait upon the canons, and also find decent surplices, and black tippets, lined with fur, for use in the church.' The tippet is a short cloak hanging down the back from a neck band. Anything lined with fur would have been pretty welcome, given the building had hessian in its window openings. There is only one illustration in the Edington Cartulary. It is of the warden, Walter de Sevenhampton, and two chantry priests receiving the advowson of Colleshulle (Coleshill, then in Berkshire) from Bishop Robert Sarum on 22 March 1358 (EC.512). The drawing, which was probably made by a scribe in the Salisbury chapter much later, shows the kneeling recipients in floor-length cloaks with very long pointed hoods and long pointed shoes protruding below.

These are just the things that the Archbishop of Canterbury, John de Stratford, complained about in 1342, to quote *Scenes and Characters of the Middle Ages* by the Reverend E.L. Cutts (1930). He chastised the clergy for growing beards and long hair and dressing as laymen, with brightly coloured normal attire, excessively long sleeves, hoods and tippets of 'wonderful length' and pointed and slashed shoes. Cutts claims that by the 1360s it was the clergy, following the luxury-loving lead of the pope and prelates in dress and lifestyle, who contributed to public disaffection with the Church in England. Incidentally, remember that at the double west doors we discussed whether a bishop could be depicted without tonsure? Just look up at the east window hood mould stop on the north side: the masons depicted a bishop with long hair.

To quote a document in the Edington Cartulary (EC.23, 29 March 1358), using the Janet Stevenson translation, 'All the brethren shall wear grey tunicles, and scapulars of the same colour shorter than the tunicles and with hoods of suitable size. They shall have cloaks of the same colour reaching to the ankles. When the rector and brethren go on journeys they shall wear wide round hats of the same colour. They are not to wear any linen garments, except drawers, next their skin. They may wear shirts of linsey-woolsey next their skin and shall sleep in tunicles of wool or linsey-woolsey. In addition to the brethren, there shall be two secular priests who shall serve the parishioners in the nave of the church and administer the sacraments to them while the brethren are occupied in celebrating the divine office . . .' What these two were to wear is not directed. The scapular, possibly with an origin in Roman fashion, is generally defined as two narrow pieces of cloth over the shoulders, held by cross straps front and back. Chambers prefers the word 'tunica' for Janet Stevenson's 'tunicle' and believes it was an undergarment with tight-fitting sleeves. He also believes the form of scapular in use then had a large cowl attached to it. Today we think of the tunicle as an over-the-head garment, open at the sides and sleeveless. They are usually decorated with wide braid in simulation of the scapular, and worn by the sub-deacon when there are three celebrants at Solemn Eucharist. 'Linsey-woolsey' was material woven from hemp thread.

The appointment of two secular priests was a change from the days of the warden, when the chantry chaplains had care of the souls of the parishioners at Edington and North Bradley. Mention of administration of the sacraments to parishioners should not be read to mean communion in both kinds. The laity had been denied wine for probably a century by 1358, not being holy enough!

The Buckler Paintings

I am going to digress slightly. First, the story of the Buckler paintings, which I have just mentioned for the second time. The west end exterior view was referred to when we were outside – for the clarity of the label depiction of a bishop beside the west doors. In 1995, during the NADFAS church recording here, seven Buckler pictures given to the parish by the late Ralph Dudley were examined. He had bought them at an auction in Malmesbury in 1952, paying between £2 10s and £7 10s each for them. At first sight they appeared to be sepia print copies, and comparison was made with a photocopy of a Buckler original held in Devizes Museum. The museum holds some 650 paintings by Buckler father and son, who were commissioned from the first decade of the nineteenth century by the Colt-Hoare family of Stourhead to document all buildings of significance in the area.

The comparison showed certain differences. Trees were larger and cattle were drawn in different areas. The dates on Ralph's set were from the 1820s, and on a visit to the museum great excitement ensued when they were identified as a set of original, though faded, watercolours. There were no internal views in the Devizes collection, yet three of ours are. One I've mentioned (the chancel) and the other two are rather mundane, being of the Cheney and south transept monuments. The paintings came back from the London conservator in time for display at the fortieth music festival in 1995. It is thought that the Watson Taylor family saw the Stourhead collection and ordered our set shortly after they purchased the estate around here in 1820. With that estate came responsibility for the chancel; it had been thus since the Dissolution of the Monasteries. In many places the landowners gained the whole ecclesiastical building and did horrendous things to them. We are fortunate that our nave and transepts continued to serve the parishioners.

Chancel Responsibiity

Let us take a break in the south-west corner, and on the way we can see the split in responsibility reflected in the wording of a brass plaque of 1891 in the north aisle regarding the restoration:

> To the Glory of God, the repair of this church was undertaken by a committee consisting of The Right Reverend the Lord Bishop of

Salisbury, The Venerable the Archdeacon of Wilts., Simon Watson Taylor Esq., The Right Hon. W.H. Long MP, Alexander Mackay Esq., George Watson Taylor Esq., The Reverend Arthur Baynham, The Rural Dean, The Reverend Francis Warre, Canon of Salisbury, Treasurer. In 1890, The Reverend George E. Long, having been appointed Vicar, became Treasurer. The church was opened for divine service by the Lord Bishop of Salisbury on September 1891. The cost of the work, not including the chancel, was £6535, towards which sum Mr Simon Watson Taylor and his sister Miss Isabella Watson Taylor were the largest contributors. Mr Watson Taylor also repaired the chancel at his own entire cost. Architect: Charles E. Ponting FSA. Builder: James Burgess. Vicars: Henry Cave-Browne-Cave (deceased 1890), George E. Long. Churchwardens: George Lewis, John Tyler.

It is a relief to see these two churchwardens' names, for it was often the practice to put their initials and the date on work completed. When we were examining that blocked doorway outside at the west end of the north aisle, I saw one of you point to the initials 'JP and WP 1891' rather crudely on the blockwork that sealed the window in the doorway. Had they been GL and JT, I would have had to claim it was a restoration repair to earlier blocking – when the brethren no longer needed to talk to women through it! Perhaps I still do, for it looks relatively recent. From here you can see the quarter-round structure in the north-west corner that I mentioned when outside that doorway.

Cade's Rebellion

All finished – let's go back to the chancel to examine the doorways. Why do they look as they do? Possibly because of the murder of the Bishop of Salisbury here in 1450. To explain this we have to consider the historical background – which includes eventual peace between France and England, treason and rebellion.

In the reign of Henry VI (1422–61) initial English victories in France were reversed by Joan of Arc. Cardinal Henry Beaufort, several times Chancellor of England, was convinced that peace with France was needed to end the Hundred Years War, but was long opposed in this by the king's uncle, the Duke of Gloucester. In 1443 the then Chancellor John Stafford, who owed his promotion to Beaufort, eventually bowed to his views. Aged forty-eight, the Earl of Suffolk (who had spent fourteen years fighting in France) was sent to negotiate peace. The resulting Treaty of Tours was very unpopular, particularly because the king was to marry Margaret of Anjou, with the return of Anjou and Maine to her father. This completed the loss of all territory in France that had been in English hands, except Normandy and Calais.

For mouthing opposition to the marriage Gloucester was arrested, charged with high treason and then found dead in his bed in 1447. His supporters blamed Suffolk (now a duke) for the fact that in 1449 English troops were in full retreat across Normandy, with Rouen (where Joan of Arc had burned at the stake just eighteen years before) lost. Suffolk's impeachment resulted in the king having to banish him from the realm for five years. On 1 May 1450 Suffolk sailed from Dover, but off Calais ships intercepted him. Some sort of trial happened and, lowered into a small open boat, he was beheaded. The perpetrators, who dropped his body on the beach at Dover with his head on a stake, were never identified.

It was widely thought that those who hired out the craft used in the ambush feared for their lives. Led by Jack Cade, they rallied support for rebellion in Kent without great difficulty. Cade called himself Captain Mortimer and must have had military experience for the prowess he showed. By mid-June 22,000 men were encamped in battle lines on Blackheath. Embassy to find out their demands resulted in an eloquently presented list of grievances. Concerns included that those who lost France should be punished, that the Crown manage its finances better (not rewarding debtors with undeserved honours), and that the aristocracy should stop using corruption to thwart the wishes of electors for seats in Parliament. Although 22,000 men may not sound that many, in 1450 it was 1 per cent of the population of England, perhaps 3 per cent of the able-bodied males.

The Murder of Bishop Ayscough

The rebellion was accompanied by outbreaks of violence in the southern counties, with the best-known incident starting in Salisbury and culminating here. Of Cade's demands, the sympathy hereabouts may have been for repeal of the Statutes of Labourers, which fixed wages for workmen, and that Richard, Duke of York be brought back into favour from exile in Ireland. The focus of discontent was the Bishop of Salisbury, William Ayscough, who had been consecrated in 1438 and was a frequent absentee. His family was identified with Lancashire, though he was almost certainly of a Bedale/Lincolnshire line. His worst offence was to have been Henry VI's confessor. The bishop fled Salisbury pursued by a mob led by a popular brewer: he was probably trying to reach Lancastrian sympathizers, perhaps at Southwick Court or Farleigh Hungerford Castle before going on to Bristol.

At Edyndon, on 29 June 1450, the 'Bisshop of Salisbury was slayn of his parrishens and peple . . . aftir that he hadde saide Masse and was draw from the auter and lad up to a hill ther beside, in his awbe and his stole aboute his necke; and ther they slow him horribly, their fader and their bishop and spoillid him unto naked skyn and rente his body shirte in tom pecis'. Some of the brethren died with him, and Jackson notes the plundering of the bishop's carriages, he having fled 'taking 10,000 marks (a mine of money in that age)'. A mark was 13s 8d.

There is another local connection to Cade's rebellion – John Stafford. In 1432, while Bishop of Bath and Wells, he was created Chancellor of England, a post he held until January 1450. In 1444 he was consecrated Archbishop of Canterbury. Another of Henry VI's preferments was to add 'lord' before chancellor after Stafford officiated in 1445 at the marriage to Margaret of Anjou. He was probably an illegitimate son of Sir Humphrey Stafford of Southwick Court, North Bradley, by one Emma of that place – who afterwards became a nun in the Holy Trinity Priory at Canterbury. Also in 1444 a legitimate son named Humphrey, like his father, was created Duke of Buckingham. John and Buckingham rode out to Blackheath, and in the archbishop's name offered a pardon for all but Cade. Rejection led to a hastily gathered army being sent under two cousin relatives, both named Sir William Stafford, one of Grafton and the other of Somerset. They found Blackheath deserted and fell into an ambush near Sevenoaks, where both were killed.

Cade marched on London, and found many to welcome him. Troops mutinied and many dignitaries were killed before people decided Cade had by mid-July outstayed his welcome. A pitched battle for London Bridge ended in pardons from the archbishop being accepted by most rebels from the intermediary, the Bishop of Winchester. John died at Maidstone in 1452 and the duke (a staunch Lancastrian in the subsequent Wars of the Roses) at the battle of Northampton in July 1460.

By August 1450 Cade had been killed near Haywards Heath and John Stafford, with the Archbishop of York, was starting to try unpardoned renegades. They abandoned this when standards of revolt were raised around Canterbury. There was an attempt to punish the Wiltshire rebels, some as local as West Ashton. This was also abandoned when many in the county rose in arms. However, Richard, Duke of York returned in January 1451 and started on 'a harvest of heads'.

The Chancel North Door

Of events here, the mob is said to have blamed the bishop for foisting 'that French woman' upon England. Another version of uncertain date has the mob unable to get in, shouting 'Death to the bishop; death to the king's confessor' – and then the eventual breaking down of a door.

Well, one early communion here I was looking at the south doorway and noticed that the ashlar courses were different to east and west. The same was true of the opposite wall to either side of a jumble of stone blocks for the width of a doorway. After the service, examination of the recess outside revealed that the east side had interior moulding which was missing to the west. Also in the roof of the recess there are ribs running diagonally, as though part of a deeper canopy vaulting of a space now blocked up. The ribs of this vaulting in the near right-hand corner are cut away, and the conclusion must be that this is the rebate for a rectangular outward opening door.

Back inside, armed with a large sheet of brown paper, I made a template of the outline of all the blocks that comprise the small doorway in the next bay west. Of this Brakspear wrote that 'there was originally an ornamental stone seat, in the middle of the west bay on the north side, that may possibly have been intended for the founder when he was present, and this was done away with to accommodate the quire of the Monastery'. He felt that 'another vestry was afterwards built on the east side of the north transept, after which the earlier and inconvenient chamber was taken down'. Whether he was thinking that, with the seat removed, this became a doorway into the new vestry he does not make clear. Certainly Ken Rogers in the first 1980 edition of the *History and Guide* assumed that the inner evidence of a doorway meant there always was one in the west bay, adding 'built up so cleverly that no trace is visible on the outside. It may have led into a sacristy.'

The cut-out template offered up against the jumbled stones of the middle bay was found to fit exactly but for two blocks. Leaving the latter aside for the moment, the conclusion must be that the outside recess and the door frame inside once comprised a canopied outwards opening doorway from the chancel. The position of the consecration cross on the outside shows that there was no exterior building for it to have led into in 1361. I doubt there ever was such an ecclesiastical building there, and the chiselled weather-mould on the north transept's east wall is probably from a shed or some such, when the Mansion House garden stretched up to the walls of the church. No, some one deliberately blocked up that doorway and moved the internal architrave frame west one bay,

Last seen 1450 (?)

presumably because they valued the decoration. Later the decoration was chiselled away when stalls were put in, lining the western bay.

Surely the most likely time for this shift is shortly after the dreadful events of 29 June 1450, particularly if this was the way the mob gained access. Remember, at the recess outside I asked you to note one continuous block of the massive plinth stone. If you think about blocking up the doorway, that stone could not have been inserted from the exterior while leaving the external recess architrave in place. The alternative is that it was inserted from the inside while the inner architrave frame was being moved. Is it not surprising that such a huge block should have been specially carved for this purpose? Surely it was more likely to be at hand, possibly from demolition of the outer walls of the south vestry. I hinted at this when we looked at what remains of that vestry. But if that demolition happened at the same time, then the south door would have become an access directly to the exterior – so why was that door not dealt with in the same way as this north one? For all we know it may have been: it does appear, remember, that a door out of the east wall of the north transept was also blocked up at some stage. And when we look at the 1850s sketch I mentioned just now you will see that the west doors are not visible from the inside. There are other blocked-up doorways, of course, that we think led into domestic buildings.

The symmetry of two doors opposite one another is normal in fourteenth-century design. The chancel north door probably just led into the garden of the warden/rector's house. Indeed, the discovery of a well with steps down to it within 100ft of this exit probably locates the second messuage that we talked about when at the northwest corner of the church.

The two blocks I mentioned as not matching the outline are of exactly the same 10in height, and located so that whoever shifted the north door frame could lengthen the engaged triangular protruding column shafting either side of the ogee arch. (You can see that column decoration on the south door.) They needed to do that because the frame was now at the lower floor level in this bay; this meant that the ogee decoration no longer reached the string-course. The gap was filled with a trefoil top-piece, and you can see where the wall was recessed to help secure it. The crocketed pinnacles to either side would have looked very truncated without the extra shafting. Interestingly, you can see on the extra stones the crayon or charcoal lines for the protrusion, rather as we saw on that profile we looked at on the south aisle piscina bowl.

We noted that other church doors from the outside were inward opening and strong-backed. The south vestry, we can assume, had no external door. If the mob failed to enter the domestic buildings, then entry via them into the church through the north aisle and transept was denied. There is perhaps evidence that they did not enter those adjoining buildings in the surviving glass. Apart from the east window in the north transept, nothing but fragments of early glass remain – other than on the northwest side towards those domestic buildings, evidenced by the plain parapet.

So we can imagine the crowd doing their worst by breaking glass, trying other doors, prising out the outside consecration crosses and throwing in flaming objects wherever they could. Coming round the east end, success with this north chancel door perhaps saved the east window of the north transept, or was there a fear in destroying the resurrection scene it depicts? Once in, priorities turned to murder and pillage.

Two years later the brethren petitioned that their house had 'sustained intolerable damages through the sons of perdition who dragged William, late Bishop of Salisbury, from the monastery and slew him and breaking down the houses and buildings of the monastery, took and carried away their goods and jewels'. What is the betting that the theft included brasses (among them those from the Cheney and other monuments), more consecration crosses, and that the vandalism included breaking statues?

We can imagine the surviving brethren, probably some of them grievously wounded, surveying the damage and picking up the only two broken figures in the chancel worth saving. There they are in their wrong niches! These westernmost four niches should have held, nearest the altar, St Matthew – gospel side, St Mark – epistle side, and coming west, similarly St Luke and St John. We know which the survivors are from the allegorical animals at the ends of the scrolls from the left arms: the four evangelists were symbolized by, in order, winged depictions of man, lion, ox and eagle. You see we have John on the north side (not much of an eagle, more a pigeon) and Mark on the south. Where should they be? Mark closer to the sanctuary and John across to the south. But had the brethren put both on the south side it would have looked a bit odd!

Other Chancel Observations

Cast your eyes up and you will see those long hooks, two each side, from which hang candelabra. They may have been here in 1450 beyond reach of the thieves. They possibly supported the Lenten veil. This gauze sheet obscured the sanctuary during much of Lent, until the events of Passion Week had Jesus in public view. An aperture was opened during mass for the reading of the gospel and during the giving of communion. This was based on St John 12.36: Jesus, after telling

the crowd that the Son of Man must be lifted up, 'went away from them into hiding'. Thus this custom was somewhat different from the covering of crosses. It died out at the Reformation, but has had occasional revivals in both the Roman and Anglican churches.

Incidentally one hook supports the lamp that burns white when the reserved sacrament is in the aumbry. It was given by the parents of Ivor Clark, a lad who was a fellow server in the 1960s before he joined the Army. He was killed in an accident in Germany. The central lamp is thought to be Spanish, and was gifted by Ralph Dudley who bought it from Blissland church in Cornwall.

While necks are craned, notice that the niches terminate as corbel supports for the beams of the original ceiling. Indeed, you can see the outline of the timbers on the stone probably from the ingrained dirt of thousands of generations of spider's webs. This is particularly marked in the southeast corner and behind you there in the west corners, where the corbels are on long engaged shafts, not niches.

Both these corner shafts have supporting figures seemingly pushing up with their backs, like the one my friend attributed to being an allegorical depiction of the master mason. These are a long-haired and bearded male and a dainty female with ringlets. I doubt the latter celebrates the first female master mason of the fourteenth century! They are on the sides one would expect – male on the gospel side. Look up, and the window stop figures comply fore and aft, with the male nearest to the high altar.

To have so many female depictions in the decoration is most unusual for the fourteenth century. So many in the chancel is, I suspect, more to do with celebrating parenthood in the royal family, rather than a bishop's partiality! However, you will note the number without head covering, and with bare arms and low-cut dresses. What thoughts did these ladies evoke in the celibate brothers after 1358? Did any succumb?

In her splendid 1978 bestseller *The Distant Mirror* Barbara Tuchman tells of a pope in this period amassing his fortune through such services as legitimizing hundreds of the celibate clergy's children a year. Her view of the sexes at that time is epitomized by the elderly Menagier de Paris, who wrote to his fifteen-year-old bride that 'It is the command of God that women should be subject to men . . . and by obedience a wise woman gains her husband's love and at the end hath what she would of him.' When we were outside at the northwest corner I read you part of EC.23 about the contacts of the brethren with women. It goes on to talk about the avoidance of assignations:

> None of the brethren shall leave the precincts needlessly after Compline, a rule which must be firmly observed by all. The Rector shall take care not to allow any brother to make unnecessary journeys, but if a journey is necessary, let the time needed be assessed and a date assigned for his return. If a brother is not seen leaving, he shall be suitably punished and his leave of absence cancelled.

Who went into such detail? Bishop Robert Wyvil, acknowledging the house to be 'suitable for the introduction of canons, now decrees that the brethren placed therein shall profess the rule of St Augustine and observe the following ordinances which he makes with the agreement of William, Bishop of Winchester, and of Salisbury chapter'.

As I nip back inside the communion rail, I can mention that St Edward the Confessor up there on the east wall introduces some realism: for Roman Catholics, he was the saint invoked to intercede for unhappy marriages and separated spouses.

The Brissett Taylor Monument

More ladies in despair here on this memorial on the north side of the sanctuary. Some have felt that the commemorated person is perhaps receiving more female attention in the afterlife than he

received before death – for Sir Simon Richard Brissett Taylor, Baronet, was a bachelor. He died on 18 May 1815 aged thirty-two, and his sister Martha appears to have organized the erection of the monument before her death in 1817. Everything is life size, and I suspect the weepers are Martha (supporting his hand) and his other sister Elizabeth.

Their grandfather, as Patrick Tailzour, had gone to Jamaica from Borrowfield, Scotland. He married a Martha Taylor there and changed his surname to hers. Maybe it was through her family that he became a merchant in Kingston.

The father of the three children, John Taylor of Lyssons Hall, Jamaica, became a sugar-planter and was created a baron in 1778. John married Elizabeth Gooden of the same island, and our Simon was only three when he succeeded to the baronetcy in 1786.

Patrick and Martha had other offspring. An elder brother to John (I will call him Uncle Simon) took charge of the upbringing of his namesake nephew. Born in 1740, Uncle Simon went to Eton, and his career in Jamaica started as an attorney for absentee sugar-plantation owners. From 1763 to 1810 he was active in local politics, representing Kingston initially and then St Thomas in the Jamaica assembly. He became a good friend of Horatio Nelson, who spent thirty months there in the late 1770s, much of it recovering from malaria caught in Nicaragua. Both being eligible bachelors, they indulged in many mistresses, Uncle Simon acknowledging a growing number of illegitimate children right up to his death in 1813. As Chief Justice of the Court of Common Pleas and Lieutenant Governor of the Militia, he was noted by General Nugent, the governor from 1801 to 1806, to have the most extraordinary manners 'and lives principally with overseers of estates and masters of merchant ships; but he has had an excellent education, is well informed and is a warm friend to those he takes by the hand. He is also very hospitable and civilised occasionally, but is said to be inveterate in his dislikes.' The governor's wife wrote in 1806 that he was 'by much the richest proprietor in the island, and in the habit of accumulating money so as to make his nephew and heir one of the most wealthy subjects of His Majesty. In strong opposition to Government at present and violent in his language against the King's Ministers, for their conduct towards Jamaica. He has great influence in the Assembly . . .'

Much of Uncle Simon's writing is in the Cambridge University Library and with the Institute of Commonwealth Studies, University of London. Professor Byrd of Rice University maintains 'that his letters form the richest correspondence I know of, bearing on politics and society – black and white – in the British Atlantic world of the late eighteenth century. His observations on slave life in Jamaica – especially when one considers the limits of his perspective – are often keen. In his time, Taylor frequently meant his correspondence to provoke, and many of his letters still do just that.' To Lyssons, he added another five plantations and three cattle ranches, involving five hundred slaves and two hundred cattlemen.

Surviving is a 1809 letter from our Sir Simon, aged twenty-six and back in England, to his uncle: 'The very distressing accounts you will receive by this packet concerning the abolition of the slave trade make me very unhappy as I greatly fear the uneasiness it will occasion you may be prejudicial to your health, it is certainly most extraordinary that the Government of this country should be so bent upon the destruction of the West Indies colonies but it is yet to be hoped they will see their error and that some remedy may be applied before it is too late . . .' Emancipation of slaves came in 1838.

Other letters indicate sister Eliza was by then also back in England. In 1805 she had married William Mayne against Uncle Simon's wishes, and was cut off by him. Her husband was the son of a failed banker and had only enough funds to enter the Army. He served as a captain in the Life Guards at the battle of Waterloo, 1815.

Sir Simon enjoyed his inherited wealth for only two years. It passed to Martha, who died two years later, and so on to Anna Susannah Watson, a niece. In 1810 she had married George Watson, and at the time of the inheritance George and Anna added Taylor to their surname. You have heard of the Watson Taylor family before, and will do so again.

But back to this memorial. You have just learned how Martha came by deep pockets, and she needed them – for this monument is by Sir Francis Chantrey. Note the tell-tale 'Chantrey SC'.

Francis Legatt Chantrey

Chantrey was born in 1781 of humble background. At sixteen, confident he had ability, he cancelled his indentures and tried securing portraiture commissions in first Dublin, then Edinburgh, and aged twenty-one in London. He exhibited pictures at the Royal Academy from 1804 and in 1808 his first piece of sculpture – the head of Satan. Recognition came with the commission for four colossal busts for Greenwich Hospital – the admirals Duncan, Vincent, Howe and Nelson. In 1811 the likeness in an exhibited bust brought the great and the good to him for similar treatment. He went to Paris in 1814 and Rome in 1819, visiting the studios of Canova and Thorvaldson and ordering the finest marble.

Monumental design gave Chantrey great satisfaction. His first masterpiece was 'The Sleeping Children' for Lichfield Cathedral, an 1817 work that portrays two young sisters asleep in one another's arms. He became an ARA in 1815 and was elected a full Royal Academician in 1818. His output was immense, amassing him a huge fortune. Honorary degrees came from Oxford and Cambridge and a knighthood in 1835. Mounted statues included Wellington outside the Royal Exchange and George IV in Trafalgar Square. His William Pitt the Younger stands in Hanover Square, his Joseph Banks in the Natural History Museum. Overseas, his George Washington is in the State House at Boston, Massachusetts, his Sir Thomas Munro in Calcutta, Elphinstone and Babington in Bombay and Canning in Athens. His Earl of Malmesbury is in Salisbury Cathedral. Along with artists J.M.W. Turner, Raeburn, Lawrence, Wilkie and Constable, he is credited with making early nineteenth-century British art pre-eminent in Europe.

Thus we have an early sculpture here, probably before he employed assistants to execute much of the work in his design. It probably cost at least £1000. Martha Taylor's outlay contributed to the huge estate that Chantrey gave to the Royal Academy in his will, having no children. It was largely used to purchase great works of British fine art, which in 1898 moved into the new Tate Gallery.

Given the dates, some have suggested that this monument was originally erected elsewhere and moved here after the Watson Taylor family bought Erlestoke House in 1820. Whenever, we have no knowledge whether it hid from our view anything that was previously against the north wall of the sanctuary.

Easter Sepulchres and William Wey

This would have been the site of the Easter Sepulchre, usually an arched recess with protruding canopy and exclusively used in churches that observed the Sarum Rite. In it from Good Friday to Easter Day were placed a wrapped crucifix and a pyx containing the consecrated elements of bread and wine – the body and blood of Christ. Concealment was commonly with intended burial cloth and personal apparels of very expensive cloth (such as cloth of gold) against the dreaded day. These were draped over the canopy.

Speaking of cloth of gold, there is a lovely frontal for the high altar which is used at festivals (*see back cover*). It was designed by Sir Ninian Comper for Colombo Cathedral, Ceylon, where Ralph Dudley was bishop's clerk in the 1940s. It came back for repair but the estimate was too much for the cathedral. Later Ralph suggested its purchase by fellow servers and friends as a memorial to Ivor Clark, whom I mentioned just now.

Sepulchre construction was most often of wood, and surviving stone ones are rare: they usually date from the fourteenth and fifteenth century. Some survive because the gentry created a memorial for themselves in this prestigious position by making it double as the Easter Sepulchre. The nearest to here are perhaps Bampton in Oxfordshire and Holcombe Burnell in Devon. Candles would have surrounded the sepulchre from Good Friday evening and a vigil of priests and parishioners sustained until the first mass of Easter Day, when the sacred elements were brought out – in symbolism of Jesus leaving the tomb of Joseph of Arimathea. At the same moment all crosses that had been veiled or covered for the same period were exposed. Finally the crucifix from the sepulchre was removed and publicly unwrapped, then carried in joyful procession. Are there any remains behind Sir Simon's monument?

The hunt for something even grander in the same vein has long been pursued here – a chapel of the Holy Sepulchre. The evidence for it stems exclusively from the writings of William Wey, who became a brother at Edington probably in 1463. Born in Devon in 1407 and a Fellow of Exeter College, Oxford, Wey became a founding Fellow of Henry VI's new Eton College. He died at Edington in either 1470 or 1476.

While with Eton, he went on pilgrimage in 1456 to the shrine of St James the Apostle at Santiago de Compostela in northwest Spain. He subsequently went on two pilgrimages to the Holy Land, in 1458 and 1462. He wrote the record of these journeys in the library at Edington, noting that his first expedition to the Holy Land meant absence from Eton for thirty-nine weeks. His Itineraries (as the books are called) are now in the Bodleian at Oxford, along with a 7ft long map of his eastward journeys. In the 1458 journal he notes that he bought various objects in Jerusalem and entrusted them to the galley-master for transportation to England, along with bits of stone that he had chipped off at the sacred sites. What a vandal!

On the flyleaf Wey lists what he gave to Edington – 'to the chapel made to the lyknes of the sepulkyr of our Lord at Jerusalem'. It indicates he constructed something more elaborate than a typical Easter Sepulchre. There were hangings for it, including curtains of blue buckram and 'a clothe stayned with the tempyl of Jerusalem, the Mounte of Olyvete, and Bethleem'. The large map and another of the Holy Land with Jerusalem at the centre are mentioned, as are 'a number of bordes containing measures of the Holy Sepulchre itself and other places' as well as paintings of the chapel at Calvary and the church in Bethlehem. The leaflet on sale in the church about the 1458 pilgrimage states that 'In the Chapter House here were representations, made in boards, of the Church of Bethlehem, The Chapel of Calvary, Mount Olivet, and the Vale of Jehoshaphat.' Chapter House? surely it must have been in the domestic buildings to the northwest.

What I have just told you is enough for those at Winchester to tease us: 'Have you found the only known rival to our Chapel of the Holy Sepulchre?' Of course we do not know whether any of the gifts from William Wey had a realizable value. With him dead, the brothers may have sold them, for it was only eleven years since they pleaded poverty after the 1450 sacking.

Winchester's Holy Sepulchre is in the north transept. It has brilliantly coloured paintings of about 1170 on the walls, probably commissioned under the patronage of Bishop Henri de Blois; they were only revealed in 1963. They include the Entombment, the Vigil of Mary Magdala and Mary the mother of James and Joseph, the Harrowing of Hell, the Entry into Jerusalem, the Raising of Lazarus, and portraits of various prophets. Why does de Blois ring a bell? The St Cross black and silver de Blois foundation.

Now: today's last flourish. Fold back this sanctuary carpet to reveal the floor slabs. Nearest the memorial is one listing those interred early on in the Watson Taylor vault below. Top of the list is Dame Elizabeth Gooden Taylor, who died in 1821. She was Sir Simon's mother – a widow for some thirty-three years. Next on the list is Anna Susannah Watson Taylor, who died in 1853, the inheritor of all that Uncle Simon wealth.

I am not going to dwell on the other slabs now, but just note among the surnames Powlett, Long and Lewis. Today we have skipped around madly on dates, as the points of interest on our tour have made it necessary. Tomorrow our guest will tell you of the research he did here in the library in the 1530s, putting into historical context what probably happened after William de Edyndon's last visit in 1362, probably to dedicate the side chapel to the memory of his brother John. It will all be tidily in chronological order. Ponder as you leave what may have happened to Wey's little chips of stone. It's lovely to think that, adding to the ambience here, there are perhaps fragments of the Holy Land under our feet.

Day Two

Good morning. Without more ado, may I introduce Nicodemus Fellowes, reader clerk to John Leland during the examination of the libraries of religious houses in the West Country in the 1530s.

Another Heavenly Guest – 1350s to 1550s

Salutations. This is my first time back, and how sad it is to see the disappearance of the rector's house, various chapels and the complex of library, chapter house, dormitory, refectory and so on. At the Dissolution we envisaged some secular use being found for such buildings, and Edyndon was initially better provided for than most. May I say I never was a religious man – so I speak dispassionately of what I found here.

John told me to call the brethren Bonhommes. I start at the beginning of William of Edyndon's chancellorship. Of that time, the first thing I noted was that most clergy and common folk virtually hated the papacy. I need not dwell on this, as you've been made aware of the situation. Secondly there was disillusionment with the clergy by worshippers and the non-committed public alike. John always said that the latter were nowhere more fervent than in the West Country.

The 1350s were violent times, with troops returning from the first phase of the Hundred Years War, fresh from being urged to commit awful atrocities. They formed themselves into companies that roamed England, demanding protection money and carrying out retribution for failure to comply. This was very unsettling, as was the uncertainty that surrounded the enforcement of the law regarding employment: the various Statutes of Labourers were flouted by landlords under the growing burden of taxation. They were desperate for workers, so they had unscrupulous agents out and about who offered more than the stipulated wages. Statutes couldn't protect those who responded to the agents from being pursued by their feudal masters. More and more families took to an itinerant way of life, always watching out for the pursuer – not least further outbreaks of the plague. Because of Bishop William's secular position, first as treasurer and then as chancellor, the situation tended to reflect on the Church, already suffering from public belief that the priesthood realized the pestilence was spread by human contact, and had been withholding access to confession in the last rites for that reason.

The latter was certainly not true of all clergy, but as locally as St John's, Yeovil, when the Bishop of Bath and Wells held a thanksgiving service in 1349 to mark the passing of the plague, it was interrupted by 'certain sons of perdition' who kept him and the congregation besieged all night until rescue came.

Hence it is not surprising that Edyndon church doors were strong-backed from the outset, and the height of all windows above the ground may have had security in mind. It will not have escaped you that the vestry windows were the lowest, and that is where the 1450 mob attacked successfully.

There was also some muttering about the youth and lack of training of clergy after the plague. There would have been some suspicion of chantry priests here, who in 1358 took on the closed life of Augustinian canons overnight and no longer communicated with the public. This church was most probably open-plan then, certainly with no seats for parishioners, and with up to seven altars – chancel high altar and five or six for the original chantry purposes. Local people and travellers drawn from the Bath–Sarum road to this novel building would have been free to wander at will, dogs and all, in daylight hours. How unpopular would the brethren have been for reserving parts for themselves, perhaps by roping them off, when the chancel and chantries were in use for their services?

Other than in abbeys and major churches that observed the Rite of Sarum, there was generally simplicity in worship. This was true of most of Britain and France; it was probably true of the previous church at Edyndon. Some might have been to Salisbury Cathedral and seen everyday services that involved three, five or even seven deacons and sub-deacons, and two or three thurifers and crucifers. Up to four priests in copes acted as cantors. Multiple altars were censed at most daylight services, and even at matins (immediately after midnight) vested priests offered incense at the high altar. Processions were frequent, with those before high mass especially magnificent. In addition to carried candles there were normally two on each altar and more on major festivals and feast days, some standing on the ground and others suspended from the roof. Following the Sarum Use meant emulation of all this elaborate ritual to the maximum degree. While it was undoubtedly a great spectacle the first few times one experienced it, to the impoverished laity it probably seemed excessive and wasteful, if not downright insincere in hard times. The brothers here had to adopt it.

However, few would not have made private devotions and respected the climax of the mass in the act of transubstantiation: bread became the flesh of Christ and was lifted above the head of the celebrant (the elevation symbolic of Jesus's place above all men). *EC.23 shows that the moment was marked by a bell for total silence, and the brethren then prostrated themselves. Similar elevation of the wine in the chalice was a relatively recent innovation.* All the brethren would have partaken of communion with the bread, but probably only the celebrant of the wine, perhaps joined on major festivals and feast days by the deacon and sub-deacon. By the 1370s the laity, if confessed, was usually only offered communion of the shared bread once a year, at Easter.

The Black Death recurred in 1361, 1368–69, 1371, 1375, 1390 and 1405, though perhaps with less devastating sweeps across England. Keeping track of financial liabilities and feudal allegiances in these times became a nightmare, particularly with strange political edicts like that about knighthood which has been explained to you. An earlier one was almost as extraordinary: in 1337, on pain of death, all sport was banned except archery, and the debts of all workmen who agreed to make bows of yew and arrows of ash were cancelled. What happened to the poor person who was owed a debt by someone who accordingly changed employment? It would be surprising if long bows and arrows were not among graffiti here, and a good example is down low on the west wall of the south transept.

By 1370 the calibre of the clergy had declined further, as families saw no merit in sons becoming priests. However, plague deaths rather than a lack of (or bad) leadership was the biggest emptier of the nave. Depleted congregations could not provide the living for the incumbent, so many priests left to find more lucrative positions such as chantry chaplain, or opted out of life and into the monasteries. It is recorded that of 376 rectors whom one bishop instituted to benefices in lay patronage only 135 were in holy orders. In another diocese of 193 parishes visited more than a third were held in absentia.

The Effect of Protestantism

The Bishop of Bath and Wells urged his flock, if on the point of death and unable to 'secure the services of a priest, then they should make confession to each other, as is permitted in the teaching of the Apostles, whether to a layman or, if no man is present, then even to a woman'! Small wonder that many began to rethink their faith – not to women priests, but a less idolatrous faith; more in English than Latin. John Wyclif, Master of Balliol and absentee Rector of Lutterworth, started it in his 1374–6 lectures in Oxford. He argued that a sinful man (the Pope in mind) had no authority over fellow men. The corollary, that ecclesiastical abuse of property justified deprivation by the secular authority, appealed to John of Gaunt, Duke of Lancaster. He was coming to prominence with the fading health of both his father Edward III and his elder brother, the Black Prince.

Gaunt had become influential with the lords when he replaced William of Wykeham as Chancellor of England in 1371 with a succession of non-ecclesiastical persons. By 1375, following Wyclif's line, he was encouraging nobles to claim back from the Church what their ancestors had given.

Feeling secure with Gaunt's backing, Wyclif went into full cry against the practices of the church, denying that the priesthood held any essential part in the route to salvation, rejecting excommunication, confession, worship of relics and saints, indulgences and pilgrimage. All that was needed was reading of scripture in one's native tongue and no sacramental worship. Denial that the priesthood could achieve transubstantiation stuck in the gullets of quite a few potential supporters, and for a while he played that down. But common people and lower clergy were won over to what was called Lollardy.

For some reason Lollardy was particularly strong among those associated with the wool trade in Wiltshire and Gloucestershire. A further influence locally was Lancaster's nomination of the senior official on his staff since 1373, Ralph Ergham, for Bishop of Salisbury when Robert Wyvil died in 1375. How better to get at the Sarum Rite!

The steward of the household of the Duke of Lancaster, Sir Thomas Hungerford, moved into the manor house at Farleigh Montfort (some 10 miles northwest of here) in 1369 and fortified it. He became bailiff to the Bishop of Salisbury and was knighted in 1376. He was speaker at the Bad Parliament, meeting January to March 1377. This was totally compliant to Gaunt's wishes, though it acted on petitions that only Parliament should be able to annul statutes, contrary to the recent practice of the duke. Bishop William of Wykeham had his wealth confiscated, could not come within twenty miles of the court and had to stop work on the cathedral.

But by June events had so unravelled that Gaunt fled from a London mob to the protection of Joan (the widow of the Black Prince for less than a year) at her Kennington home. With her influence as Princess of Wales and mother of the future king, she ordered the Convocation of Bishops to stop trying to decide whether Wyclif should appear before the pope, as the latter had demanded. The crowd dispersed; Wyclif went on his way, free to preach. Wykeham enlisted the help of Alice Perrers, the king's mistress, to secure himself a pardon from Edward III just days before the king died on 21 June 1377. To the papacy Wyclif remained a heretic – now receiving protection by the state in England.

On 16 July the twelve-year-old son of Joan was crowned Richard II. However, Lancaster was largely a spent force and unable to fulfil the regent role he had probably aspired to for the last decade. The new king restored Wykeham's temporalities and work on the cathedral nave restarted. Whether he regained his share of the brothel is not recorded, but it was perhaps fitting that his surviving mitre was found much later to be part of a lady's girdle of rather earlier date, set with enamels of animals. Could it have been a present from William de Edyndon?

The aim of Lollardism, to allow personal familiarity with the Bible for the masses, failed largely because Wyclif could not achieve a timely translation of even the New Testament before he died in 1384. In 1399 Parliament compelled Richard II to stand aside in favour of John of Gaunt's eldest legitimate son, Henry IV. The Earl of Salisbury and two of Joan's sons by Sir Thomas Holland, the Earls of Kent and Huntingdon, were executed for plotting the restoration of Richard II in 1400. The House of Lancaster was thus established in the year Gaunt died.

The aftermath was an accommodation between Church and State to stamp out firstly Lollardism and secondly the sense the populace had of being able to exert 'people power'. They were largely successful with the former, with the first heretic burned in 1410; with the latter, however, despite the failure of the Peasants' Revolt (which I'll not go into), the common folk remained more self-assertive and questioning than ever in the past. Typical is the action of six parishioners here in 1428. John Rowere, William Newman, Stephen Taylor, Richard Smith, Robert Panter and John Danyell chained themselves around the Tenhyde Cross in objection to paying more than a penny at weddings, churchings and burials. They were arraigned on 20 June before Bishop Neville in the chapel of his manor at Ramsbury, but effectively only cautioned.

Probably the conduct of services changed little here throughout this turmoil. We know the names of all the brothers here in 1382, and clearly several were local Wiltshire men or from neighbouring counties. Their number was then eighteen. This was when their rules for succession were applied, with the death of John of Ailsbury. They elected three candidates and Bishop Ergham selected Thomas Odyham. Another of the three, Thomas Lavynton, lived long enough to succeed him. We know that because he was rector when the bishop visited in 1400. His name arises in another document I'll discuss later. *The incumbents list, previously referred to, does not mention him!*

The previous visitation had been in 1390, two years after Ergham left to be Bishop of Bath and Wells; the Bishop of Salisbury was John Waltham. Some records say it was not the bishop but Archbishop Courtenay who visited. Courtenay had started such parochial visits in 1382 and met opposition (after visiting Rochester, Chichester, Bath and Worcester) from the Bishop of Exeter. Excommunication of the latter and appeals to Rome ensued. The king intervened in Courtenay's favour, but this apparently didn't deter the Bishop of Salisbury from objecting to the visitation of parishes in his diocese. However, I can find no record of a 1390 visitation.

Richard Mitford replaced Waltham in 1395 and conducted the visitation of 1400. It was classed as generally satisfactory. There was some lack of discipline, with reminders to attend services, behave better in choir, refectory and cloister, keep to the vow of silence and avoid absence without reasonable cause. The biggest rebuke was the need for better care of the archives. There was no mention of Lollard influence or financial problems.

William of Edyndon had done a great favour to his foundation by securing total exemption from taxation by the state. This was enshrined in a royal charter of 1359 from a grateful Edward III (EC.29), which was confirmed by Henry IV, Henry V and Henry VI on their accessions. I have found no document from Richard II's reign, but clearly there was no interruption. The rector attending convocations must have met increasingly jaundiced eyes from his counterparts at other religious houses. Finally, in 1441, the exchequer felt that the nation should no longer be honouring the memory of Bishop William thus, and the rector was summoned for non-payment of a clerical tenth. Interestingly, one of the judges was an Ascough; the same name as the Bishop of Salisbury murdered here nine years later. The outcome cannot be established, but the possessions of the Bonhommes increased in 1444 when John Stafford became archbishop and gave them a nineteenth manor, that of Baynton from the Rous family. In 1452 they were again excused a clerical tenth on grounds of their poverty, after the 1450 sacking.

You've heard about the death of Bishop Ascough, but perhaps not been told that I found recorded that 'The body of him was buried in the House of Bonhoms at Hedington and on the spot where he was killed there is now a chapelle and hermitage.' *Jackson notes that villagers in the nineteenth century 'used to show, as the scene of the murder, a spot where they pretended that the grass grew so rank and strong that cattle refused to eat it'. Many books give Edington Hill or Golden Cap Hill to the east as the site of the chapel. Certainly a cistern up there still has a stone base. But going back to the original account of the episode, a 'hill there beside' is more likely to be the one opposite the chancel, where Ralph's Seat is today. Send for Time Team!*

You've also heard about the try-on over the high cost of entertaining those on the road through here in 1394. It was included in a letter to Bishop John Waltham from those appointed to inquire into a petition from Thomas Odyham to confirm them in the rectory of Kyvele (Keevil, east of Steeple Ashton) 'because their revenues are much diminished by plague and the burdens of hospitality and because property worth forty marks yearly and more was not amortized at the death of their founder . . .' The brethren basically secured what they asked for. (EC.217–23)

Another financial story I discovered dates from 1408. The newly elected Bonhommes rector Thomas Culmer wrote to John Brekevyle, Prior of Mottisfont. He cited the former rector, Thomas Lavynton, as having failed for twelve years to receive the 26s 8d a year previously paid to Edyndon by the prior for his plurality as incumbent of nearby King's Somborne, north of Romsey. The case went all the way to Westminster, with Culmer winning on 12 April 1410. The attorney for the prior took the line that the church was held in perpetuity to the prior personally and his bishop had freed him from all payments. That argument failed now, but was to become all too familiar and successful by the end of the fifteenth century when used by local gentry to gain parish tithes rather than allowing them to go to the monasteries. The argument was that these gentry needed the money to finance their appointees to minister to the parish laypeople. Sadly, by 1500 this money corrupted many gentry, who pocketed it as reward for former outlay and did little more.

Local Boy John Stafford

I mentioned John Stafford, and I know you've heard of his role in Cade's Rebellion. I want to go back one archbishop to Henry Chichele (1414–43). He was first involved in state business when sent with Sir John Cheney to Pope Innocent VII in Rome in 1405. In 1409, as newly consecrated Bishop of St David's, he accompanied the then Bishop of Salisbury, Robert Hallam, to the Council of Pisa set up to stop the rivalry between the pope in Rome and antipope in Avignon. Both were deposed and Alexander V was elected to Rome. Those who were deposed refused to comply; chaos followed.

The young Henry V came to the throne in 1413, and set about increasing the persecution of the Lollards. Sir John Oldcastle had helped the Crown suppress a Welsh revolt, and had married the heiress of the barony of Cobham. Though a friend of the king, when his sympathies for the Lollards were revealed he was summoned as Lord Cobham before the Lords. His refusal to attend, his arrest and escape ended in insurrection and massacre.

The royal councillors and Archbishop Chichele decided that the unrest at home and restless disposition of the king could be focused overseas by reviving the old claim of Edward III to the Crown of France. The archbishop obtained agreement of the clergy to a grant of two tenths for the war (Edyndon did not pay, of course), and further replenished the state coffers by selling certain lands belonging to alien priories; it was virtually their dissolution. Rome was in no state to complain. The 1415 victory at Agincourt made it all worthwhile.

Like Chichele, Stafford was in a difficult situation regarding Henry Beaufort, who seemed to be favoured by the papacy. Beaufort was the second son of John of Gaunt and his mistress in France. Born there, he and other siblings of the relationship were legitimized by Richard II and Parliament. In 1398 he became Bishop of Lincoln, and four years after his half-brother became Henry IV he was made chancellor. In 1404 he resigned that post when consecrated Bishop of Winchester, possibly because he was opposed to war. Henry V made him chancellor again in 1413 but he resigned in 1417. Pope Martin V proposed to make Beaufort a cardinal in gratitude for his contribution to the 1414 Council of Constance, the next after Pisa. Archbishop Chichele objected, and the king refused to allow him to accept. When Henry V died in 1422 Beaufort and the uncles of the baby Henry VI became joint regents. In 1424 Beaufort resumed the chancellorship for two years before falling out with the other regents. The pope partially extricated him from England to be papal legate for Germany, Hungary and Bohemia as a cardinal. However, until his death in 1447 Beaufort, still Bishop of Winchester, meddled in English politics, taking contrary positions to other powerful advisors to the king and always wriggling out of traps they set for him. *Remember John Stafford was chancellor from 1432 to 1450.*

From my studies I believe that, despite high office, Chichele and Stafford made a conscious effort to limit involvement in the machinations of court and Parliament, Crown and papacy in the second quarter of the fifteenth century. They concentrated on bringing a new stability to middle England and in particular to rural life. As new opportunities arose for education of the sons of the middle class, they saw the springing up of a different local gentry, which meant merit could be the criterion for who held sway in a village or town community. The new gentry were encouraged to deeper involvement in their local church, and not just in the traditional publicizing of their wealth with benefactions. They were encouraged to force minions to attend services and lend weight to the priest's promise of damnation for listening to heresies elsewhere. Possession of a New Testament in English remained a crime punishable with branding as a heretic. Equally, though, they felt the common man's preparedness to question his faith needed better explanation from the pulpit.

You've heard that Cade's Rebellion resulted in no bloody retaliation. This and other aspects of the 1450 event show how successful Chichele and Stafford had been. The demands of the rebels did not involve any call for religious reform, showing that Lollardism was virtually dead. They asked for the repeal of the Statutes of Labourers, but little else related to the social condition of employees vis-à-vis farmers and landowners. The Peasants' Revolt had sorted that out. Thus a French observer found that England in the 1470s, of all the countries he had known, was 'the one where public affairs were best conducted and regulated with the least violence to the people'. For the rest of the century kings changed and the peerage slaughtered one another, but the battles affected only small areas of the country and the rest carried on living contentedly.

In 1463 Wey must have made all at Edyndon feel a closer identification with the Holy Land and the life of Jesus. Clearly there was investment in the furnishing of the church, as happened to some degree almost everywhere. This depended, of course, on the whim of the gentry, making for some discrepancy not just in furnishings but in religious observance between neighbouring parishes. The skill of the carpenter blossomed, with rood screen, reredos, Easter Sepulchre, misericords and sometimes even seating for parishioners. Here we still have the pulpitum of about 1495, a more effective screening from the parishioners of the brethren at worship. Being wood and textiles, of course, these furnishings were equally easy to remove.

Such discrepancies put the bishops on their mettle to provide guidance for the poorer qualified incumbents regarding standards of churchmanship, common practice in hearing confessions and sermon content. Caxton's first printing press was not built until 1476, so the cathedral and monastic scriptoria worked overtime.

Incidentally, there must have been seating for the brethren from the outset, because the 29 March 1358 letter states: 'At vespers, matins and the other canonical hours on great feasts, half the choir shall sit during one psalm and half during the other psalm, but on other days all shall sit during the singing of the psalms.' I loved another bit: 'At all the canonical hours a bell shall be rung first to summon for as long as it takes to say a Hail Mary. After a suitable break for the brethren to answer the calls of nature, another bell shall be rung to summon them to gather in the church.' *(EC.23)* I digress.

The second half of the fifteenth century saw the gentry increasingly wishing to be remembered with monuments in their parish churches. John Stafford's mother Emma died in 1446 and he had her buried in North Bradley church with a fine monument. *There is still a floor slab to her memory.* I cannot shed light on whether your south transept monument and Cheney monument date from then. It's highly likely that in addition to the pulpitum you'd have had a rood screen by 1500 between the westernmost tower columns, extended with screening across both aisles. Thus the brethren could have come and gone to their chancel chapel without contact with others. The rood screen would have had two doors in it to permit processions at major festivals to pass to and from the chancel. One door would have served as access for a brother to conduct duties towards the parishioners and chantries. Certainly within a decade or so, if not sooner, a nave altar would have been placed in front of the rood screen.

Mention of Emma reminds us that John's father is mentioned in EC.48 and 49. They refer to a squabble between those responsible for the North Bradley

The pulpitum from the chancel

chapel and the Grevyle family who had a chantry chapel in their house at Southwick. The relevant section describes the Edyndon rector 'admitting to the vacant perpetual chantry in the chapel of the manor of Suthwyk, Richard Lakynton, chaplain, whom Humphrey de Stafforde, knight, patron of the chantry, presented to the Rector and Convent on 5 June 1397'.

Congregations responded positively to the initiatives that I've mentioned. A surprisingly genuine interest by even the humblest souls appears everywhere in the records; a desire to understand more of what the liturgical year and associated ecclesiastical rubric and Latin really meant. They needed little motivation to become supporters of initiatives to add vitality to worship. Religious processions outside church, religious bonfires at sites given new religious significance, and the placing of statues of Our Lady and new and old saints at street corners became the norm. Guilds were formed to organize the celebrations of particular feasts, that of Corpus Christi especially being elevated to new importance. Plays and carols, both imported ideas, fulfilled a new and vital teaching role in this movement.

Holy Week involved unique features for laypeople, with Good Friday a day of deepest mourning. All went barefoot to church and crept on knees to kiss the base of a crucifix, which was held by the priest dressed in his mass vestments. There was no mass to follow, but the priest, having shed his vestments, carried the host in a pyx (consecrated on Maundy Thursday) and the kissed cross, now veiled, to a sanctuary. In many churches this was an Easter sepulchre, as I believe Graham has told you.

A race now started to be buried as close to the main altars as possible, rather than in the side aisles or churchyard. Of course the new gentry were the winners. It had long been the practice to bury children as close to the walls of the church as possible. All this led to the destruction of many space-consuming chantry chapels with altars, and erection of enclosed seating areas so that well-to-do family members could worship over the interments of their relatives. These screened enclosures commonly restricted the view of the nave altar, and it seems that side aisles were cleared and squints provided, where appropriate, to allow the perambulating congregation a view of the sacrarium. Preaching in English became an increasingly important expectation, and screened enclosures may explain the introduction of the first high pulpits. From 1500 onwards people further down the pecking order were allowed to provide bench seating for their families. Bench-ends became a carpenter's extravaganza. Singers were pushed into lofts above the screens, which were also strengthened to take the new status symbol, a small organ.

Thus not only were the monasteries assailed with ever-increasing taxation, but they also lost the initiative for ordaining what should constitute the spirituality of the laypeople. The reduction in demand for their intercessions on behalf of the dead hit them badly. The printing press reduced the workload for their scriptoria. They continued to own great tracks of land and remained important economically, but gifts and fees for services virtually dried up. Their initial reaction was to become more reclusive, but as we shall see more desperate measures were needed.

Morale in religious houses fell. We have an example of this at Edyndon. In 1502 a brother, John Hortone, was accused of twice breaking into the rector's house. The previous year it was alleged he stole silverware worth £13 10s (an indication of the worldliness of the incumbent). The second time he allegedly took 'a book called Byble' worth £20. Thirty years on I pondered these values as incredibly high, but thought of the labour of handwriting that book in Latin, probably with lavish illumination. Most such books surviving the Dissolution were destroyed later in the Reformation. *The finest survivor (in the British Library) is the priceless missal of Sherborne Abbey. With its inclusion of many coats of arms of Somerset families it bears witness to their new-found importance in the production of books for use in worship in the early fifteenth century.*

Wyclif must have been laughing from his grave. So much of his philosophy was coming to fruition in England, with the common man devising his own ways to salvation. Then a Czech priest, Jan Huss, who had come under the influence of Wyclif's writings in 1403, preached that the Roman Church had to clean up its act (even though he didn't agree with everything he translated). Excommunicated, he set out for the Council of Constance in 1414, but was not given safe conduct. The council put him on trial and convicted him; he burned at the stake in 1415. This was all good publicity and Wyclif's writings were more widely translated, causing a long simmering that boiled over when in 1517 Martin Luther openly denounced the sale of indulgences. Radical moves for change happened very quickly throughout the continent. Further medieval abuses were denounced, and failure by the papacy to respond led to rejection of its unyielding authority. Luther, Zwingli and Calvin rapidly moved to the creation of new systems of doctrine, organization and practice, which was given the title Protestantism.

The Influence of the Reformation on the Monasteries

In England we knew about what was happening on the other side of the Channel. There was relief that the papacy was distracted by it and not interfering in the way the Church was evolving, less radically, here. The reclusive tendency of the monastic houses couldn't last, because their former self-sufficiency was only viable given a certain level of income. Now they had to earn a living by such things as taking in lodgers ('corrodians'), providing education (often supplementing their own poor ability with an employed schoolmaster), turning guesthouses into hostelries, copying secular manuscripts and leasing out facilities such as corn and cloth mills. They bought their food and fuel instead of growing it and let non-residents in as staff. The size of the community at the gates grew *(much as William of Edyndon may have speculated would happen)*.

Though the monks and nuns had become much more worldly, they could not afford time for the necessary estate administration. Gradually they started to lose personal control as they appointed the equivalent of today's land agents. In many abbeys, particularly in towns, they no longer provided a priestly service to the community. They no longer allowed processions on Sundays (or even at great festivals) through the screen to the high altar in 'their' chancel. Instead they urged the gentry to pay for a vicar who would provide pastoral care and take masses at altars outside the screen. The laymen of the Name of Jesus guild, who now sustained a Jesus altar in front of the screen, saw it become the main parish altar, with no one wishing to see the high altar any more.

Edyndon had not turned into a town and I found no sign of a vicar, but the Hungerfords were rapidly growing into that land agent role. Closeting the high altar behind screens made the ritual more mysterious, and less personal to the layman in the nave. In some larger churches (possibly here) without a vicar, a system was devised in which a previously consecrated host was elevated at altars outside the screen just a fraction later than elevation at the high altar. Another new initiative, aimed at increasing the feeling of involvement, took place at the start of the mass. The giving of the peace had always been a symbolic enactment of St Matthew's demand that, before coming to the altar, if 'thy brother hath ought against thee, leave there thy gift . . . and go away; first be reconciled to thy brother and then come and offer thy gift'. In the earliest church the peace was symbolized by the sex-segregated congregation embracing those of their own sex. In Europe the kissing of idolatrous objects was linked to this reconciliation with a pax board. By the end of the fourteenth century the vessels in which the bread and wine would be made flesh and blood took on a lasting significance of representing Christ's body at all times, and in the fifteenth century a form of communion for the laity developed in which the celebrant kissed these vessels and then a pax board (often a piece of blade bone shaped like a paten and inscribed with a holy symbol), which was then brought outside the screen and passed down, so that all present kissed it.

The laity were also appeased at the other end of the mass, in order to strengthen a sense of community. Each family in turn brought a loaf to be blessed by the celebrant, and at the end of the service this 'holy bread' emerged and was divided between all the laypeople. Some pocketed a morsel as a good-luck charm for the coming week.

However, such initiatives by the clergy backfired: people felt that they made Jesus a condescending figure. They turned to greater veneration of the Blessed Virgin Mary as 'theirs' as against her son, who was identified with the priesthood. In consequence the gentry supported lady chapels outside the screen by refurbishing old chapels and even building new, always associated with private devotion of the laity. Typical is Westbury church, unlike Edyndon in a town and beset by many factions. The original Cheney chapel of around 1370 was demolished, all but one window, and rebuilt by Sir John Willoughby during the reign of Henry VI (1422–61). Initially named the Broke chapel, it became the lady chapel. This church has two other surviving chapels – the Mauduit chapel and the chapel of the Holy Name, built originally as the Rous family chapel.

This veneration by the laity of the Blessed Virgin Mary started in about 1425 and was tolerated because it had never been part of Lollardism; had it been, then the Church would have had to stamp on it. It was a convenient vehicle for letting the laity have its head, unfettered by the Church hierarchy, thereby protecting the hierarchy to a degree from disillusionment. Indeed, there was admiration of the devotion of monks and nuns; laypeople wished they could emulate them. In the 1430s the bishops called for wider access to the Lay-Folks Catechism, which was written in Latin. Ability to recite its Paternoster, Ave Maria and Credo in Latin were examined during confession. It was John Stafford as Bishop of Bath and Wells who first had this catechism translated into English, and he ordered a copy for every church in his diocese. Instead of being censured for it, on his death-bed in 1443 Chichele wrote to Rome recommending Stafford as his successor (without mentioning the heresy, of course!).

Books setting out the monastic methodology for devotion began to be copied for purchase, based on a seven-fold division of the day – a Book of Hours. Though everything in them had to be in Latin, a fondness grew of the fifteen gradual psalms (120–34) and seven penitential psalms (6, 32, 38, 51, 102, 130 and 143), one psalm overlapping the groups – 130. Their recital for the dead rather than the mass became popular, and of course surreptitious copies of the Richard Rolle translation into English were around. Included in the Book of Hours was a Little Office of the Hours of the Blessed Virgin, the subject matter of which was amenable to explanatory illustration with beautiful wood-block prints.

Supplementary religious treatise and poetry in languages other than Latin slowly became available. When there was no outcry about such writings in French (for a limited readership among the gentry), English was tried. By 1500 Richard Rolle had become a saint and the Book of Hours was in English. The few Latin versions that survive (called prymers – derived from the first daily devotion being Prime) frequently have favourite poems in English handwritten into them. The Little Office of the Blessed Virgin Mary is invariably the most thumbed. Other female saints basked in a new light, like St Katharine of Alexandria (of the wheel torture fame) and St Margaret of Antioch (swallowed by a dragon, which exploded when she made the sign of the cross). By the early sixteenth century horror was a powerful influence.

The Bonhommes would have seen John Stafford grow up and perhaps been involved in his religious upbringing through their responsibility for the chapel at North Bradley. He had a softly-softly approach that some felt amounted to pusillanimity. For example, when Reginald Pecock, Bishop of Chichester and a determined adversary of the Lollards, investigated the mendicant orders and exposed grave faults in their practices, and became an advocate of reinforcing the Roman supremacy, his treatise was sent to the archbishop. He expected action but nothing happened.

Despite all the problems I've outlined for the religious houses, some still managed to command respect as powerful centres of spiritual life into the sixteenth century, with many worthy souls still joining and intent on improving their reputation. However, some smaller houses closed or changed into educational establishments. Jesus College, Cambridge, was until 1496 a nunnery that had a reputation for licentiousness. The house of the Black Augustinian Canons at Longleat could not make ends meet, and in 1530 handed its lands over to the Carthusians at Hinton Charterhouse. Here at Edyndon I discovered there were problems with two brothers running away on separate occasions. The bishops, led by John Morton, Archbishop of Canterbury 1486–1500, took steps to get rid of any depravity. In 1489 Morton obtained a papal bull authorizing him personally to visit certain monasteries that were exempt from diocesan supervision. This enabled him to take vigorous action against St Albans, where he insisted on a clean-up of abuses within sixty days.

In 1462 the different constitutions of Canterbury and York had been reconciled and the advent of the printing press enabled York, Hereford and Salisbury, towards the turn of the century, to print their own versions of the liturgy (still in Latin) in considerable numbers. Printers in Salisbury did overtime, leading to ever wider adoption of the Sarum Rite in the south and in Wales. It even spread to the continent. *It was strictly followed in parts of Portugal and north Spain into the twentieth century.* The liturgical calendar kept changing to reflect devotional fashions, with new votive masses like 'The Crown of Thorns', 'The Five Wounds', 'The Visitation of the Virgin' and in the 1490s 'The Transfiguration of Christ' – according to Luke chapter 9 the supernatural form in which Christ appeared to three disciples even before his death.

However, in 1511 it suited politically to side with the pope. France looked intent on seizing the pope's domains, which would have made it dangerously powerful. England joined Spain and Germany in the Holy League to thwart this. Wolsey became Archbishop of York and chief minister in 1515. In gratitude for his assistance the pope made him a cardinal and in 1521 bestowed on Henry VIII the title 'Defender of the Faith' for having personally written of the value of the seven sacraments against the attack of Luther. *The title is used by the sovereign to this day.*

Cardinal Wolsey set out plans to found colleges at Oxford and Ipswich and applied pressure for funding, with the result that twenty-nine monastic houses 'voluntarily' closed, handing over their residual wealth in the period 1524–29. However, in 1529 Wolsey fell from grace for not completing in the king's favour the inquiry into the legality of his marriage to his brother Arthur's widow, Catherine of Aragon, before the pope withdrew the jurisdiction to Rome. Into power came Thomas Cromwell to deal with the pope's refusal of an annulment. A major clash with Rome looked on the cards, and the possible reaction of religious houses was of concern. Immediately after Henry married the evangelistic Anne Boleyn bigamously on 25 January 1533, John Leland was tasked with establishing what antiquities were held by the cathedrals and religious houses. That the Dissolution occurred hampered our work, and we did not complete the task until 1546.

The Crown's apprehension proved well founded, for in 1533 Cromwell was told by Sir Walter Hungerford that the prior at local Hinton Charterhouse said he would never recognize the Boleyn marriage. Incidentally, Anne was the daughter of Sir Thomas Boleyn, Earl of

Wiltshire, holder of the title after a succession of Staffords onward from the son of Humphrey, first Duke of Buckingham – *remember that Humphrey's role in Cade's Rebellion*. Anne's mother was higher born than Sir Thomas, being Lady Elizabeth Howard, daughter of the second Duke of Norfolk.

I hope I have given you a background picture of the state of the monasteries and nunneries that we were to investigate. We were of course all agog as to what would happen next. On 23 May 1533 the new twice-married archbishop, Thomas Cranmer, declared the previous royal marriage null and void. On 1 June, Anne was crowned queen consort. On 7 September a daughter Elizabeth was born. On 23 March 1534 Parliament passed the Act of Succession invalidating Mary, born of Catherine, in favour of the children of Anne. Rome launched sentences of excommunication on Henry VIII and the archbishop. Inevitably, Henry responded by having Parliament pass the Act of Supremacy in November, making him head of the Church in England. All the Somerset Carthusians vowed martyrdom over this loss of the pope's supremacy. An oath of allegiance was, therefore, required of all houses, as was payment of all income for the year from 1 January 1535 to the new head of the Church.

The Clock Strikes Eleven

The Dissolution

The Valor Ecclesiasticus was an exercise to assess the sum due. Large numbers of income assessment commissioners were appointed to draw up an income statement of all houses by 30 May 1535, with severe penalties for deception. Sir Walter Hungerford was the commissioner for Hinton Charterhouse and here, with Sir Edward Baynton commissioner for Stanley and Malmesbury Abbeys.

Edyndon, with income of £442 (£7 from their ecclesiastical courts including Tenhyde), was ranked eighth of the thirty-one religious houses remaining in Somerset and Wiltshire, behind Glastonbury, Malmesbury, Bath, Wilton, Amesbury, Montacute and Muchelney. It was well ahead of Cleeve (£155), Lacock (£168) and Stanley (£177). Numbers of monks/nuns in the latter were seventeen, nineteen and nine respectively. The Bonhommes were just thirteen in number, including John Ryve as rector.

Early in 1535, the itinerary for the summer progression of Henry VIII and Anne Boleyn around the West Country was published. A Nicholas Poyntz of Winterbourne (northeast of Bristol) was on the list, and he had 350 men construct a new wing at his Acton Court for the visit, thereby earning a knighthood during the stay. Also on the list were the Paulets at Basing in Berkshire and Sir Edward and Lady Isabel Baynton at Bromham, 10 miles from Edington. Having been joined by Cromwell, on 4 September the royal party went from Bromham to Wolfhall near Burbage, home of the king's lecherous friend, Sir John Seymour. (As an example, he had two children by a son's wife.) His daughter, Jane, had been at court since 1530 as maid of honour to Catherine of Aragon and then Anne Boleyn. Where and when an affair between Henry and the Catholic Jane Seymour began is unclear, but it was common knowledge by February 1536.

In summer 1535 a set of four visiting commissioners were tasked with checking the spiritual rather than temporal state, looking for laxity, scandal and abuses. They started in the West Country, and it was their early findings in the smaller houses that gave the excuse for Cromwell as the king's spiritual vice-regent to present a bill in early 1536 whereby all houses with an income of less than £200 were suppressed. All their property had to be gifted to the head of the Church and arrangements made for their numbers to be integrated into larger houses. Ostensibly the money was a war chest against Rome's plans for military action against England, and certainly the finest ships of the fleet, *Mary Rose* and *Henry Grace de Dieu*, were virtually rebuilt by 1540.

A new department handled the receipts: this was the Court of Augmentation. Dissenters were executed; there was a sigh of relief among those who survived. I felt that to Rector Ryve it seemed to be a sensible rationalization, given the recent monastic changes. The Augustinian canonesses of Lacock were spared the first suppression by paying a fine of £300, probably through the good offices of Sir Edward Baynton, whose sister Elizabeth was a nun there, and his first cousin, Joan Temmes, the abbess. But what would the visiting commissioners eventually report about Edyndon? They knew what Cromwell wanted to hear, and many wrote of scandals beyond belief; but some seem to have been more honest. From September 1536 these four commissioners went to the university towns, and then had a period examining friaries that had been exempt from the 1536 Act of Suppression.

The first visiting commissioner to come to Edyndon was John ap Rice (Rees), a Welsh lawyer. Was it coincidence, I thought, that the Edyndon Romsey manor farm had been leased to a Meric ap Rice for forty-five years in 1531? Was that too early for there to have been a bribe? Anyway, John reported from here on 23 August 1536, and enthused about the well-conducted house at Lacock! 'At Edyndon we found the Rector a man of good name, but not so his brethren. The youngest, who has confessed an unnatural crime, partly for lack of age and want of good will to continue, has been discharged of his coat.' Quickly following was a second commissioner, the young lawyer Thomas Legh, whose insistence on being royally received and his contemptuous attitude were reported by Rector Ryve to ap Rice. He protested to Cromwell, probably to no effect.

Meanwhile, the Court of Augmentation appointed its own wealth collection commissioners, one for each county; for Wiltshire it was Sir Henry Long. Each had to form a team to verify sale of assets and wind-up payments for each of its suppressed houses. Diaries were complicated by the need for each team to include one of seventeen auditors of the court and a regional receiver, besides local gentry. The receiver for Gloucestershire, Wiltshire, Bristol and Hampshire was Sir Richard Paulet, who secured William Berners as auditor.

The rector here, John Ryve, died in May 1538. Illustrating the loss of control by the bishops, Sir Walter (as of 1536 Lord Hungerford of Heytesbury) wrote to Cromwell: 'The Bishop . . . has power to admit one of three whom the brethren of the house shall present to him. I desire your Lordship to write to the Bishop in favour of a friend of mine whom the brethren have nominated – Sir Paul Busche . . .' Bush had become a brother only eight years previously and was already corrector. He became rector.

The four visiting commissioners continued around the country from 1537 to 1539, visiting the larger religious houses and making it clear that Cromwell meant what he had said in a letter of early 1538. Heads of houses were to put in the stocks anyone who did not trust Cromwell's word. They were to keep their houses in good repair, for the king 'does not intend in any way to trouble you or devise for the suppression of any religious house that standeth'. The Bonhommes apparently made a gift of the advowson of North Bradley to Cromwell in 1538. Was this because they were unable to pay demanded taxes, or because of gratitude for the letter, or under pressure from Lord Hungerford for a sweetener that would put him in a good light? Many saw the writing on the wall, and 150 houses voluntarily surrendered in 1538 and early 1539, knowing that Cromwell was very disappointed in the rate at which money was coming in from the first suppression. The inevitable second act came in mid-1539, and those who held out were charged with treason. This resulted in three great abbots, Glastonbury, Colchester and Reading, suffering horrible deaths.

Edyndon, at one stage unsure that their brand of Augustinian canons counted as monks, was a voluntary surrendering. It happened on the afternoon of 31 March 1539, after Hinton Charterhouse had surrendered in the morning. It was to Visiting Commissioner Sir John Tregonwell, a Cornish lawyer who had been involved in negotiations for the Catherine of Aragon annulment.

In the interim Anne Boleyn was executed, in May 1536 (with Sir Edward Baynton much involved in the framing of charges). Henry's third wife Jane Seymour produced a son. Her brothers, Edward and Thomas, saw the prospect of becoming regents. The king was urged to declare Princess Elizabeth a bastard.

Post-natal complications led to Jane's death in October 1537. Another blow to Cromwell, now called vicar-regent, took place when he and England's first married archbishop – Cranmer – thought it opportune to write a Bishop's Book setting out the regime under the new head of the Church. (Cranmer's first wife died, but he hid from the king that during his embassy to Germany in 1531 he had engaged in clandestine meetings with the noble hierarchy that supported Luther's way ahead assuring them of Henry's sympathy. During this activity he was befriended by Osiander, the Protestant reformer whose niece he made his second wife.) Unfortunately the draft that Cromwell and Cranmer produced leaned too far towards continental Protestantism, and was returned by the king with page after page covered in corrections. Henry produced the statute called the Six Articles and had Parliament pass it in 1539. It declared as necessary the doctrine of transubstantiation, communion in one kind only, celibacy of the clergy, vows of chastity, authorization of private masses and continuance of auricular confession. He was still a perfectly orthodox Catholic – and he was going to take some convincing that Cranmer and Cromwell's iconoclastic onslaught on the cathedrals and churches was in the new Church's interest. Thus, with arguments that England needed allies lest France and/or Spain formed a Holy League to invade, they proposed his marriage to a daughter of one of the Lutheran princes. If the result was successful she might sway him towards the church they foresaw. Holbein was dispatched to paint the possibilities, and a flattering miniature of Anne of Cleves had the desired result. Aged twenty-five, she was married to Henry VIII on 6 January 1540. Cromwell, who had been created a baron in 1536, was made first Earl of Essex on 18 April. But success was short-lived.

So who got what out of the Dissolution? For some time Lord Hungerford had been sweating over whether he would be offered the Hinton Charterhouse and Edyndon estates. His concern was that his third wife had smuggled a letter to Cromwell complaining that he had imprisoned her in one of the castle towers of Farleigh Hungerford with little to eat or drink, in the custody of his chaplain (William Bird) who had tried to poison her. To his great relief Tregonwell gave him the opportunity to purchase the former but not the latter. Within weeks, however, while Hungerford was away in London, a Sir Thomas Arundell of Wardour Castle 'despoiled and carried away a great part of the church and buildings'. Hungerford complained to Cromwell, but was shocked when he was suddenly arrested early in 1540, along with his chaplain. He was charged with harbouring a traitor, as Bird had sympathized with the Pilgrimage of Grace, an insurrection in the north of England against the loss of the pope's supremacy.

The king quickly tired of Anne of Cleves, and on 10 June 1540 Cromwell was arrested. There was no apparent charge or trial. Cromwell had always been Hungerford's patron, and with his fall the bitter Lady

Hungerford pursued her vengeance. Her husband was charged with unnatural vice against his son. Hungerford became the first person executed under the Buggery Act of 1533, and was beheaded on Tower Hill alongside Cromwell on 28 July 1540. Hungerford's lands were confiscated by the Crown.

The change of attitude towards Cromwell and his supporters stemmed from Henry VIII meeting Katherine Howard (daughter of the marriage of Joyce Culpepper to Edmund Howard, a son of the second Duke of Norfolk) in May 1540 at Winchester House, Southwark. You've probably heard of this large palace, home to the Bishops of Winchester for over 500 years. It had a long river frontage and a park of some 70 acres. *The last bishop to live there died in 1626. In 1642, when the episcopacy was suppressed by order of Parliament, the palace was converted to a prison for Royalists. It was returned to the see with the Restoration, but was in such a bad state that it was let out as tenements. The site was thereafter built on, and it was thought that no early structure remained standing until a fire in 1814 revealed the rose window of the great hall, 13ft in diameter, in a warehouse in Clink Street. Thought to have been built by William of Edington, this window and much of the west wall of the hall are very well displayed today.*

Katherine Howard became wife number five, only to be beheaded in 1542, chiefly for alleged dalliance with a relative, Thomas Culpepper. Then there was Catherine Parr, who outlived Henry VIII. But I must continue telling you who obtained what in Wiltshire.

Tregonwell bought Milton Abbey and its huge estates for £1000, and made the cloister his family home. Sir Henry Long moved his home from Draycot Cerne to South Wraxall, north of Bradford-on-Avon, after acquiring the estates of Bradenstoke Priory, northeast of Chippenham. Sir Edward Baynton acquired Stanley Abbey and demolished it. He used the stone, along with materials from Devizes Castle and a royal manor at Corsham, to turn his manor house into Bromham Hall, which was almost as big as the Palace of Whitehall. *The hall was demolished on 5 May 1645 in the Civil War.* The site and many of the estates of Lacock went for £783 in 1540 to Sir William Sharington, who knocked down the nunnery – all except the cloisters, which he converted into a house. *It survives almost unchanged today. Sharington is remembered for supplying Thomas Seymour with underweight gold coins. In 1549 he was imprisoned, but Thomas was executed before the trial and Sharington was freed after paying a heavy fine. He died in 1553 and has an early Renaissance tomb in Lacock parish church, in the northeast corner of the lady chapel on the north side of the chancel. In line with what Nick just said, this chapel was built at the end of the first quarter of the fifteenth century.*

The 1535 inventory for the Bonhommes shows the following rectorships under their control: Edyndon, North Bradley, Market Lavington and Keevil in Wiltshire, Buckland and Coleshill in Berkshire and Newton Valance in Hampshire. Many of the smaller holdings of land had disappeared, but nineteen manors remained. The thirteen in Wiltshire were Edyndon, Tenhyde, Baynton, Bratton, Imber, Dilton, Bremeridge, North Bradley, Bulkington, Market Lavington, Eastcott-in-Urchfont, Eastrop and Kingston Deverell. *Bremeridge is perhaps the only one not easy to find on a modern road atlas: it is west of Westbury.* The other six manors were Tormarton in Gloucestershire, Alvescot and Westwell in Oxfordshire, and West Ilsley, Buckland and, the most valuable, Coleshill in Berkshire. In 1532 three chief stewards were recognized for the majority of these – Sir Henry Long in Wiltshire, Sir John Briggs in Oxfordshire and Nicholas Willoughby in Berkshire. The advowson of Keevil went in 1541 to the Dean and Chapter of Winchester, perhaps as a mark of the William of Edyndon connection. *They still make the presentation to that living.*

Most religious houses deteriorated rapidly because the lead was stripped off the roofs and sold. Tewkesbury Abbey and Edyndon were among the few where the main monastic building doubled as the parish church, and they survived intact. By 1540 the land areas of Edyndon and Tenhyde had long been divided principally into 'Rector' and 'Romsey' domains by ownership. That year the Abbess of Romsey was given licence to alienate Edyndon Romsey and Tenhyde Romsey to Sir Thomas Seymour, who was granted most of the Bonhommes estate by the Crown. In 1544 he also received Lord Hungerford's estates.

His older brother, Sir Edward Seymour, had in 1536 acquired the estates of Maiden Bradley Priory, whose head was said to have had six children. He made the site his principal home. With the 1539 Dissolution he obtained the estates of Muchelney and Amesbury, some of the Stanley lands, the estates of Easton and Monkton Farleigh and much else farther afield. Tenants were very much in demand.

I now come to the first person named Baynton with a direct bearing on Edyndon. It was Sir Edward's second wife Isobel who took the tenancy of the converted domestic buildings here from Sir Thomas Seymour. She was born Isobel Leigh, child of the second marriage of her mother Joyce, born Culpepper. Remember I mentioned Joyce just now in her first marriage to Edmund Howard, during which she bore Katherine Howard, Henry VIII's fifth wife. Sir Edward Baynton (married to Isobel in 1531) had been vice-chamberlain of the queen's household from early 1533, to Anne Boleyn, Jane Seymour and Anne of Cleves. After Henry

VIII married Katherine Howard in 1540 her half-sister Lady Isabel Baynton became lady of the privy chamber until Katherine, as I said before, lost her head in 1542. Indeed, Sir Edward and Lady Baynton were custodians of Katherine when she was banished to Sion House while charges were compiled. Sir Edward died in France during the 1544 invasion that captured Boulogne.

Some say that Lady Isabel Baynton sought the tenancy in 1545; others say it was 1548, jointly with a Sir Henry Hastings (probably just a trustee), after a William Popeley vacated. Whichever, Thomas Seymour was not the landlord for very long.

Henry VIII died in 1547 and Edward Seymour became regent with the title lord protector to the infant Edward VI. Immediately Thomas Seymour married the king's widow, Catherine Parr. Catherine loathed her new sister-in-law Anne, née Stanhope. This Anne and her sister Elizabeth (married to the son of the late Thomas Cromwell) had been about the only friends of Jane Seymour when Queen. Catherine suspected them of now starting a rumour that her husband Thomas was having an affair with the teenage Princess Elizabeth, Henry VIII's daughter, and planned to become a widower and marry her. Whatever, the ex-queen, Catherine now-Seymour, died in September 1548 after childbirth. In 1549 widower Thomas, first Baron Seymour of Sudeley, Lord High Admiral, took advantage of popular discontent and plotted to overthrow his brother: he was arrested and executed for treason. Brother Edward was executed in 1553, but not before the Edyndon estates passed to Sir William Paulet, already Baron St John since 1539, made Earl of Wiltshire in 1550 and first Marquess of Winchester in 1551. *The Paulet seat, Basing House, was burnt to the ground by the Parliamentarians in the Civil War. In William and Mary's reign the sixth marquess was made Duke of Bolton, still holding the Edington estates.*

Back to the Bayntons. By his first wife Sir Edward had a daughter Bridget, who married Sir James Stumpe, son of William Stumpe, a wealthy clothier in Malmesbury. Sir Edward Baynton was able to arrange William's purchase of the abbey there for little over £1500. My boss, John Leland, recorded this, adding: 'Stumpe was the chief causer and contributor to have the abbey church made a parish church. At the present time every corner of the vast houses of office that belonged to the abbey be full of looms to weave cloth in . . .' Knighted, William made a home in the abbey buildings. He died in 1552, having seen his daughter-in-law Bridget die in 1545 and his widower son next year marry his stepmother-in-law, Lady Isabel Baynton. Why she needed the tenancy of the Edyndon estates thereafter might seem a puzzle – for

Sir James Stumpe had a home at Charlton, near Malmesbury, and after his father's death one in that town. *James died in 1563, and there is record of him leaving her the lease of Edington and all the plate left in the house. Isabel died in 1572. Perhaps the answer lies in the desirability of keeping in with Paulet, who blew like the wind about religious matters to stay in high office – he was lord high treasurer 1550–72. An avid Catholic in 1532 when he was made comptroller of the royal household, he saw things Henry's way, then became a Puritan under Edward VI, Catholic under Mary and was 'reconverted' under Elizabeth, persecuting alternately whoever stood for the opposite. Incidentally, could the fact that Tinhead has a Charlton Hill today have anything to do with Sir James Stumpe's involvement here?*

I can see that coffee is ready and I'd love a glass of water, if you would like me to tell you more about Paul Bush.

I was particularly fond of Edyndon and its library. While working over at Hinton Charterhouse I stayed in its lovely monastic guesthouse cum tithe store cum wool and cloth sales office in Norton St Philip. *The George today.* When I fell for a wench who worked there we decided to offer our services as secretary and housekeeper to someone I greatly admired – Paul Bush. That kept us in touch with Edyndon and the area, because his family acquired the lease of the manor of Dilton, and his brother John became steward of the Edyndon lands in west Wiltshire.

Paul Bush

Born of a local family in about 1490, Paul Bush was educated by the Bonhommes when they started teaching. He had potential, and his family let him join the community on the understanding that the rector would send him to Oxford. He obtained his degree in 1518 after studying at the Augustinian college, and stayed on, acquiring a reputation as a scholar, author and poet. He came back and became rector, as I told you.

At the Dissolution Bush did very well compared with the other brethren. The corrector, then John Scott, only received a pension of £10 a year, others only £2. Not only did Bush get £100 a year, but also the former monastic manor house at Buckland and some houses at Coleshill. He chose to go to the latter and we had one of the houses. Life was very pleasant, until suddenly in 1542 the king sent for him. He came back and told us he was to be the first Bishop of Bristol: Henry VIII had promised he would honour England's second city with the creation of a new diocese during that 1535 tour of the West Country. To make it a viable size, Dorset was to be added to the see. Paul was not all that enthusiastic for it meant giving up his pension for a more paltry salary.

Perhaps that was what lay behind Henry's manoeuvre!

Archbishop Cranmer's wife had been slipped back to Germany when he was elevated. The archbishop was highly influential with the lord protector and achieved legislation in 1548 that allowed his wife back. Bishop Paul took this as a sign that he could marry Edith Ashley, an affair we had known about for ages. Mary's accession to the throne in 1553 and the restoration of Roman Catholicism meant that a commission was on the point of passing a sentence of deprivation over his marital state when, in 1554, he decided to resign. He became Rector of Winterbourne (remember the Poyntz family home improved for the royal visit – Iron Acton Court), where a blind eye was turned to his marriage. The irony was that Edith died later that year.

As his secretary for all those years, I can tell you that Bishop Paul was no radical and didn't blow with the wind. He put God first in his life and was respected for it. In his last years he wrote against the 'rash fantastycall myndes of the blynde and ignorante' in defence of the mass and about authority within the Anglican Church.

Paul Bush died in October 1558, months after Queen Elizabeth was crowned. We all lobbied hard for, and achieved, a fitting monument for him, one which respected his married status. You can see it still in Bristol Cathedral. He is depicted as a cadaver (skin draped over a skeleton). "The plaque says he was last provost of the Bonhommes." I have no idea how that happened. I should add that Bush fared better than the married archbishop. For twenty-three years Cranmer survived and achieved much of value to the Church of England, but Queen Mary was instrumental in his being burnt at the stake in Oxford in 1556. *Bush's will survives in the cathedral records, and we can see that he lived well in his last years from the many possessions listed. These he bequeathed widely, including to those who had served him here.*

The same year a few local people fared little better under Mary's reign. A lady from Edyndon was taken to Salisbury for declining the kiss of peace as in the restored litany. She was arraigned alongside a lady of Salisbury who refused to raise her eyes at the elevation of the host. They did penance, but others died for nonconformity. John Maundrell was a Bulkington farmer who in Henry VIII's time had been accused of speaking out against certain church ceremonies, and did penance in Devizes for it. Now, he and two others interrupted the vicar during a service at Keevil church. Taken to Salisbury, penance was not an option and they were burnt at Bemerton – *just seventy-two years before George Herbert was parson there.*

One or two things have come up in conversation. Graham has told me that in the nineteenth century a Canon Jackson claimed my boss

John Leland recorded burials here of Sir Richard Penley who gave West Ilsley to the monastery, of Sir John Rous of Imber who gave Baynton, of an executor of Bishop William's will called 'Blubyri' and of a Willoughby. He also guessed that obits for Gereberd and Thomas Bulkington must have meant they were buried here. Well I have no recall of those details.

The water was wonderful and someone just told me the vaulted well is still there – *above where the stream flows under Great Woods*. Gather the lead pipe to the church has gone – not surprisingly. And now, Graham, I must go.

Post-Dissolution – The Domestic Buildings

Now our guest has departed, let us turn back to the history of the monastic domestic buildings. After Isabel Stumpe died in 1572 her son Henry Baynton (born 1536) took on the lease. Many books claim that it was not Henry but the eldest son of Sir Edward Baynton by his first marriage, Andrew, who was involved in the lease and subsequent damage, but he died in 1563. Confusingly, Sir Edward had sons named Henry by both his wives. His second son by his first wife was Edward (1517–93), who inherited the Bromham pile from Andrew – more on him in a minute.

A survey of the Edyndon buildings survives in the library at Longleat. It was made shortly after Thomas Seymour was executed in 1549, and states they were 'not yet defaced; the Hall with all houses, buildings, barns, stables and other houses of offices all covered with tyle, The Frater and Cloyster covered with ledde'. Nick spoke of cloister, and here it is again; not passageway.

To digress on several scores. The monument to the son, Sir Edward Baynton, in the southeast corner of the family chapel in St Nicholas's Church, Bromham, is well worth making a detour to visit (as guidebooks often say). Supported on rods projecting from the north wall is his helmet, decorated with a griffin, as in the device above the family coat of arms. His gauntlets also used to be there. This Sir Edward's first wife was Agnes ap Ryce, daughter of Sir Griffith ap Ryce and Lady Catherine Howard, another daughter of the second Duke of Norfolk. The latter was aunt to her namesake, who became queen consort, and also to Anne Boleyn. Bells ringing with the name 'ap Rice'? Sir Griffith was Welsh, his seat Carew Castle, Pembrokeshire. An article on this Sir Edward notes him selling 'his family's share of "Whitleigh", the ancient property of the Mauduit, Molines and Hungerford families', in 1571. This is intriguing as these names arise heretofore, and Mauduit is mentioned in the Edington Cartulary: more research is needed, perhaps.

That lease to Bayntuns (they had changed the spelling by then) expired in 1593 and the Paulets were informed that the buildings (including Tinhead Court) were in a shocking state. We know that a sale of stone had happened in 1585, for three cartloads were sold to the undyed-broadcloth-weaving Whittaker family. The stone doubled the size of their timber-framed Becketts House in Tinhead, which still stands today. One author believes demolition started in 1579.

The Bayntun son claimed a right to assign the lease to his wife, but the then marquess disputed this, and his letter of 20 July 1593 to the Keeper of the Great Seal includes reference to the damage: he had 'presently plucked downe the said howse, and hath so spoiled the same, as one thousande pounde will not reedifie it'. We know the marquess was on friendly terms with Sir John Thynne, who was building Longleat House, and it is probable that the fine Mansion House here, which the Lewys family occupied in 1629, was emulation in about 1600 to the extent that his purse would allow. In 1598 the marquess had made leases with two of his four illegitimate sons, John and William, on property here. A year later a house of unknown state in Edington was occupied by William Jones of Keevil, a man of some wealth who that year bought Brook Hall, Westbury, and a share of its estate measuring 280 acres. More on the earlier history of that building anon. One of those two sons, William Paulet, was living in Edington in 1603, perhaps in the new mansion. It seems he remained here until his death in 1629, which is the year when the Lewys family took the leasehold.

Anne Lady Beauchamp's son Richard Lewis (another spelling change) took the lease in 1664 and stayed until 1694. In 1665 he acquired the lease of what John Paulet had held. In the eighteenth century the main branch of the Pawlett family came back (amongst other change in spelling!) to live in the Mansion House. They included Harry Powlett, second son of the second Duke of Bolton, who became fourth duke and ninth Marquess of Winchester in 1754 and a privy councillor in 1755. He died in 1757. His son became the sixth and last duke and rose to be Admiral of the White in 1775. Both were buried at Basing.

The Clock Strikes Noon

Back to the Sanctuary

Let's look at the memorial slabs under the carpet again. This time these names will mean something more to you. Here is Lady Catherine Powlett, wife of the fourth Duke. And here is a Long family member, and there Richard Lewis, whom I just mentioned. Next to the Taylors, of Jamaican sugar plantation connections, is an odd coincidence; a reverend gentleman by the name of William Roots who died in 1830. Do you remember a novel called *Roots* by Alex Haley about a slave family in the United States? It won a Pulitzer special award in 1977 and was the basis of a successful television series by the same name. The brass plaque here is the already mentioned Anne Lady Beauchamp.

And now, standing by his floor slab just outside the sanctuary, it seems apposite to read some highlights of a lecture given by Canon Ralph Dudley to the Society of the Friends in 1988:

> ... I was inducted here as perpetual curate of Edington. A rector always got all the rectorial fees in the Middle Ages; a vicar who did some of his work was given part of the fees. A perpetual curate was given no fees at all, so there was nowhere for him to live either and perpetual curates were paid by the family who owned the land in Edington. Sometimes they lived in the Priory House over the wall here and the perpetual curate was also regarded as their chaplain which was useful on occasions.
>
> When the Pawlett family lived there in the seventeenth century (they were a peculiar lot) [eighteenth century?], one of them had an ailing wife, but he also had a girlfriend named Lavinia Fenton who was the first Polly Peachum in *The Beggar's Opera*. She was reputed to have lived at The Grange [in Inmead], which is a much older house than it appears from the front. He [Lieutenant-General Sir Charles Pawlett, 3rd

Duke of Bolton] went on a tour of Europe, hoping that his wife would die at any time, so he took Lavinia with him and also his private chaplain who was presumably the perpetual curate of Edington, so that he could get married as soon as he heard of the death of his wife. There is still a room at the end of the Priory House called the chaplain's room. Another of them trained his footmen on half-raw meat so that he could run better in front of his coach, carrying a lantern in one hand and a pole in the other to get the brambles out of the way. They made a road further along the Plain called Coach Hollow. [It runs up the escarpment this side of The Lamb in Tinhead.]

Lavinia was probably the illegitimate daughter of a naval lieutenant named Beswick. A waif born in Charing Cross, she became a child prostitute. When her good looks were recognized and she made an appearance at the Haymarket Theatre in 1726, aged about eighteen, she took the name of her mother's then husband, one Fenton. She became a great London beauty, and was captured by Hogarth in a painting of a Polly Peachum scene, with the duke visible in the box. They had three children before their marriage in 1751, all of whom died young. The duchess survived her husband, and references say she moved to Greenwich and died in 1760, being buried in St Alfege's Church there. So how come Canon Jackson in his 1882 notes on Edington wrote: 'In a vault in the church is a brass coffin-plate with this inscription "The most Illustrious Lady Lavinia Dutchess of Bolton, Dowager of the Most High Puissant and Noble Prince Charles Powlett, late Duke of Bolton . . . Earl of Wiltshire, &c. Died 24th January 1760. Aged 49 Years"?' A slight underestimate of her age, perhaps!

> Two parish priests covered a period of about a hundred years between them. William Roots [who was here from 1786 to 1826] lived in Warminster because of the absence of a house here. He was also curate of Erlestoke, but he was paid so little that he refused to take more than one service on Sunday. He rode over on horseback. He had to come for funerals of course, and in the churchwardens' accounts there is payment for 'a shed for Mr Roots to stand in' when he came over for funerals. It was a sort of sentry box set alongside the grave on wet days.

That puts me in mind of Penelope Carew Hunt's draft for the Parish News of July 1986:

> Soon after Canon Dudley arrived . . . in 1955, he appealed to the Parish Council to help find another piece of ground to be an extension to the

churchyard . . . finally a piece of orchard, owned by Mr George Drewitt was bought . . . and consecrated on 3 June 1986 . . . The Bishop, The Registrar and the Reverend Bird, suitably gathered under a large black umbrella, paced the boundary of the Ground after the Bishop has stood upon it, and with his Pastoral Staff marked upon the ground the symbol of our faith . . . Roger Pepler (who as Chairman of the Parish Council has spent much time bringing the provision to the parish) petitioned the Bishop 'Reverend Father in God, we ask you to consecrate this ground for the burial of our people.'

Let us quote from Ralph again:

> He [of the shed] was succeeded by Samuel Littlewood who was here for fifty-three years [1826–79]. He was an extreme Evangelical and, though his father was a friend of Garrick and Siddons, he regarded the stage as evil. One of his granddaughters, Gertrude, committed two terrible sins according to the family. First she became an actress and secondly a Roman Catholic. It was she who provided me with many details about Samuel Littlewood. She presented a portrait of him which is in the parvis. He was the last man in England to wear a beaver hat!
>
> In time the Watson Taylors built the lovely old vicarage, in which I lived for many years, but they kept the building and made Samuel pay rent. So out of £40 per annum he had to pay £16 rent; so he only had £24 to live on with his family in the 1830s. One Watson Taylor went bankrupt through gambling and could then pay him nothing at all. There was a long case in the House of Lords to try to get his stipend for him. Samuel produced long sermons, some of which are in print. The church used to be full of box pews in those days. People did not necessarily go to sleep while he preached his long sermons. He had a very loud voice so they did not get the chance, but in his days they used to play cards during the sermon. In his latter days the church decayed very considerably . . .

Mention of such a meagre salary puts in perspective a June 1836 notice sticker bill that I found among the possessions of Miss Penelope Carew-Hunt:

> Whereas, on the night of Saturday, the 21st May last, a WHEAT RICK belonging to Mr Mark Butler in the Farm Yard, at Tinhead, in the parish of Edington, Wilts, was Feloniously, Wickedly, & Maliciously SET ON FIRE by some evil-desposed Person or Persons at present unknown, and totally consumed, together with a LARGE BARN and other FARM BUILDINGS, HIS MAJESTY, for the better apprehending & bringing to

Justice the Persons concerned in the Felony has been pleased through his SECRETARY OF STATE to offer a REWARD of ONE HUNDRED POUNDS . . . And as a further Encouragement an additional Reward of £250 is hereby offered . . . such Reward to be paid upon Conviction. Apply to Mr Henry Pinnegar, Solicitor, Westbury.

There was a Butler's Farm on Ordnance Survey maps as late as 1924 adjacent to Becketts House. £24 a year to live on compared with a £350 reward is thought-provoking. It is interesting too that in my days as PCC treasurer over 160 years later the church paid its insurance through Pinnegar Finch & Co., solicitors of Church Street, Westbury.

Back to Ralph:

After him came the Reverend Henry Cave-Browne-Cave. He does not seem to have been very popular, partly because all the box pews were removed and partly because the row of lime trees along the front were reported by the architect to be pushing their roots under the south aisle, so they were removed. He quarrelled with at least six of the local farmers and all six of them died one way or another in one winter. He was so unpopular he was allowed to have nothing to do with the church restoration. Canon Wall, Vicar of Melksham, was put in charge and, if the committee were to meet in Edington, they had to find days for their meetings when Henry . . . was out of the village. However, he built the parish hall with money he raised.

The person transcribing Ralph's lecture notes apparently had as much difficulty with his handwriting as I have experienced. Francis Warre was Vicar of Melksham from 1876, tying in with the wall plaque I read to you, though he is not listed there as leader, only treasurer.

Of Charles Ponting Ralph writes:

He . . . was a very conservative architect so there was no Victorianisation of this church . . . When he first came to look at it, he found everything in a very dangerous condition, just as it is 100 years later. He said the [south transept] tomb should be sandbagged as the roof might fall on it at any moment. The Cave-Browne-Cave family were very loyal. One of his daughters became a nun. The other one, Irene, whose monument, a lovely stone, is in the floor of the north aisle, always took a great interest in the church and paid for a new entrance to the vault under the chancel, which could then be used as a vestry. She also left all her money, amounting to £4000, which paid for the restoration and improvement of the organ a few years ago.

That Watson Taylor vault is beneath our feet, with many of the side chambers emptied of their coffins and still in use for vestry purposes. In one chamber is a fine white marble tomb chest with lotus motifs and at each corner sugar cane plants. The inscription reads: 'To the memory of Simon Taylor Esq. of Lyssons Estate in the island of Jamaica, who died on the 14th April 1813, aged 73 years. Also to his brother Sir John Taylor Bart., who died on the 16th May 1786, aged 41 years.' Uncle Simon and our Simon's father are buried side by side at Lyssons, so was this monument brought from Jamaica?

"Did you know there was a 640-ton ship called the *Simon Taylor*, which was built in 1824 and wrecked off the south coast of England in 1849. As well as plying to Jamaica, it was used as a convict ship to Western Australia." British slaves!

The crypt does not extend under the sanctuary. Down its centre are several worn floor slabs, which are probably those of Bonhommes brethren. As I said before, they presumably came from the original chancel floor. When I first arrived in 1963 I remember Ralph telling us of the movement of the mostly lead coffins into the two eastern bays and of their sealing with breeze-blocks. The workmen inadvertently lifted the lid of one lead coffin in his presence. Amazingly, the face inside was perfectly preserved for just a few seconds, before the skin collapsed to finish like talcum powder on the skull.

Ralph loved his ghost stories, including the coach and horses on the B3098 at the top of Monastery Road, and several people seeing the lights on in the church at night and hearing singing. At twilight on one occasion a Miss Cunnington at the Monastery Gardens saw two men walk across the near corner of the Weir Field carrying a ladder. Suddenly they ramped down into the ground, and when she insisted a dig took place at the spot two skeletons were found. There was a door in a house that regularly unlatched itself, and a blood stain in another: whatever was done to scour it, it reappeared. Ralph knew Lucy Read in the village well but I do not recall him relating her ghost tale.

Lucy died in 2000. Her writings tell of her grandfather finding himself accompanied by a panting black dog when walking from Edington to Tinhead in the pitch dark. It made no response while with him, nor when he called after it when it disappeared near The Lamb. He was convinced that this was a ghostly experience associated with the story of a horseman who was racing to meet a wager and broke his neck in Coach Hollow. The headless ghost and dog have long been said to cross the B3098 from the hollow on moonlit nights.

Ralph was also a believer in dowsing. On one occasion I found him in church with an expert, seeing whether a pet theory applied: that Anglo-Saxon churches were built where two streams at different underground levels crossed, one running roughly east/west, the other north/south. Somewhere down the nave they found a T-junction, which proved nothing.

That is enough of that! Let us look at the railings next. They are Laudian in origin, though not in this configuration. They result from a directive to reverse the puritanical actions of the Reformation after William Laud became Archbishop of Canterbury in 1633. Nicodemus told you how the Court of Augmentation should have meant that anything saleable here would have gone. If it did not cause the disposal of artefacts as this was to be recognized as a parish church, then measures under the iconoclastic onslaught should have done. I say 'should', because how individual priests and congregations reacted, and how enforcement was applied, were variable.

The measures started little more than three years after the Act of Supremacy, with orders in 1538 to remove religious shrines and venerated relics. Many of the latter were within stone altars, which therefore disappeared. Statues were next to go, and then in 1547 removal of all images in wall paintings and window glass was ordered. Limewash did not cost much, but replacement plain glass was a different matter. In 1548 the remaining chantries were dissolved and their endowments were confiscated. The chapels, once without altars, were allowed to remain the property of their families with further interments allowed, as Nicodemus explained. Prebends were confiscated.

With Edward VI on the throne the pace quickened, with many days of celebration banned. In 1549 the first prayer book in English was issued. In 1550 all remaining altars in traditional positions had to be removed: a simple chancel screen was to remain to protect the chancel from the secular activities that were allowed to increase in the nave. Behind this screen a rectangular table was to be erected lengthwise down the chancel. The communion service in the new prayer book kept the congregation in the nave until the offertory, with the priest in a reader pew. Armed with their offerings, the priest then led the congregation into the chancel. They dropped money in the huge oak chest at the chancel entrance and filed into tiered stalls, facing inwards to the long table where the communion took place. In our case these stalls might already have existed, since the days of the brethren. *Remember that EC 23 quote about sitting during the psalms.* Church registers were ordered to be kept of services. They were to be stored in a chest with three locks, one each for the priest and two churchwardens. It was only to be opened with all three present. In 1552 a second prayer book was issued, more puritanical in tone and banning the use of vestments.

Queen Mary put everything into reverse, before Queen Elizabeth came to the throne and ordered the status quo in every church to be kept while reconciliation between the sharply different factions was sought. The first injunction was that every church was to have a chancel screen, but none was to display the rood on the top. (Remember we saw its form on the chancel reredos; the crucified Christ with St Mary and St John on either side.) For many this meant building anew, and to save money the choir and organ were no longer to be in the loft in any church but in the nave. They moved to the west end, initially on a raised platform, but gradually, because of space constraints and as orchestras became more common, musicians and singers moved into a gallery.

Under Charles I, Archbishop Laud introduced an aggressive High Church policy in order to achieve uniformity in all churches. Concerned about lack of respect for the altar, he ordered in 1635 that high altars be erected at the east end of the chancel, screened on three sides by railings to keep people and their animals from approaching it too closely. Anne

Lady Beauchamp complied. However, this altar did not become the focal point of the communion service until well into the eighteenth century, largely because that service took a back place to matins and evensong. For over a century most churches only celebrated the Eucharist once a month, apart from at the major festivals, which were now very few in number. It was not Ponting who had the railings made into a communion rail right across the chancel, for that article in The Antiquary says they were thus in 1882. You can see that a section to the south of the gates is of later workmanship than the rest.

To jump ahead a bit: given these dates for change start after 1633, it is interesting that the font cover's elaborate design should be dated 1626. What I have said about inward facing stalls explains the removal of the decorative stonework around the blind doorway in the west bay of the north wall – chiselled away for stalls. Clearly they did not extend as far east as the south doorway. And this ties in with the rectangular table having stood central to the lower floor level – the level then and now. That Canon Jackson, writing in 1882, mentions the blind doorway probably means the stalls disappeared well before the box pews. Incidentally, the two pairs of stalls on this side of the pulpitum are not original to this church. The seats are misericords. Lift one and you can appear to be standing while perching on the folded seat. Two have traditional carvings when you lift them – a dragon and a griffon, I think.

"But wouldn't the great Lewys monument have been right in the middle of the south stalls?" No: remember I said that it was up in the sanctuary until 1901. (You can see evidence that there was an accident when it was moved: it is badly cracked down the centre – see the fracture on the legs of the figures.)

"So unless the sedilia and piscina were part-mutilated during the 1450 sacking, I suppose we must put their present sad state down to her ladyship." Many, including me, would agree that there is surely enough detail remaining for the church to accurately restore them.

Anne Lady Beauchamp erected the marble and alabaster Lewys monument shortly after her second husband's death, I suspect. The 1630 date of the passing of Sir Edward Lewys is lightly etched on the slate at the back, but hers was just painted on over thirty years later. (Remembering his origins, is the slate Welsh?) The paint has faded, but we know the date in 1664 is 25 September, from the floor plaque I pointed out in the sanctuary. As you can see she had five children by him: Edward, William, Richard, Robert and Anne. I will leave you to sort out which is the girl, and also the arms on the shields.

Several references have Anne immediately marrying Sir Henry Glenham, of an East Anglian family, and having five more children before he died in 1632. No one has said where she lived during that marriage.

As we have seen, Anne was more highly born than the 'Right Worshipful Sir Edward Lewys late of the Vane in the countie of Glamargan, Knt. one of the Gentlemen of the Privie Chamber to Prince Henry and after to King Charles I', to quote his credits on the slate. Thus she rests as the higher of the two effigies.

Miss Inger Norholt restored the monument in 1966, and subsequently gave a report to the Friends of Edington Priory. This included her discovery in Glamorganshire that the 'pathetic remains of this once splendid house [The Vane] are still to be seen close to Caerphilly'. I also spotted a hamlet named Van in Montgomeryshire, the county where, as I said earlier, Sir Edward Lewys had estates.

Do you notice anything odd about the cherub or putti offering a crown of glory? It has two right hands. The crown is of wood, the stars of lead, and the article in *The Antiquary* suggests it is a replacement, the original 'having been stolen or lost'. Could that have been because Anne removed such a Royalist symbol during the time of Oliver Cromwell? Certainly some have thought the crown alludes to how close this couple were to royalty. Not only had Anne been the wife of Edward Seymour, the great-grandson of the brother of Queen Jane Seymour, uncle of King Edward VI, but her husband's grandmother was Catherine Grey, sister of Queen Jane Grey, who in 1553 nominally ruled for just nine days in a bid to prevent the accession of the Roman Catholic Mary Tudor. Anne's mother was Lady Margaret Howard, a descendant of Lady Elizabeth Howard, mother of Queen Anne Boleyn and grandmother of Queen Elizabeth I.

One day an American lady was photographing one of the boys on the front here. She claimed to be a direct descendant of him, and said that he was an early governor of one of the thirteen English colonies there. You might have thought the fourth child from the left was a little girl, from the dress with leading reins, but that was what boys wore until about the age of six. Also note that the protruding end of the hilt of Sir Edward's sword is a piece of Ralph Dudley's handiwork. The blade is an earlier repair in painted pine.

Miss Norholt found that the feet of the lion at the bottom of Sir Edward's effigy and part of the western drape had been sawn off. She repaired them and replaced the sword on the eldest boy, only for it to be stolen. The cherubs on the top had been smashed into many pieces and poorly re-assembled. She did a better job. Sadly the praying angel on the eastern end of the plinth will never fly again, for nothing was done about its clipped wings. Talking of things sawn off, notice how the crocketed pinnacles on the evangelist's niches have one crocket projection cut away. Scaffolders, I would guess, are to blame there. Another outstanding repair job!

As we are about to leave the royal family chantry, what better description for 'family' than this one-liner on the front of the monument: 'Since children are the living corner-stone, where marriage built on both sides meetes in one, while they survive, our lives shall have extent, upon record in them our monument.' It is sad, therefore, that floor slabs in the chancel tell us that two of Richard Lewis's daughters did not survive till their first birthday. Richard was MP for Westbury and in 1682 High Sheriff of Wiltshire. Some see the pen of George Herbert in that inscription.

Into the west side of the supporting structure for the monument is set a floor slab, which Canon Jackson tells us was by the blocked-up doorway before the first-floor upheaval (*see page 87*). It reads 'Here lieth John Allambrigge, clk, sometime chaplain to the Right Honorable Anne Lady Beauchamp who dyed . . .' The rest is mutilated. Why does he not appear on the incumbents list? And where was the slab for seventy years to 1901?

Looking back when the sun is out, we have a wonderful dappled colour on the walls and floor from the window in the middle bay. It depicts Faith, Hope and Charity, with their emblems, and is by Thomas Baillie and Co. of London. It is a copy of the 1770s west window in the chapel of New College, Oxford, designed by Sir Joshua Reynolds and painted by Thomas Jervais. And just look who the inscription tells us it is dedicated to – Elizabeth Mayne, widow of Colonel Mayne, second daughter of Sir John Taylor, Baronet. She who is probably a weeper on the Chantry

memorial and he who fought at the battle of Waterloo.

I cannot leave without mentioning the plaster ceiling. Jackson writes that the chancel was 'formerly ceiled with stone, having the arms of Bishop Edingdon on the bosses. The present ceiling was substituted by Mr Joshua Smith, of Erlestoke, in about AD 1789.' It is decorated, not with William's arms like Buckland but with mitred heads. I am not sure there is any evidence for the stone ceiling. As I noted before, the shadow shapes above the corbels look just like the timbers in the nave. Smith also put on a copper roof, which is quite spectacular if you look down from the escarpment.

So where does Joshua Smith fit in? Jackson tells us that the will of the fifth Duke of Bolton charged the estate in 1763 with payment of all his debts, and then assigned them to trustees to the use of his brother, the sixth duke, Harry Powlett. The testator died in 1765, and during Harry's lifetime the trustees sold the Edington estate of 4094 acres for £72,100 to Peter Delme of Erlestoke. There were legal complications as the fifth duke had left some of the estate to his housekeeper assuming she would have no male heir. She did, and Delme never completed a conveyance. In 1782 Joshua and Drummond Smith purchased the estate out of Chancery and it took an Act of Parliament in 1784 to sort out the title.

Joshua was MP for Devizes at the turn of the century, and increased his land ownership to 8000 acres with purchases in Coulston and Erlestoke. He knocked down most of the Mansion House here and used the stone to build a grand house, Erlestoke Park. Two rooms with seventeenth-century plasterwork ceilings were left, and a rainwater collection box on the north side of The Priory still bears the Paulet arms of three daggers. Jackson also tells us that there was an inn called the Three Daggers over in Tinhead on the main Salisbury road, already closed in his day. We referred to it when speaking of turnpike coach roads.

It was the executor of the will of Joshua Smith who sold the 8000 acres to the executors of Uncle Simon Taylor in 1820 for 250,000 guineas, with settlement to Anne Susannah Watson Taylor. This Anne and her husband George extended the estate as far as Urchfont. In 1830 they lavishly entertained at Erlestoke the Duchess of Kent, Princess Victoire of Saxe-Coburg-Saalfeld and her eleven-year-old daughter, the future Queen Victoria. That year Parliament passed the Regency Act by which Victoire, ten years the widow of Prince Edward, fourth son of George III, would act as regent if Victoria came to the throne still a minor. Such stays in the country kept Victoire away from the then king, William IV, who loathed her to the extent that he often said his deepest wish was to live long enough to see that regency unnecessary. In 1837 he succeeded – by less than a month. Did Victoria's visit include a Samuel Littlewood sermon or a guided tour here?

Second Day – After Lunch

Three things to notice before we finally leave the chancel. First is the end of this south pew, which has a shield-shaped representation of the early sixteenth-century seal of the Bonhommes which is in the British Library, there lozenge-shaped. The Blessed Virgin Mary and Child are at the top for Salisbury, then Peter and Paul for Winchester, with Bishop William holding his crozier at the bottom. Ponting has added the shields of Bishop William and Bishop Robert Wyvil to either side at the top and copied the seal's inscription – 'Commune Rectoris Conventus de Edyndon'. That supports the theory that the head of the house here was called rector. On the opposite bench end there are finely carved acanthus leaves. There is a leaflet by the south door, *The Estates of Edington Priory*, by the former librarian of the history faculty in Oxford, J.L. Kirby – with the seal reproduced on the cover. He was another of the lecturers to the Friends, in 1965.

Second are these two marble, or are they granite, slabs in the doorway of the pulpitum; they are over the original steps down into the Watson Taylor crypt. I have told many visitors that at the restoration they were turned over to hide the ring-bolts by which they used to be lifted for interments, but when

I checked I discovered there are no ring-bolts. It must have been quite an undertaking to raise them without some such arrangement.

Finally, this side of the pulpitum is Ponting's deduction of what the original c. 1495 structure must have been like. Floor level change caused no scarfing at the bottom of the new wood this side, but just look at that on the doors, which are original. They had 1ft 2in cut off when the floor was raised, and you can see the new wood that was added when it went back down. There are two carved double ogee design panels facing inwards at the ends, which may be earlier in date.

Right, let us go through to the north transept. "Wait, what about the little organ here?" It probably dates from the late nineteenth century. Above the keyboard is a silver plate engraved 'Alexr. Mills/ Organ Builder/ New York'. We know it was in a Christian Science chapel in Bristol before Ralph Dudley acquired it and gave it to Edington.

At Last out of the Chancel!

Look back at the original side of the pulpitum. Splendid carving, and what a rich patina. Notice that there is a groove around each aperture as though the whole may have been glazed originally. Canon Jackson tells us that the screen in his day was 'beautified with the Royal Arms, the Commandments, and Creed and the date 1788'. That 1882 article in *The Antiquary* states the arms as being in the centre and as dated 1783, besides adding the Lord's Prayer to the displayed texts. The loft above, both say, had been accessed by steps (Jackson) 'now closed up . . . in the corner of the north transept' . 'Beautified' is a matter of taste, for a surviving photograph shows no panel over the doorway; to each side was one almost square panel with a narrower one outboard. The questionably seventeenth-century (possibly German) wooden statues of St Mary and St John are thought a Ralph Dudley acquisition, finally placed here in 1991.

That early photograph is from the crossing opposite the porch door and shows the raised chancel floor with four steps up to it. The pulpit is one column nearer the tower pillars than now, with a reader's desk beneath and everywhere box pews. It also shows the emergency strappings and supports for the roof and columns of the nave up against the tower.

My wife and I helped the executors of Ralph Dudley's estate clear his home over at Southwick. Antique experts and a succession of book dealers went through his effects, but the final clearance had to be into a skip. I put aside two objects for closer examination. One was a small

Before and after the 1887-91 restoration

leather-bound book, 4in by 2in. It proved to be, to quote: '*The New Testament of our Lord and Saviour Jesus Christ. Newly translated out of the original Greek: and with the former translations diligently compared, and revised, by his Majesties speciall command. Printed at Cambridge, 1628.*' His Majesty was Charles I.

The second object was much more significant to the history of the church – a pencil sketch by the second wife of Samuel Littlewood, Ellen. Ralph had covered it in perspex and bound the edges with passe-partout (grained gummed paper). I recommended to the Parochial Church Council that it should have its importance written on the back and be placed on the inventory for the clergy living in the new vicarage. This was done, but one occupant and it was never seen again. Fortunately both the Wiltshire County Council archive and yours truly had poor photocopies.

Ellen's drawing shows her husband facing west about 3ft back from the top of the sacrarium steps. There is no nave altar, no black and white flooring, but the worn central floor slab of a brother is eastward from his heels, in the same position as today. The high box pews come east as far as the rear of the western tower pillars. At the west end the bottom foot or so of the west window is obstructed by a musicians' gallery on five columns. The wall is continuous across the back under the gallery. The two and two wall plaques you see either side of the doorway were shown equidistant on the wall.

I noted that a photograph from outside, of around the same time as Ellen's drawing, showed the double doors were still visible, if impossible to open. The situation is referred to in the *Trowbridge Chronicle* of 1880:

> The present condition of Edington Church is most lamentable; the wet penetrates through the roof and walls, and in many places the floor is green with damp. Some portions of the building are insecure, notably the west end, where the great doors are walled up to sustain the west window over. What we dread is that restoration will sweep away much that is interesting. We trust however that all the old stained glass of which so much remains, will be preserved and not treated as North Bradley, close by, where it was much smashed out with a hammer, because it was firmly fixed.

So that is how the arms of the monastery that Canon Jackson told us were there in the east window were lost.

In the Littlewood drawing the aisles have Jacobean plaster ceilings, just as in the nave. If you look up at the apex of the north wall of the north transept you see a date of 1663 and beneath a bowl of what look like

tulips. *(An article in* The Antiquary *of 1882 states the south transept had an identical apex with additionally the initials ND.)* Some have put forward the idea that the benefactor for the new ceilings made a fortune out of 'tulipmania'. I would like to think that it was Anne Lady Beauchamp doing rather more than just looking after the chancel – doing penance for having indulged a love of tulips or for damaging the sedilia?

Tulipmania perhaps deserves some explanation. It was a phenomenon that began among the Dutch bourgeoisie in which the prices of bulbs for the recently introduced tulip reached extraordinarily high levels, and then collapsed – in the first speculative economic bubble. A striped red and white 'Semper Augustus' bulb sold in February 1637 for 6700 guilders (then about £600) – equivalent to the value of a house on Amsterdam's smartest canal, as well as a coach and four. Six months later the bubble had burst. A less extreme version happened throughout Europe: hundreds of people made a fortune; thousands lost theirs. The story goes that one merchant mislaid an Augustus bulb in his warehouse, only to catch a sailor eating what he thought was an onion. The sailor spent months in jail.

Back to the subject in hand. In both the photograph and the drawing the western tower pillars and other arcade columns carried heavy memorials. As you can see, Ponting removed all but two of these on aesthetic grounds and to lighten the load they contributed. He moved most of them to the north transept. I will not dwell on any of them except the smaller one now on the north wall. This is to Edward Price, who died in 1806, and Sarah, his daughter, who died aged twenty-seven in 1799. They are said to be 'of Tinhead Court in this Parish'. This is the only reference I have found in the church to that building, and indicates that something habitable was left after the destruction by the Baynton son. Indeed, it was occupied by an Edward Carpenter in 1607, when it was said to be moated and with an ecclesiastical barn. When we first came to Edington in 1963 there was a fine barn of Tudor brick along the north side of Court Lane down from Shore House, which had earlier been Shore's Farm of about 100 acres. A wayward bulldozer, and the barn was gone.

There are a number of things to see from the north transept. In the aisle there is the double doorway from the domestic area of the monastery, still with a strong-back. Neither those doors, nor the door to the roof, have original woodwork. There is a blocked doorway in the north wall beneath the indistinct painting referred to by our first guest (*see page 57*). Then east wall, there is the no-longer blocked door (*see page 13*). Three of these openings employ a four-centred arch, which is stronger than a segmental arch. This is necessary because of the weight of the stonework above the opening.

GFL

Note the extent of the chiselled-away string-course, niche and piscina, presumably done so that wood panelling could be inserted behind the lady chapel altar. In its place is the seventeenth-century dark oak reredos, which was behind the high altar in the chancel until 1936. Some have suggested that Joshua Smith gave it because, as a salvaged chimney-piece from the Mansion House, it did not suit his new house at Erlestoke Park. The two sections of rail in front are thought to be Jacobean and came from Bradford-on-Avon Priory.

Look up and to the west at that strange window of one main light, five tracery lights and two eyelets. In the c. 1360 lower tracery, on the left, it depicts a seated gold angel wearing a brown robe and hat, with a part-obscured hand organ, and on the right a gold-winged angel with gold encircling nimbus and a draped yellow robe holding a part-obscured lute. A vicar here, the Reverend Neil Heavisides, suggested the left-hand figure might be St Jerome because the hat might be a cardinal's and the organ a book. St Jerome is credited with being the first to translate the Bible into Latin. On the north wall we have glass of the same date. The intact tracery design is based on simple crosses. Beneath this, down to a horizontal line, the glass is crocketed pinnacles of whatever formed the subject matter of the main area. Surely all those corbels and roof levels outside must have some connection with the loss of the stained glass below?

Panning round to the east wall we see the crucifixion window. As I said before, it is amazing that this survived when so much else outside the protection of the domestic buildings disappeared, presumably in 1450. The different degrees of discolouration and the irregular loss of painted detail have been put down to the difficulty that the glaziers had in obtaining quality coloured glass in the middle of the Hundred Years War. The best at this time was produced in France and not available. What could not be produced in England is said to have come from Hesse and Lorraine, particularly the blues and yellows.

The filling of all windows with highly coloured glass had become the aim by the late twelfth century for those wealthy enough to afford it, copying the French. The glass was coloured by adding metallic oxides while molten. Sheets were produced by blowing the glass into a cylinder, lopping off the ends, slitting it lengthwise and allowing it to fold out flat to cool. Some think that the growth in the use of a home-made grey glass called 'grisaille' was an economy measure, but it probably arose in England because our weather meant there was less light than on the continent. If you have been to Chartres you will know the feeling. On a bright day you are blinded on entry until your eyes are accustomed, and on a dull day you grope around in any case. That

there was grisaille low down in this window would be entirely logical – to light this dark northeast corner altar; not that the glass you see is original.

It is worth bringing binoculars to look at the very fine features in these windows. Look at the beauty of the sad face of Jesus's mother. This painting in black used a process centuries old, involving application with a brush of a suspension of copper or iron oxide mixed with finely pulverized glass in a gum and wine or urine flux. Before firing, the painting was covered in a little ash or quicklime. If you do bring binoculars, compare the standard of painting of the leopard's heads between the west window of the south aisle and those in the north aisle. Remember it arose before.

As we step back, look at the north aisle window above the doorway. It is the best preserved of these, with border decoration of the traditional lions for England and along the bottom fleur-de-lis, reflecting that Hundred Years War claim to the crown of France. See the yellow and black decorations on the plain glass of the diamond-shaped panes, called 'quarries'. There are ten different designs in what survive and I expect they were in all the church's windows that did not display a Biblical story. Imagine the beauty of the sunlight coming in through them. This yellowing is a fourteenth-century improvement in glazing techniques brought about by the discovery that on applying a solution of almost any silver salt to the surface and firing it, the glass was stained yellow. The intensity of colour depended on the strength of the solution and firing temperature, the darkest being nearly ruby coloured. At Edington it is to be seen in these border panes and quarries as well as on the mitre and robes of the saints in the clerestory windows.

GFL

A couple of pictures now. The Virgin and Child on the west wall is said to be a Victorian copy (of little merit, according to an art dealer – but they always say that!) given by a couple named Taylor at the time of their wedding in 1962. The wife wrote in 1985 that it was inherited by her husband from his grandfather, a vicar in Worcestershire in the 1880s. Older, probably, is this smaller version of the same subject on the plinth of the pulpitum. Written on the back is 'From a church close to the field of Waterloo. Brought home by Lt. W.B. Strong, the 44th Regiment, grandfather of the Reverend G.E. Long, Vicar of Edington, 1890–1910.'

"What about that secure-looking chest beneath the picture?" It is an Armada chest. Unlike most of the chests around the church we know where it came from: in 1958 Devizes Museum was unsure whether its floors could take the weight! It probably dates from the sixteenth or seventeenth century.

An extract from the *Wiltshire Times* account of the restoration tells us that 'The restoration of the nave altar necessitated the removal of the ringers from the ground floor of the church. By means of a specially designed bell stage, the bells have been raised some 14ft without exercising any increased strain on the tower as they still bear on the same low part of the walls, the ringing loft being contained within the bell frame.' The ceiling afterwards looked no different. In 1967 that wooden bell frame had suffered so much weakening by death-watch beetle that to ring was declared unsafe. A metal frame was substituted.

The restoration account also tells us that this cupboard against the northwest pillar was fitted 'with an apparatus to enable one person to chime them from the floor of the church. The clock and its machinery for playing 'God save the Queen' on the bells have been put into order.' Ralph Dudley was an expert at playing tunes on 'the apparatus', used it as a call to service, and had the servers ring the angelus on it during the Eucharistic prayer.

Remember the floor slab in front of the nave altar? You can see from here that the light shows up the indent that its missing brass causes in the carpet. It is of a priest, probably in a cope, and interestingly was reused probably three centuries later to mark the burial of an Emma Long. Just her name is enclosed in a simple lozenge, with no date. The processional candlesticks were given in memory of a young server, Dennis Bray, who died in 1968.

Look up at the northwest tower pillar. On the southwest-facing side of the shaft do you see some chiselling away of the stone? Ponting left that because he believed it showed the height of the rood screen. An old postcard shows how Ponting left the sacrarium, with a screen right across behind this same nave altar fixed to the tower pillars and similarly down the sides, to the extent of the first bay in the arcades. Those side sections of the screening are still in place, with the original sole sacrarium door in the southern one. In the screen behind the nave altar was a reredos of five painted panels set in the screen. They were painted by Miss Eleanor Warre, daughter of the Canon Warre I have mentioned. In the far right panel she drew William of Edington holding a model of the church and showing it to William of Wykeham, depicted before he became a bishop.

I believe it was either Ralph or his predecessor who wished to have access right round the nave altar, probably so that it could be censed – not that Ralph ever celebrated from behind it, facing west. The reredos found its way to Christ Church, Blakenall Heath, Walsall. The short sections of screen were joined and placed in the second bay of the north arcade, screening the organ: you can see the join. Incidentally, in Ralph's day servers came and went through the access door, never between the pillars and the altar except during the service.

I am sure that Eleanor's painted figure of our William inspired the designer of the appliquéd banner that stands here (*see front cover*) – though this time the church model is in William's other hand. The banner dates from the ministry of the Reverend Francis Henry Sprent, 1924–29. The other four banners that are around the church, Blessed Virgin Mary and Child, St Katharine, St George and St Giles, were made in Ralph's time by Mrs Gwenyth Luce, sister of Admiral Sir David Luce who lived at the Monastery Gardens in the 1960s. As the first submariner to become First Sea Lord, he resigned along with the Navy Minister when Denis Healey as Defence Secretary cancelled the building of two aircraft carriers. Luce was on the Dieppe Raid in 1942 and was chief staff officer to the naval forces for the D-Day landings in 1944.

Mulberry-coloured kneelers here in the south transept pay tribute to the armed forces. These, together with those in the nave and in the lady chapel, were all worked by parishioners and Friends in the 1990s. The St George's altar dossal (the drape behind the altar) bears a worn crucifixion embroidery bought in about 1960 in Ipswich by Ralph Dudley, and described then as 'very old'.

The Clock Strikes Two

The South Transept Monument

And so we come to this colourful monument. For many years this has been known as the Baynton Monument; yet the caption under the Buckler watercolour of the monument calls it 'The Monument in the South Transept of Edyngdon Church'. 'Baynton' would surely have been included if that name had been in use in 1826. While Ralph Dudley frequently followed convention, he advocated 'Beckington Monument' many times. Sir Harold Brakspear was in favour of 'Bulkington Monument'.

Monument in the South Transept of Edyngdon Church Wiltshire.

Perhaps the Baynton name is attributable to the writings of Edward Kite in 1860 (remember, he wrote of slabs with the arms of Bishop William). It probably stemmed from the foliage and barrel features of the monument and the practice I have referred to before of taking your name from the place of your family home or your favourite location. Kite perhaps saw 'Bay' and 'Tun' as being the closest site to fit the criteria: the manor Baynton was just beyond Tenhyde.

However, the Edington Cartulary refers to people with the name 'de Baynton' only some long time before rebuilding here. We have seen Isobel Baynton as the first bearer of the name to crop up around the well-documented period when the Bonhommes were here, and that only after the Dissolution. All these names beginning with 'B' and ending 'ton' have been guesses based on a combination of just two features of the monument. These are the supposed letter 'B' on its three monograms, as on the effigy's barrel, and that rebus of greenery sprouting from the barrel (tun) in eight places – top shield, two tomb chest front panels and five badge bosses under the protruding edge of the chest slab.

A rebus is effectively a visual pun. Its use goes back before William the Conqueror's time in some coats of arms, as a play on a family name. It has been thought in the past that the species of greenery here had to start with a 'B' to achieve the pun. That is now discredited, as I will explain in a moment. The speculation for 'bay' is obvious: 'bec' was medieval for 'branch' – hence Beckington; 'boc' was 'beech' and easily corrupted to Bulkington. 'Bolkynton' occurs as a benefactor and local witness to documents in the Edington Cartulary and, as I said earlier, in obits; there is nothing like Beckington, though. A *Wiltshire Notes and Queries* article, by E.T. Morgan during the First World War, suggested another candidate, an abbot of St Augustine's Abbey, Bristol, William Burton. He is said to have retired to Edington in 1536 and died here. Adding to his credentials is that he inserted a rebus of branches emerging from a barrel in a reredos beneath the east window in Bristol; but as we shall see this is not the only place that that rebus appears.

It has already been mentioned that the interregnum warden here in 1358, Walter de Sevenhampton, stayed close to Bishop William to be one of the executors of his will. In the Bishop's Register four executors are named. It omits the first of those given by Canon Jackson – Nicholas Kaerwent, Rector of Crundale, John de Bloebiri, Rector of Wytteneye, Thomas Hungreford, William's seneschal, Walter de Sevenhampton, Rector of Alresford, and John de Corfe, Rector of Collyngeborne Abbast. It was this Thomas de Hungerford, who endowed an obit for himself and witnessed several documents in the Edington Cartulary, probably while living at Heytesbury before the family moved to Farleigh Hungerford as previously mentioned. But perhaps of most interest was one who subsequently became a brother here: John de Blebury. Again I have already mentioned him: according to John Leland he was buried here. There is another spelling of his name: in an early version of the church guide Ken Rogers wrote that 'Leland also named a John Bloebury, a brother, as benefactor with a chantry.' I shall return to him; but for now I just ask you to note that his initials could be those on the two monogram bosses here under the chest slab.

The monument includes the figures of St Peter and St Paul, holding their symbols of keys and sword respectively, in corner niches. Does anyone recall seeing those symbols crossed? Yes – on the arms of Winchester diocese on the chancel reredos. Winton, as I told you, is the Latin signature of Bishops of Winchester. Thus one can see the rebus as vine (synonymous with wine/Win) and tun/-ton, again alluding to a Winchester connection. That rebus actually appears in a ceiling boss of c. 1530 in Bishop Langton's chapel in Winchester Cathedral, the greenery coming from the bottom of an upright barrel. That the south transept has been identified as the chantry for William and the Bishops of Winchester, not just by me but by Ponting, might suggest a very strong Winchester connection. However, I have to tell you that I believe the monument was originally erected somewhere else. But again, when a move was necessary is there significance in the fact it was placed here?

Let us examine the rebus more closely. The stem is clearly twisted in not only the top but most other depictions. Would not twisting be more likely to be associated with a vine rather than trees like bay or beech? If you look at the western front panel there are indications of side greenery, which might be tendrils like a vine. A vine leaf is clearly the motif of the frieze at the top. One must admit, though, that this decoration was widely used without Winchester association, many claiming that it symbolized peace in medieval times. Of the rebus at the top, someone has written that the leaves look as though of oak. Oak in French is 'chêne', leading to speculation that the rebus refers to Middleton Cheney – a place with Gilbert de Middleton and William de Edyndon connections. Or is this a clergyman member of the local Cheney family of whom we know nothing? Remember that we heard earlier of a Sir John Cheney, who accompanied Henry Chichele to see the pope in Rome in 1405.

Whether this monument is of 1380 or 1480, the Bonhommes were in, and answerable to, the Diocese of Salisbury not Winchester. All those documents quoted earlier had Salisbury's authority, not directly Winchester's. Bishop William is the focus for their connection with Winchester. The names of brethren show no such connection except for John Bloebury. But in any case would such an elaborate monument befit someone who never became rector?

Many commentators have noted the similarities of this monument to the Cheney tomb in the south arcade, which can perhaps be dated to c. 1425–50 – more of this anon. Besides the vine scroll similarity, there is the format of the chest with a panelled front, with identical cusping to our panels here, the remains of crested parapeting, the angels holding shields, the vaulted ceiling, the sides decorated with canopied niches and the outside buttressed and pinnacled. However, so are many other surviving monuments in other churches, dated over a span of nearly two hundred years from 1370; that of Thomas Corniche, who died in 1513, is a good example at Wells.

In 1995 one of the greatest experts on mouldings and vaulting paid a visit to Edington. I told him that most commentators had dated this monument as later than the Cheney. Was there anything in the mouldings to confirm that? At a first glance he said he could see nothing that would not have been in vogue by the late fourteenth century. However, he stressed they would have been commonplace for a century or more thereafter. He felt that more study of other survivor monuments might be needed to say that the form of this one, and in particular the curved shape of the opening to the canopy above the slab, could be that early. Purely on shape, I would only point to the arch over the doorway in the north aisle (original to the 1350s rebuild) and to one in the cloister arcade at St George's Chapel, Windsor, by John Sponlee, built 1353–56. That arch even has spandrels as here. *Spandrels are the corner infill circular decoration.*

Some experts, the visitor an exception, think the pendant drop form of vaulting on the Cheney could not date from before 1450, making the simpler form of vaulting on this monument perhaps the earlier of the two. Is that difference in the bay above the effigy's heart deliberate, to make a sort of cross, or did the carver go wrong, improvise and say 'To hell with it, no one will ever notice.'

The sunburst rose was one of our visitor's reservations; he thought it first arose with ceiling bosses in Tewkesbury Abbey, employed, it was said, as a Yorkist victory symbol after the 1471 battle there. Others, I

EAST   WEST

read, put it later, as a symbol of reconciliation of the House of York with
the Tudors in 1485 with the crowning of Henry VII. An authoritative
television programme changed all that, indicating that it was a symbol
of the Blessed Virgin Mary from as early as the thirteenth century. For
even longer the rose had been associated with womanhood, the petals
having an anatomical connotation into which I will not go! The sunburst
rose is to be seen in the window that I mentioned at Buckland along
with Bishop William's arms – likely to be fourteenth century.

The visitor, like many others, saw nothing to indicate that the effigy
does not match the rest, or is of a different date. But perhaps his most
interesting observation was that, without more research, he doubted
any abbot or prior, let alone the head of an obscure Augustinian order,
as here, would have been depicted with such a resplendent cushion to
lay his head on. This and the gold and silver leafed tassels, the whole
grandiose design and use of gold and silver in the motif decorations
pointed to great wealth spent in veneration of someone much more
significant. Remember that the Bonhommes petitioned in the 1390s
about their destitute state, and again after the sacking in 1450. This
perhaps points to construction either early on in their existence or in
the late fifteenth/early sixteenth century; if, indeed, it was they who had
it built. Certainly the figure is an ecclesiastical person: note the tonsure.

Several experts have commented that most wall-side monuments did
not have the effigy finished to the same standard of carving to the rear
as to the front , which showed. Ours is of the same standard throughout,
with an equilateral triangle on the hidden end of the barrel. This was

the symbol of the Holy Trinity, again pointing to this being a clerical gentleman. Was no expense spared, or was the effigy once in a position where it was seen from both sides? The rear wall configuration looks to suit a tablet plaque rather than a viewing point. That the plaque is no longer with us is consistent with the removal of metal from elsewhere, which we put down to the sacking in 1450. Sadly I cannot point to any surviving metal from the hundred years after that date, which would have weighed construction in favour of an early date. Would that we had the plaque, for it might tell all!

It is generally accepted that the interest in regularity and rectilinearity of patterns in the West Country during the fourteenth century, provided the conditions necessary for the development of the fan-vault. Tewkesbury's Trinity chapel of c. 1375 and the Gloucester cloisters built 1381–1412 exhibit such vaults, springing, it is thought, from the ideas incorporated in the tomb of Hugh Despenser beside the Tewkesbury high altar: he died in 1349 and his wife in 1358. Both have fine effigies and the tabernacle canopy is delicate work, – like putting all our chancel niches into one pile. It probably dates from the 1360s, therefore.

Let me make clear why I think the monument has been moved. Here it is against what is otherwise a continuous flat wall. The majority of it is recessed into that wall, though the frieze and end panels are not. The east

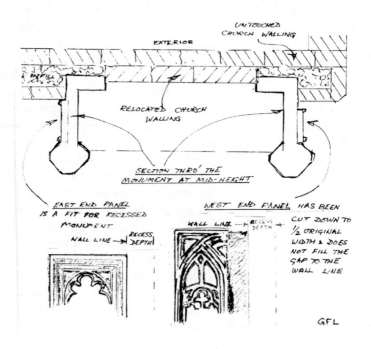

end has a near perfect panel to suit what protrudes when the monument is thus recessed. That is not true of the west end, where an amount of the original width of the panel has been discarded. Measurement shows that the whole panel there would have reached back to the recessed depth.

You can make up all sorts of configurations of walling for it to have been against in its previous location, but perhaps its overall length is the most interesting. It would fit between columns in the nave arcades. If opposite the Cheney monument, was it part of the screening for the brethren's access to the chancel? However, if it is a monument to the founder of the Bonhommes or a brother it is much more likely to have been in the chapter house or other domestic area. A logical time for it to have moved is when its previous location became unsuitable, perhaps when the monastic domestic buildings were decommissioned or demolished because of the Dissolution and its aftermath. But also remember the possible 1450 vestry connection with the burnt stone found inside this memorial.

Incidentally, the stone we see where there is a blank wall under the canopy (where I guessed a plaque may have been) is of blocks that were in the original front face walling. Imagine the installers of this monument in this location – whenever that was: they have to make a recess. Break up one 5in thick facing block and prize out adjacent ones; pile them over there. Take out the infill and cut back the bond-stones through the wall. Will the monument be load bearing? Better think about a lintel and keep the recess narrow. Better support the cut bond-stones and lintel by lining the recess with those blocks in the pile there in place of the infill. Perhaps no need to fuss about which stones, or whether they go in back to front, as no one is going to see; because even where there is that opening at the back of the monument under the canopy it is going to be covered by a metal plaque. Do you see the thinking?

We can be very sure this is what happened because one of the blocks picked at random to line the recess has inscribed lines on it, part of an architectural drawing on the original wall that was destroyed in this installation. We know that because the drawing design is identical to two others either side of it. The particular block is that dressed one, left centre in the plaque space – see the scribed arcs and radial lines up to the top right corner.

Note some other things. The two lead plug holes into which dowel pins on the back of the plaque must have been pushed – at the top there. Notice too that the plaque was smaller than the space left for it at the top: see the touch-up paint on the stones for an inch or so down.

Round the east side see the mutilation done to the consecration cross. These observations all add up in my view to a rushed job of re-siting, not original workmanship to match the elaborate design of the monument. If you were designing a monument to go here, would you thin and weaken the church wall beneath a window?

When the chest was opened in 1995 it contained rubble (some burnt), including carved mouldings like those around windows in the nave and the aisles. Most were slightly inaccurate, perhaps making them rejects (because of carving errors) or apprentices' pieces. There were also worn encaustic floor tiles dating from 1300 and earlier. In the 1960s it was found that there was a vault under the tomb. Its contents were examined in 1988 and identical tile fragments were found. They are in Trowbridge Museum. Apart from indicating that the tomb chest probably never contained a body in this location, we can learn little from these emptyings – except to surmise from the fragment dates that the spoil came from the infill in the dismantled wall when the recess was cut, and that this operation involved opening the vault.

The experts' conclusion on the vault, which is offset relative to the monument, was that it pre-dated our monument. Against outside walls was a common place to bury children; and their bones were found. If the monument was originally built here, then that cuts down the window for the vault's construction to within fifty, at most a hundred years of 1361.

Returning to the effigy: we are looking for a cleric. The names of most of the early brethren and rectors are known. James Brazier's research for his PhD in 1992 gave an appendix of all known obits and chantries here (sixteen in number). As you can guess there is a Bulkington, but no Baynton. There is John Rous, and another author, Rachel Tyler, has suggested that this Imber family was dying out in the early fifteenth century. They had maintained a chapel at Baynton with its own incumbent. With the blessing of John Stafford they gifted the manor estate to Edyndon, as we noted before. She suggested that our monument might be his memorial, the rebus recalling his gift of Baynton. That he was not a cleric she justified by referring to a recorded custom at Lincoln Cathedral, in which laity were shown in effigies with clerical appearance – the ultimate accolade for faithful beneficiaries. We have also seen how members of the laity were often appointed to fill vacancies in clerical positions, but that did not seem to be the case with John Rous. Canon Jackson noted that in 1428 he was accused of inciting inhabitants here not to pay offerings to the church at certain services. Previously he had frequently appeared before the bishop's court in Heytesbury, accused of Lollardy and heresy.

RICHARD II's BADGE
IN WESTMINSTER
HALL. MANY OTHER
EXAMPLES EXIST,
inc. ADJACENT TO
EDWARD II's TOMB
AT GLOUCESTER.

THE EDINGTON
S. TRANSEPT
MONUMENT BOSS.
UNDERCOAT RED
ON BODY. GREEN
ON FOLIAGE.

NB
RICHARD II
1377-99

GFL

There are two other possible clues about date. The couchant animal on a boss of the chest slab has been noted by some as a paschal lamb, but the symbol of the king at the time of construction was often incorporated in such a way. The Reverend Charles Boutell's *Manual of Heraldry* of 1863 (at least twice updated) tells us that a couchant stag is likely to be the badge of Richard II (1377–99); he shows examples in Westminster Hall. This stag badge came from his mother, Joan, the Fair Maid of Kent, but hers was white: this one is red! Only undercoat is left. The monument has what appears to be an elaborate mason's mark inside on the east wall by the barrel, but we can learn nothing accurate from it, if indeed it is of the monument builder. The trend with time was to more elaborate marks and certainly this is more elaborate than most of the sixty or so that I have recorded on our rebuild masonry.

The second clue is lettering. Knowledge of this has increased over recent years. In April 1987 Dr Blair of Queen's College, Oxford, wrote to us that he had compared the boss monograms with the specimens of letterings published by H.S. Kingsford in *Epigraphy of Medieval English Seals* (1929): 'I am now convinced it can only be interpreted as "XB" based on a seal of 1461.' No one argues with the B, but others suggested the first letter could be I or J. Professor J.D. Burnley of Sheffield University, writing in August 1993, notes another similar X of 1399 in the same reference, widening the date perspective. He was more intriguing about the barrel monogram, certain it is a W. He did not exclude the possibility that the boss monograms may also be Ws. Of a Chaucer text of 1415 he writes that there are 'versions of the capital "W" with traces of a cross on the first as well as the second and third uprights'. This

Edington's Chantry, Winchester. c. 1375.
Corpus Christi College, Cambridge MS 61. c. 1415.
Church Window, Welborne, Norfolk. c. 1430.

S. TRANSEPT MONUMENT
Barrel.   Bosses

kind of W is 'script known as Textura, which was developed during the thirteenth century, but continued to be written throughout the fifteenth century'. I suspect he meant fourteenth century, not thirteenth century.

Burnley was convinced enough to look for other W attributions, probably in ignorance of many of the other clues that I have discussed. He pointed to two Bonhommes rectors, 'William Godwyn (good wine), 1450–64 and William Newton (new barrel), 1464–post-1479'. However, he concluded, 'William of Edington seems to me to be very much the prime candidate'. Experts never agree. They need only have looked at William's chantry chapel in Winchester to find the closest of matches to the W on our barrel. The date of that chantry is put at within fifteen years of his death, that is pre-1381. I have done my own collation of lettering from dated windows and brasses and favour a date between 1380 and 1450. This ties in with Macklin's 1969 assessment of monumental brasses: 1350–90 – letters became more rounded, derived from Lombardic shapes; 1400–60 – more upright and largely composed of straight lines; from 1460 – more rounded and legible but less neat and even.

If this monument is the brethren's commemoration of the sponsor of the church and founder of their House, then the obvious question is why is he not depicted with a mitre as at Winchester? Similarly commentators on the Winchester effigy are curious that there is no crozier. Pure speculation on my part rests on four holes in the effigy and slab, three of which I was unable to stop those who replaced the effigy last time it was off from filling with hard cement. Have you seen the tomb of the Black Prince in Canterbury Cathedral? Remember the prince's helm and armour arrayed along the top on metal rods. What if the boss monograms are JB for John Bloebury, executor of William's will? He came to Edington thereafter, and what more natural than that he became the driving force behind the brethren in emulating the cathedral by building the finest memorial they could afford. It is not unreasonable to imagine that he was in a position to bring a real mitre, crozier and perhaps other artefacts used by William of Edyndon, so perhaps the effigy was adorned with a crozier on metal rods set in the holes I mentioned and a mitre on or over his head. Even if the monument was not achieved during John Bloebury's life, there is no reason why it should not have happened at any time up to the Dissolution, as and when wealth permitted.

There are no coats of arms on the Winchester chantry and none here. Of course there may have been on that plaque, along probably with all those other things we have agonized about – his family name, his place of birth and family tree, and even an account of the positions he held. We must console ourselves with that tribute around his tomb chest at Winchester, very likely written by William of Wykeham. It is in Latin, of course, but in English it reads as follows: 'Wilhelmus, born Edyngdon, is here interred. He was a well-beloved prelate and Winchester was his see. You who pass by, remember him in your prayers. He was discreet and mild and of much sagacity. He was a watchful guardian of the English nation, a tender father and protector of the poor. To one thousand, three hundred and fifty, add ten, five and one, then the eighth of October will mark the day of his death.'

A few monks at Winchester may have baulked at that tribute, but there is support for it in twentieth-century assessments of William. Sir Arthur Bryant wrote: 'Never . . . had England seemed so thriving. Her nobles and commons – knights, franklins and merchants – were united behind her sovereign, and under the administration of his discreet chancellor and former treasurer, William of Edington, Bishop of Winchester, the governance of the realm was conducted more smoothly than at any time before.'

One last clue I must tell you about is highly disputed. William was first prelate of the Order of the Garter. Contemporary paintings of events involving garter knights are unanimous that in the early days the blue of their attire was much lighter than the deep colour we associate with the Order today. There is no indication that Miss Pauline Plummer and Ralph Dudley knew this when they wrote of taking a paintbrush to a watercolour palette and painting the outer garment on the effigy the blue you see today. They did this because during her brilliant restoration of the monument in 1966 Miss Plummer found that blue in original paint under gold leaf. She claimed that any paint elsewhere had oxidised to a grey, which she felt had led many to think the effigy must be of a member of the Bonhommes.

Ralph knew that cloth made at Beckington was always said to have been blue in colour. He also knew that the Reverend George Long (remember him as incumbent on the restoration plaque) had found documents in Winchester or Romsey that stated a priest Thomas de Beckington was buried here. They may explain Ralph's leaning to the attribution of Beckington. After his time the Beckington cloth colour was proved correct when medieval dye material was found between floorboards during restoration at Shawford Mill near that village. But back to the effigy: subsequently spot checks have found no ancient colour pigment anywhere on the clothing, just red and green on the pillow. It seems illogical to me that clothing would not have been painted.

If sunburst roses on front panels and bosses denote the Blessed Virgin Mary, then that might indicate a connection with the Order of the Garter – which was established 'to the honour of Almighty God, the glorious Virgin St Mary and St George the martyr'. Here we may be quoting Bishop William's words in drafting the constitution; but where is St George on the monument?

So, should we discount the Baynton attribution on the evidence presented? I think so. We could do that by echoing Buckler's title and calling it simply the Edyngdon Monument, or does that smack too much of thinking it is for our William?

The colour is fantastic and consistent at the top, but at the bottom there are some very bright patches. It looked nothing like this before Pauline Plummer started her restoration. She covered the monument in foam, which was impregnated with chemicals of some sort, and left it for ages. When the wrappings came off the grime was gone, and it looked even brighter than it does today: it was as if colour had been drawn back to the surface of the stone. The conservation team decided that limited areas at the bottom with very little original paint, owing to dampness over the centuries, should be repainted to what was thought to be the original colour intensity, just to give an idea of how brilliant it must have been. Unfortunately this included some areas on the front panels which have had an on-going problem with damp; this has caused effervescent salts to leach out. They have been sent off for all kinds of treatment and damp course membranes have been introduced. The deterioration is evident still, but is at a much slower rate.

Over the top it looks as though some of the sandbags were never removed, but I am sure that is not true. Why is the domed effect so crudely finished? It is unfortunate that we can see this: originally the top edge had parapetting on it to hide the doming from sight.

Scratchings on the west end panel have already been noted. Among them are a 'WD' and interlocking circles, and along the front of the slab are names. I will talk about graffiti later, but not about these specifically. Suffice it to say that 'Ralph Aldrig' and 'Hector Carpenter' are from families that appear to be hereabouts as long ago as the seventeenth century. Remember Edward Carpenter of Tinhead Court? He will crop up again. Enough on the monument. What else here?

The wooden crucifix on the pulpitum support was carved from local elm by a parishioner, Thomas York King, in about 1992. He was a farmer who in retirement made all our communion wafers from his own wheat, using an ancient machine (from a nunnery in Warminster) which was kept down in the crypt.

William of Edyndon's Will

How timely; our verger is just passing with our beautiful processional cross, consideration of which can conveniently lead us on to William's will. The cross was made in 1924, and given in memory of members of the family of the Reverend Samuel Littlewood, namely Elijah Harrison and Julia Fanny Littlewood. Look at the number of simulated rubies set in it. The maker must have known that Bishop William apparently had no jewellery without rubies. His will shows that

Bishop Wyvil received a gold ring set with one (and cancellation of a debt). Three other friends were also left similar rings.

Canon Jackson wrote in 1882 that the will was dictated in Latin by the bishop on 11 September 1366. It shows clearly his concern for all who had cared for him in life; there is no mention of any relatives. Legacies significant to what I have told you of his life included the following: to John of Aylesbury, 'Rector of my House of Edyndon, to celebrate, and to pray for my soul, twenty pounds and a cup of silver with cover'. I hope that was not among the things John Hortone stole, or had it gone in 1450? To each brother here he gave 100 shillings; to the Carthusians 'in Selwood' 8 shillings (this was to Witham Friary, near Frome, then within the limits of the ancient Selwood Forest); to Hinton Charterhouse 3 shillings; to the church at Cheriton 20 marks for the supply of a vestment and £10 for the poor; the latter sum also went to the 'Church of Middleton near Bannebiri'; and 'to Thomas Hungerford, my Steward, fifty marks and a cup with cover'. A handwritten note of later date states that the total sum bequeathed was £3000.

Dr Highfield gives other extracts: 'And to Robert, my body servant, I give ten pounds, and to John Romsey, my barber, I give five pounds and to the boy in the bakery five pounds, and to Thomas, the carter the elder ten pounds, and to Philip and Thomas who work in the brewhouse, five pounds each, and to William, the boy who leads the first cart five pounds and to John the boy who leads the second cart five pounds . . .' Thomas Brinton, Bishop of Rochester, was to ensure that the kin of his old patron Bishop Adam Orleton were cared for, and individual sums went to all friends in high places, including Archbishop Simon Langham and William of Wykeham. 'And if there is any residue, let it be set to the work of perfecting the nave of St Swithin's Church at Winchester; or let it be given to my House and Chantry at Edyndon, if it has need, or in other pious works or uses.'

'My soul I leave to Almighty God, my creator; and my body to be buried in my Cathedral Church at Winchester in the nave at the point where the monks make a halt on Sundays and Feast Days, as they go past in procession, or elsewhere in that church, if the prior and my executors should think it more fitting.' Considerate to the last.

Encaustic Floor Tiles

B ack to more tangible things. Frank Stevens followed Brakspear as
Wiltshire Archaeological and Natural History Society president. His
presidential address asked 'How is it that . . . [these] tiles are the only form
of pottery, made in this country in medieval times, which can claim any
outstanding artistic quality?' He tells us that the technique came from
the continent and that they were made exclusively by monastic orders
for some reason. They started this industry long before the enforced
diversification of the early sixteenth century.

Square bevil-edged moulds were filled with dense and crude red clay.
After slight drying, a pattern of depressions was forced into the surface
with a wooden stamp. The depressions were carefully filled with white
slip of china clay. Various glazes had remarkable effects on firing: lead
gave a yellow tint to the white oxide of iron in the slip, and copper salts
gave a greenish tinge to the body of the tile. Lines were scribed in some
of them to facilitate subsequent fracture for fitting around edges. All
were given a depression in the underside to assist fixing, and in this
depression one can sometimes see the detailed thumbprint of the maker.
All these features were in tiles found at various places in Edington.

The extensive collection
of Wessex area tiles in the
Salisbury and South Wiltshire
Museum (SM) includes
examples from most of the
great monasteries of the
area (including Breamore,
Amesbury, Salisbury, Stanley, Lacock and Cleeve) and
from the sites where the
monks set up tileries to
supply the great houses, such
as Clarendon Palace and
Heytesbury House. Edington
is represented with four
tiles found in 1935; where
exactly they were found is
not now known. Three are
¾in (20mm) thick, said to be

from a Wessex tilery of uncertain location in the third quarter of the thirteenth century. Designs are all numbered, and our three involve two which are unique in this collection: a griffin is SM95 and two birds addorsed (turned back to back) is SM105. The fourth tile is similarly unique to here. It is 1in (28mm) thick of a stag (SM78) and thought to have been made at Kiln 2 Clarendon in the fourth quarter of the thirteenth century.

The nine pieces from the vault, now in Trowbridge Museum, include a number of fragments of ¾in thick tile made at Nash Hill, near Lacock, also in the last quarter of the thirteenth century. They are of a design in which the use of four identical tiles makes a floriated cross as a major feature in a circle. All Nash Hill designs are slightly inferior versions of ones found at Cleeve Abbey.

In 1995 there were further finds at Edington. Nine fragments came from the tomb chest here and six from the rubble side of an east/west orientated wall with semi-circular buttresses in the grounds of The Priory, which was being restored by English Heritage. Three ¾in thick tile pieces from the vault made one complete, but very worn, SM105 tile. Another three pieces from the vault make a complete, but again worn, ¾in Nash Hill quarter floriated cross design tile. The three other pieces from the vault comprise the following: another ¾in worn fragment of the same Nash Hill design; half of a 1in tile, so worn that little slip remains; and about a third of a ¾in tile of heraldic design, similar to tiles found on the site of Amesbury Abbey and dated to c. 1250.

The six pieces from the wall comprised the following: two fragments of the same Nash Hill design tiles, but 1in, not ¾in thick like the rest, one with a dark brown glaze to the body and a yellow slip (lead addition); the other a green glaze to the body and an even yellower slip (copper and lead addition). Another of the six is perhaps the earliest piece – just over half of a 1in tile, similar to tiles in the Salisbury and South Wiltshire Museum, which are said to be from Clarendon Palace and made in Kiln 1 Clarendon, which only operated 1240–44. The other three are a whole but smaller 1in tile with good green glaze, somewhat pink towards the edges, scored down the centre for halving; a plain terracotta coloured 1in tile of the same smaller size; and the majority of a tile without any edge remaining, so worn that it could be of ¾in or 1in thickness originally. Were all these pieces from the floor of the previous church?

In the March 1908 *Wiltshire Notes and Queries* four patterns of large encaustic tiles were noted as having been found in an upper room at 'Becket's Farm, Tinhead'. One was said to be incomplete but identical to one removed some years previously from Ivy Mill, Edington. The location of these today is unknown. Featured on one is a double-headed eagle with, as its body, a shield bearing a rampant lion. That makes them sound really large and not of the same period as those I have been describing. Interestingly, double-headed eagles and rampant lions survive in an old plaster ceiling at Beckett's House, Tinhead. Another tile apparently had a shield bearing 'on chief two mullets', the arms it was said of the St John family. A fragment of a St John tile was found in November 1995, close to the site of Tinhead

Court, but Devizes Museum at the time thought it was unlikely to be contemporary with the Rector of Edington being John St John (1494–1515). Remember that Sir William Paulet was made Baron St John in 1539.

Banker Marks

Changing the subject, this is a good spot to look at banker marks. Going up to a height of about 13ft I have found sixty-three in total; do look for yourselves. Here on the tower pillar there are three blocks with simple arrowheads, including one upside down as though the setter found that, when it came like this from the quarry, it fitted better the other way up. The blocks above and below those three bear a much more elaborate mark, reminiscent of some medical symbol. The east and west walls are covered in marks, including one that is normally on the top edge rather than in the middle, this italic F. At eye level on the west wall one of his is also upside down.

Adjacent is a 'fylfot' mark. I do not like to call them swastikas because of the Nazi connotation. Some like to make a distinction between swastikas, with the bend to the right, and fylfots as here with a bend to the left, but this is phoney, for bands of this decoration often alternate the bend direction. Fylfot describes a pre-Christian symbol for the sun, which was adopted into Christian symbolism to represent perfect submission to the will of God. They are prominent on Bishop William's amice at his neck in his Winchester chantry effigy (*see page 208*).

The small grid of vertical and horizontal lines on the west wall has been described as a mason's game called nine men's morris, but the game sold today under that name (to be played on the flat with marbles) is nothing like this pattern. The intersections here have indentations, but it would be difficult to fix pegs in them for a game. No, these are where one point of large compasses was placed in scribing the arcs you can see out to the right about 4ft. That there are six lines in each direction in the grid and the column arcades in the nave have six supports to the arches led me to suggest initially that the grid gave measured offsets for the amount the columns had settled in the months after build, so the curvature for the arch sections could be adjusted, thereby allowing all the arches to have their apex in a straight line. At first I could not explain

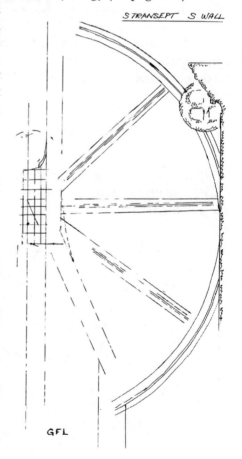

S TRANSEPT S WALL

GFL

the radial lines between the grid and the curves, unless they were for reinforcing members to the arch template.

Then as I worked around the walls another grid became obvious on the south wall. Since it did not have the six line symmetry (more like five by nine), it could not be for the other arcade. The arcs are of the same radius as on the other drawing. They clearly ran behind the monument, indicating presumably that they predate its erection; they also run across the consecration cross. It looks as though they were drawn straight on to stone before it had any coating on it, which would make them pre-1360. Of course there are amounts of white in the grooves and holes, where the coatings covered them for centuries. Interestingly, above this grid there are some shapes that may indicate the profile of the design. These are similar to the profiles in the earliest architectural drawings to survive, namely at York Minster and Wells Cathedral, which some authors say perhaps date from 1360–80. Could ours be older? Perhaps our second grid relates to transept and chancel windows. I have already mentioned a third set (one stone inside the monument): perhaps that was for the other arcade. Equally all drawings may have been for woodwork not stone. They might be the design of tread-wheels for lifting build materials up the walls and tower, or something to do with the hanging of the bells.

The Tower

If it is the latter, how many bells did they have then and what was the purpose of the grids? Indeed, did they have any bells at all initially? Remember what I said about the tower windows. Ponting wrote that 'the belfry windows were originally filled with coloured glass, portions of which remain in the tracery, and for the same reason, probably, the jambs and arches are, contrary to the usual order, deeply moulded on the inside, while on the outside the tracery is flush with the wall'. I know of no church where bells rang out behind tower glass; when bells went into our tower, the glass would have been removed. Originally no bells here must be the conclusion. Incidentally, thinking about the design of cross you could work into that tracery – surely it could not be as detailed as 'fleurie' or 'patonce'. 'Moline' is so much simpler, making it amenable to such integration.

A document from 1924 states that the belfry contained six bells then, the treble being the oldest – 1640. In 1553 the inventory was said to be four bells and a sanctus bell. When the bell frame structure was replaced in steel in 1967 it was decided to integrate the five bells from Imber church. The peal is now ten bells with a spare, the 1640 bell cast by John Lott of Warminster. He also cast two of the Imber bells in 1635 and the firm two more for Edington in 1647 and 1654. The 1640 bell is struck by the turret clock when the tenor bell is left 'up'.

The turret clock is mid-sixteenth century, and was designed to be faceless. It has an arrangement to drive a carillon machine, but that never returned from the repairer when sent there in the 1960s. Perhaps there was not much appetite in the village for the first line of the national anthem every quarter hour! My wife and I were asked in New Zealand where we came from, and on hearing Edington the farmstay owner said, 'I know it – the church with the faceless clock. Our holidays in England are spent visiting battlefields and we had to see the most important – Ethandune.'

The removed carillon machine

The Clock Strikes Three

The Cheney Monument – Cheney/ Paveley

Right, let us have another look at the Cheney monument (*see Buckler watercolour, page 45*) and talk about attributions to families from the heraldry there. You are familiar with the alleged Paveley and Cheney arms, and here we have a monument long claimed to be that of Sir

Ralph Cheney and his wife Joan, née Paveley, married in 1368. W.H. Hamilton Rogers in his book *The Strife of the Roses in the West* (1890) was convinced that the tower form of cross was the coat armour of the Paveley family. However the garter knight, Sir Walter Paveley (c. 1330–75), bore on a blue shield a gold cross patonce, according to the description in Foster's *Dictionary of Heraldry*, but the illustration of what is above his stall in St George's Chapel, Windsor, looks more like fleurette ends on a flared Latin cross. Sir John Paveley may have only displayed martlets, not a cross.

Hamilton Rogers quotes a deed dated 1361, in which Bishop William of Edyndon is described as becoming 'guardian to the heiresses of Sir John Paveley'. This branch of the Paveley family were 'Lords of the Westbury Hundred', living at 'Brooke Halle'. The site of the hall is at Brook House Farm between Rudge and Hawkeridge. The date of the deed agrees with the date given for Sir John Paveley's death, at which stage he held the title of Prior of St John of Jerusalem. His parents were Sir Reynold Paveley (c. 1293–1347) and a Miss Marmium. Sir Reynold's father was a Sir Walter Paveley, but not the garter knight if his given death date is correct. 1323 was before the Order was founded.

Sir John Paveley appears to have had three daughters, of whom Joan seems to have been the only one not already married by 1361. Isabel Paveley (died 1413) had married John de Erleigh (died 1409) and had one child, Margaret Erleigh, born at Beckington in 1387. More on Margaret in a moment. Alice Paveley had married Sir John de St Lo, who outlived her, dying in 1374. Alice died the day after her father in 1361. Bishop William was therefore looking out for just one unmarried heiress, Joan.

Sir John Paveley had first married Alice St John, who died by 1347. He then married Agnes de la Mare, and Joan was born in 1353. Lady Joan Cheney, as she became in 1368, has a pedigree claimed by some to make her HRH Prince Charles's nineteen-great grandmother, Sir Winston Churchill's eighteen-great grandmother and possibly George Washington's fourteen-great aunt.

Joan's husband, Sir Ralph Cheney, was born at Poyntington, near Sherborne, Somerset, in about 1330 and died on 11 November 1400. She died just before him. His parents were Sir William Cheney (also born at Poyntington) and Joan Georges. His grandfather was Sir Nicholas de Cheyney (died c. 1326), and there is evidence of him arranging a marriage between a John Cheney and a Joan Erleigh at the end of the thirteenth century. Sir Nicholas was a petitioner to Edward I in 1298 when Warden of the Channel Islands, and his son William Cheney also held that appointment in 1331. William was killed at Crécy in 1346. His son and heir was Edmund, knighted in 1347 aged twenty. The warden title was held by him 1358–66; he died without issue in 1376. A Nicholas de Cheney was his sub-warden in 1365. Edmund's brother and heir Sir Ralph Cheney continued the Cheney line, as we shall see, but does not appear on the list of wardens. Some of this comes from others' research into the manor of Steeple Morden, near Cambridge, given to Sir Nicholas's father, a knight from the Channel Islands, in 1248.

Sir Ralph Cheney is noted as a Member of Parliament and Sheriff of Wiltshire, probably after he moved into his wife's Brook Hall on their marriage in 1368. Joan was then aged fifteen. They had one child, William, in 1370. Several references say that this Sir William Cheney was also Sheriff of Wiltshire. Most claim he married twice, firstly to Cecily Stretche, resulting in two boys, John and Edmund, and then to the Margaret Erleigh just mentioned. They write of him being her third knight-husband, and that by her previous marriages she had become a very wealthy woman.

The various sources tie together quite well, but it all goes a bit wrong with the record of Sir William Cheney dying on 27 September 1420 aged fifty, and his first wife Cecily on 12 October 1430 at Brooke Hall! Was the alleged marriage to Margaret Erleigh bigamous?

Margaret Erleigh

Then I found a reference to another Sir William Cheney who was born in 1387 (the same year as Margaret), perhaps of a different branch of the family, who held the title of chief justice. More searching, and someone has him marrying Margaret Erleigh only a couple of years before her death in 1443. Had Margaret Erleigh then been marrying the Sir William born of Ralph and Joan (forgetting the quoted date for his death of 1420) he would have been into his seventies and she in her mid-fifties. It is much more likely that she would marry someone her own age – this other Sir William. Her first child was born in about 1410, a son John St Maur (Seymour). Her first husband died in 1415, her second in 1435. She had a daughter by the latter – Margaret Sondes (Sandys).

I am not the first to recognize this confusion. Who cares, you might say? Well, one should care if attempting to solve the dating of this monument, for we know those Erleighs that I mentioned at the turn of the thirteenth century bore arms of three escallops, and we have four escallops very prominent here on the tomb chest. The earlier marriages of Margaret Erleigh were to rather more distant families, to Sir John St Maur, born at Castle Cary, who made his home at North Molton, Devon, and to Sir Walter Sondes, born at Winchester Castle, who made his home at Andover, Hampshire. Margaret's return to Beckington on his death in 1435 seems not unreasonable.

Foster links three escallops to the Dacre family and records no arms for families named Erles, Earleys, Herleis or Erleighs (all Edington Cartulary or other document spellings possibly referring to her family). However, he gives a Sir Robert Herle in Edward III's reign bearing 'gules, a chevron between three drakes (shovellers) argent'. The chevron is common to many families, not least when red to the Staffords.

The inquisition post mortem of Margaret's estates lists one third of the manor and advowson

LOCAL FAMILIES

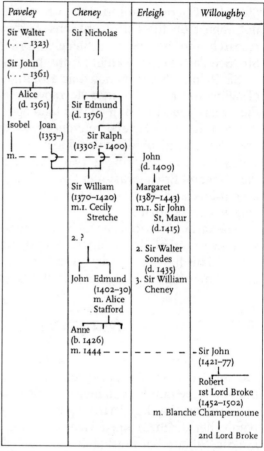

of North Molton, Devon, the advowson of Blaketoryton, Devon, one quarter of the manor of Westbury, Wiltshire, and in Somerset lands in Crudlyngcote, the manor and advowson of Bokyngton, ditto Bakkarc and Durston, the manor of Pury, and lands, etc. in Blakeford and Prestleigh. The inclusion of Westbury does not indicate which Sir William Cheney she might have inherited it from – because of former inter-marriages, like the thirteenth-century John Cheney to Joan Erleigh that I just mentioned. The spelling of Bokyngton must surely equate to Beckington, since we know she was born and lived there; although in relation to the south transept monument I said that 'Boc' equated to Bulkington. Perhaps Ralph Dudley felt this supported his Beckington attribution.

More Confusion and whence the Cheney Escallops?

Around on the northwest corner of the monument canopy we have a quartered shield. These arise as the arms of children of a heraldic heiress (living or deceased); that is, she had no living brother when her armigerous father died. The heiress occupies top right and bottom left and the child's father top left and bottom right. The conundrum is that one would not normally expect to see the arms of an offspring on a parent's memorial. Ours has the arms with which you are familiar, Cheney and Paveley, though the cross here is moline, not fleurie.

On this southwest corner of the canopy we have the vertical half division of the shield, signifying the desire of a married woman to continue to bear paternal arms, marshalled on a shield with those of her armigerous husband. The husband occupies the left side and is said to be 'impaling' the wife. Thus this shield is consistent with the attribution of Ralph Cheney impaling Joan Paveley, if cross moline can be hers, not always fleurie or patonce. The latter of course has implications for the tower window tracery.

Canon Jackson was alert to the conundrum I have just mentioned: 'in this shield the cross is quartered with Cheney, which . . . is a form usually denoting the son of an heiress'. We know much more about who died when than in his day, and I cannot tell whether Jackson was aware that Joan was the only unmarried daughter within a day of Sir John Paveley dying and could be thought of as a sole heiress. Equally he may not have known that her son may possibly have been married to the heiress Margaret Erleigh, she of the escallops. Everywhere on the monument the Cheney arms have escallops on the fusils. Equally everywhere else on it the assumed Paveley arms are cross fleurie.

The other canopy shields are Cheney on the nave side and Paveley on this aisle side, all on shields – no lozenges for Paveley. Joseph Foster illustrates the arms borne by a Sir William Cheyney at the siege of Rouen in 1418 as quarterly, blue with a gold cross patonce, opposite five fusils on red 'conjoined in fess argent, on each an escallop sable'. That is the mirror of our canopy quartered shield, quite apart from the cross type difference and the five instead of four fusils. Quadrants are usually numbered 1– top left, 2 – top right, 3 – bottom left and 4 – bottom right, with 2 and 3 the male. Perhaps masons here did not always know about that convention.

Foster lists a Cheney during the reign of Henry II bearing six lozenges without escallops and a John Cheney in Edward III's reign, four in fess each with an escallop, adding 'Rauff bore this coat within a bordure of the second'. So where do the escallops come from between these two? Ralph's father was not John, but I mentioned that his grandfather Nicholas arranged for a John Cheney to marry an Erleigh. That is possibly when there was incorporation of escallops on to the Cheney fusils. All sorts of practices probably went on in this time of war and during the Black Death, as families feared annihilation and wished to preserve their arms in some way. In 1417 Henry V was the first to try to regularize matters by disallowing the bearing of arms without authority of the Crown. The College of Heralds was founded in 1484.

One possibility, therefore, is that Margaret Erleigh, when in the money, wished to create this monument in the place that, through Bishop William, was associated with the Paveleys and thereby later the Cheneys. Her mother was Isabel Paveley. Joan Paveley was her mother's half-sister. William Cheney was therefore a close cousin, even if she was not, for a short while, his wife. Margaret did not die until 1443. Was it her idea to relegate them to the canopy and ensure her remembrance with front chest Erleigh panels? Whether she was the husband of Ralph and Joan's son or not, remember she had become a Cheney by about 1440. Hence, if construction is after that date it is logical she might place as central chest panels Cheney fusils and escallops, and likewise the rudder to one side if it is a Cheney badge. Thus the figures in the missing brasses of the Purbeck marble slab in front of you may be, I suggest, Margaret and her Cheney husband.

Of course, this slab may have replaced an earlier one of Ralph and Joan; likewise the chest panels may have been changed. Such re-use of monuments was not uncommon.

Supporting this hypothesis of a 1440s date for the chest and slab are the expert's views on the indents in the slab. More on that in a minute.

Ponting tells us he thought this 'perhaps a little later in date' than the south transept monument. In 1887 he wrote:

> This tomb extends the full width between the two pillars, which have been cut away to receive it. Both tomb and pillars bear traces of original painting, in spite of the scraping which the former has received. Against this on the nave side . . . exists the moulded stone curb of an ancient "carol" or closed chantry, and the position of a similar one can be traced on the north side of the nave.

These make the opening in the monument the entrance to just such a family enclosure as Nicodemus spoke about as more common towards the second half of the fifteenth century. In view of the intricate Paveley/Cheney/ Erleigh relationships I have outlined this may well be a communal enclosure for the three families. With homes in Beckington and Brooke Hall, west of Westbury, the probably infrequent occasions that significant family members were worshipping in Edyndon may have made this a reasonable arrangement. After all, Cheneys had a chapel in Westbury church from about 1370 as Nicodemus said (tying in with Ralph Cheney's arrival), and the Erleighs had chapels in Beckington Abbey and church.

In 1882 Canon Jackson had reservations about the attribution to Ralph and Joan: 'the . . . arms, carved on the frieze of the canopy and panels of the tomb, if intended to apply to such a match, are rather perplexing'. He believed the two pintle rudder with tiller to be a Paveley badge and knew the Erleigh arms were 'three escallops, two and one'. He recognized that for Paveleys 'more than one variety of cross is given in the armouries'. He does not mention that he knew there was an enclosure beyond the monument.

The Rudder

A tiller is what you hold to move the rudder; a pintle is the downward facing pin that engages in the eyelet gudgeon protruding from the sternpost. In references the rudder is not recognized as a charge or badge until the nineteenth century. Foster does not record it. Papworth's *Ordinary of British Armorials* quotes it as appearing in two crests: it arises initially with Joseph John Henley of Waterperry House, near Oxford, born in 1821, and later in the crest of the Scollay family in Scotland.

So can we do any better? It is boldly there in the chest panels both sides, but more significantly it is in the double ogee above the archway on this aisle side. It is not there on the other side of the archway, a clue perhaps that this was intended from the outset as an entrance to an enclosure for those identified with the rudder. We have seen that the key males in the possible attributions are all Cheneys, either Ralph or William. Thus it is logical this would be a Cheney male badge, rather than that of Paveley.

Originally a Chinese concept, the sternpost-hung rudder appears in wall paintings in place of the steering oar in Europe in the late

Top left:
Seal of Dover, 1305
(with steering oar)

Top right:
Gold noble 1344
to commemorate the
Battle of Sluys
(with rudder)

Bottom left:
Graffiti from the porch
west wall

Bottom right:
Rudder on the
Cheney monument

twelfth century. The earliest depiction in England is on a late twelfth-century square black font in Winchester Cathedral, as if on a small river or coastal craft. Depiction on coins and seals puts its introduction in larger sea-going ships between 1305 and 1344. Did a Paveley or Cheney ancestor suggest this adaptation? Was the manoeuvrability it brought a decisive factor in the destruction of the enemy at Sluys in 1340 or against a Spanish sortie up Channel in 1350, thereby bringing him fame? It is certain that, coping with the vicious tides around the Channel Islands, it would have helped Cheney ancestors. Barbara Tuchman writes of the hazards of sea travel in that century: 'Except for galleys powered by oarsmen, ships were at the mercy of the weather, although rigging had been improved and the swinging stern rudder gave greater control.'

John Leland visited Brook Hall in about 1544 during or after Willoughby occupation:

> From Steple Ashton to Brook Haule by woody ground. There was of very auncient tyme an old Manor Place where Brook Haule now is, and part of it yet apperith. But the new building that is there is of the creating of the Lord Steward unto King Henry VII. The windows be full of rudders (device). Peradventure it was his badge or token of the Admiral. There is a fayr Park but no great thing. In it be a great number of very fair and fine grand okes apt to sele houses.

One is tempted to say that 'location, location, location' was recognized even then!

The lord steward referred to is Sir Robert Willoughby, born at Brook Hall in 1452. He probably left in 1472 when he married and set up home at Callington, Cornwall, where he died on 23 August 1502. In 1483 he supported the abortive insurrection of the Duke of Buckingham against Richard III. He fared better than the duke (who was executed at Salisbury), escaping to Brittany to join Henry Tudor, Earl of Richmond. In 1485 they sailed from Harfleur and landed at Milford Haven, to go on to win the battle of Bosworth and see Richmond become Henry VII. Perhaps he rebuilt Brook Hall in order to have a mansion nearer London than Callington in which to entertain his majesty.

A hundred years later John Aubrey found 'A very great and stately old house. The Hall great and open with very old windows – but only one coat of Pavely was left.' In the parlour, chapel and canopy chamber he found and copied twenty coats of arms – 'the rudders everywhere'. The conclusion reached by Jackson in 1889 was that Leland had it wrong in thinking the rudder is 'peradventure' linked to the Willoughby family, because it is found here on the Cheney monument, which is 'of a date many years before the Willoughbys succeeded to Brook Hall'.

The Willoughby Connections

This 'many years' may not be altogether true in view of what we now know. If a chantry enclosure was the design intention for the whole complex (including the tomb chest) from the outset, then that points to a 1440s date – from what Nicodemus told us. Remember that Sir William Cheney had two boys by his wife Cecily. The younger, Edmund Cheney, was born in 1402: he married Alice Stafford. They had three girls before he died in 1430. The heiress from that union, Anne Cheney, was born at Brook Hall in 1426. She married Sir John Willoughby (1421–77) from Frampton, Lincolnshire, in 1444: he had succeeded to the title eighth Lord Latimer on his father's demise in 1437. So this Willoughby family could have been in the old Brook Hall by 1444; certainly Sir John Willoughby was Sheriff of Wiltshire in 1453. Thus the 'many years' looks dubious. John and Anne's eldest son was the future lord steward I mentioned – Robert Willoughby, born in 1452. He was created to a new barony in 1491, and we can surmise that the title Baron Willoughby of Broke refers to his love of Brook Hall, perhaps because he had just rebuilt it. He died in 1502.

At the end of the nineteenth century it is recorded that the porch of Westbury church (thought to be built in c. 1400) contained an impaled coat of arms of the rudder and those of a daughter of the Stafford family. If the porch date were out by only twenty years, then this could well mark the union of Edmund Cheney to nine years older Alice Stafford, born in 1391. It would mean Cheneys were identified with the badge of the rudder by 1420. We shall see a possible earlier date. Alice was certainly of the Southwick connection, for her brothers took the name Southwick in their titles.

Other authors think that Robert Willoughby, now ninth Lord Latimer, in the late 1480s adopted the rudder, to emphasize the title he had then received of 'Admiral to the King'. If this were true, then why would anyone erect or alter this monument when he had already based himself in Callington? Clearly, though, Robert was identified with a career in defence of the realm. Perhaps, as we shall see, he started in the Channel Islands.

The Treaty of Paris in 1259 set up two royal representatives for the Channel Islands: the English Lord of the Isles was to represent their interests at court while the Warden of the Channel Islands was intended to be the hands-on administrator, particularly regarding defence. Grosnez Castle in Jersey was built in 1330 by Sir Jean des Roches, warden 1328–30. It remained nominally the seat of the warden for many years thereafter, though of terrible defensive design: its water supply was outside the ramparts. From early on each major island had a bailiff answerable for civil affairs to the warden. As wardens became more frequently absent the position weakened and the bailiffs became more important with each French attack, until Jersey was occupied 1461–68. By 1469 Grosnez was a ruin, much as it is today. The warden title was abandoned the following year. Whatever had been the warden's badge it was going begging. Could it have been a rudder? That would fit well with aspects of what I have said, and will tell you next, about incumbents of the warden post.

Sir Robert Willoughby might have served under Sir Richard Harliston at the re-capture of Jersey in 1468, when he was aged sixteen. By 1489 he was in command of a force of 6000 men who landed in Brittany to support its duchess, Anne, against the French. Remember he had been in exile in Brittany 1483–85, so he knew the factions there well. In 1489 England was concerned that France might hold every port opposite us on the other side of the Channel, except Calais and the Channel Islands. Truces and treaties did not hold, and a fresh English army was landed in 1490 under Lord Daubenay with a fleet assembled under Willoughby, who bargained successfully for the port of Morlaix. However, the war in

Brittany finished in ignominy in 1491, with a face-saving promise to pay our expenses of £149,000 – the Treaty of Etaples. What would Bishop William have said!

The Bere Ferrers Connection

Just as Sir John Willoughby came courting Anne Cheney from Lincolnshire, so their son Robert left Brook Hall to go to Bere Ferrers (8 miles north of the confluence of the rivers Tamar and Tavy in Devon) to seek the hand of Blanche Champernoune. The village was a Saxon settlement. Henry de Ferriere, who was Master of Horse to William the Conqueror, and chairman of the Domesday Commission, c. 1086, was given estates all over England. Family members, with horseshoes their armorial charge, took possession of these various estates, and the Devon branch established their home at Bere Ferrers, with Ralph de Ferrays described as Lord of Bere in the second half of the twelfth century.

Sir William de Ferrers (died 1242), who built the present church, St Andrew's, was the great-grandson of that Ralph. How many generations later I know not, Martin de Ferrers (born 1355) apparently had no male heir. He was described by the chronicler Risden in Edward III's reign as 'a principal man in the government of this shire, was put in special trust, with others, for the defence of the sea coast against invasion of the French'. Whether he died in 1377 is not certain, but his arms are said in the church guide to have been at that date four horseshoes and five two pintle rudders with tillers. This would be well over 100 years before the young Willoughby visited Bere Ferrers. However, some caution is needed. The only evidence for the arms, being as described, is an Elizabethan bench-end carving in the church – dating from around 1558 at the earliest. A Thomas Ferrers was Warden of the Channel Islands three times, 1333–37, 1337–40 and 1343–48. Did Martin inherit the rudder symbol from that source?

In the church's north aisle is a Purbeck marble tomb without inscription, believed to be of the second Lord Broke. He died in 1521 without a male heir, so the title went into abeyance until revived in 1535 through female descent into the Greville family. A similar situation saw it pass to the Verney family, to continue to this day.

The other end of the bench provides a carving with better credentials. Here the uncoloured wood-carving is said to be identical to the arms of Robert first Lord Broke on a surviving fragment of glass from a long-gone window that commemorated his heir. The overall grand-quartered shield carving is rather basic and the church guidebook description

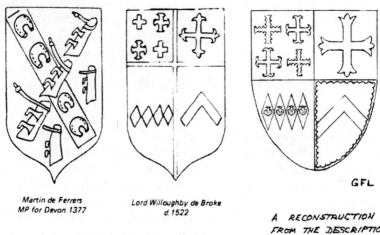

Martin de Ferrers
MP for Devon 1377

Lord Willoughby de Broke
d. 1522

FROM THE BERE FERRERS
CHURCH GUIDE

GFL

A RECONSTRUCTION
FROM THE DESCRIPTION
IN THE GUIDE
OF THE GLASS FRAGMENT

of the glass is more enlightening. The top left grand-quarter is said to
be Willoughby. It is quartered itself, with top left and bottom right an
engrailed gold cross on black and opposite male quarters of a moline
cross. I was unable to see the glass version to verify the colours, but gold
on black is given by Foster as the Ufford family, whereas he says that
Robert sixth Lord de Willoughby bore at the siege of Rouen in 1418, on
red, a silver cross moline, quarterly with, on gold, a black cross engrailed.
I think the church guide may be wrong.

I mentioned earlier that an engrailed cross is Peverell – but, according
to Foster, that was blue on gold not black on gold.

The second grand-quarter, top right, has a cross fleurie in the carving,
but the glass is said to be 'Gules, a cross patonce Or', thought Latimer.
Foster agrees a patonce cross could be Latimer, but equally it could be
Paveley. The wood carving is a cross fleurie. There is no argument with
the third grand-quarter on the glass. It is on red – four silver fusils en
fess, each charged with a black escallop. This indicates Cheney. Finally,
the fourth grand-quarter is described as on gold – a red chevron with an
engrailed bordure, thought Stafford. Foster agrees that founder garter
knight, Sir Ralph Stafford, later the 1st Earl Stafford, bore the latter at
the siege of Calais in 1347.

Additionally, the south porch roof is groined with oak beams on
which are ancient bosses displaying what the guide has described as
the arms of the Ferrers, Cheneys, Latimers and Willoughbys, including
many rudders with tillers. Unfortunately the date of the porch is not
known. It is large with a parvis room above, thought to have served as a

meeting place for pilgrims embarking for Santiago de Compostela.

So a trip to Bere Ferrers makes one feel very much at home with the shields on this monument. Its church guide also provides a connection between Sir Martin Ferrers and the first Lord Broke, which could explain the latter's apparent attachment to the rudder. This is an alternative suggestion to the ideas I have already given, of personal vanity or the Paveley/Cheney connection that we saw in Wiltshire. Remember that Robert courted Blanche Champernoune. She was the daughter of John Champernoune (died 1475), who in turn was the son of Alexander Champernoune, originally of Modbury, south Devon. Alexander had married a daughter of Sir Martin Ferrers, who gave Bere Ferrers as her dowry. In gratitude, this Alexander might well have incorporated the Ferrers rudder (if indeed they bore it), since this was probably the end of this branch of the Ferrers family. Equally it might have happened earlier through some other intermarriage between the families, though I think that the history of the rudder's introduction makes it unlikely that this happened with the known marriage of the daughter of the church builder (he died in 1242) to a William Champernoune, who died in 1304.

Incidentally, Lord Willoughby of Broke was a benefactor of Seend church, and has an acknowledgement on the outside of the north aisle with a three pintle rudder.

The Head-Dresses

Before I forget, I must talk about the head-dresses presumed to have adorned the brasses on our Cheney monument slab, *as seen (on page 182) in the view through the monument to the north transept.* They are described by Edward Kite in 1860 as 'deep clear indents of a man in armour, head on helm, feet on a lion, a long dagger at his right side, and a sword probably across the front of his body, as evidenced by the broad indent of the lower part of the left leg which include the sloping end of the angled sword. By his side, turned towards him, and slightly leaning back from the hips, his wife in butterfly head-dress and elegant gown. Four shields complete the composition.' It concludes: 'the indents show that the brasses were laid down c. 1480 . . . and it is not known who re-used the tomb for the brasses some eighty years after his [Sir Ralph Cheney's] death'.

Kite (whose recollection of slabs I have referred to before) also described 'In the pavement of the south aisle, a Purbeck slab of large dimensions, bearing the indent of two effigies (the male apparently in civil costume), with canopy and border fillet.' This is possibly also described by Hamilton Rogers: 'In the churchyard, near the porch, is a large broken Purbeck marble stone, probably removed from the Chantry within. On it are the indents of a knight, and lady in horned head-dress, under an ogee crocketed canopy, flanked by pinnacles, evidently of contemporary date with the tomb (of Sir Ralph Cheney). Above the figures are two shields, below their feet the space is powdered with scrolls, and a ledger line enclosed the whole.'

From dated paintings I am not sure that 1480 is correct, if the above authors were basing their dates on head-dresses. The horned or butterfly head-dress seems to have been in vogue in the period 1440–60. The lambrequin (a scarf over the helmet to keep it cool) appeared on brasses at much the same time, perhaps so that the size balanced male and female artistically. Thus the brasses on this Purbeck slab could have been stolen in the sacking of the church in 1450.

A final thought. The purpose of heraldry was originally to achieve ease of identification on the battlefield. This was a time of war when extraordinary measures of knighthood were introduced. We have seen that everyone with wealth was obliged to accept knighthood or be fined and ostracized: cash or honours! The new generation of knights, therefore, would be trying to achieve distinctive charges or badges – so it is not surprising that symbols not in use earlier were borrowed and new ones like the rudder were created.

Changing tack (as sailors say), a tale about other members of these two families who had good and bad fortune respectively during the Black Prince's campaign in support of Pedro the Cruel, King of Castile, against his brother, who was an ally of France. We were worried about the powerful Castilian fleet falling into French hands.

Margaret Erleigh's grandfather, Sir John de Erleigh, was married to Margaret de Brienne, a direct descendent of Charlemagne. Of a great warrior family, he fought alongside the Black Prince at the battle of Navarette, outside Najera, Spain, in 1367, but shortly afterwards was captured and held for ransom. This was so large that his wife was forced to sell most of their extensive lands in Ireland. He died of the Black Death in 1372 and is said to be buried at St George's Church, Beckington. During that battle a Sir Thomas Cheney, jointly with another knight, captured the young Bertrand du Guesclin. He received £1483 6s 4d from the Black Prince, who released the Frenchman for a ransom of the order of £8600! Sir Thomas went on to serve as Warden of the Cinque Ports, while du Guesclin was scourge of the English as they were driven back on Calais. He became Constable of France and a national hero.

That is enough on the fall-out from trying to date this monument.

The Final Lap

It is time to cross over to the north aisle; there is much to note on the way. As we start, look up at the south aisle window, level with the brass lectern. In the head there is a bluish quarry. Written on it is 'Thos. Ba . . . Plumber at Devizes of 4/'. Devizes Museum know of a Thomas Bayly in a rent book of 1746, and confirmed the script here as mid-eighteenth century.

Now turn up between the choirstalls. If you could not see the quartered shield on the canopy when I spoke about the monument, glance up now. Also confirm that there is no rudder this side above the entrance. Ponting has left the outlines of the carols, as he called them. See how narrow is the gap between them. With high screening the view from the west would be impaired. I wonder who occupied that north carol. Hungerfords?

Come up to the communion rail. Squeeze along to look at the bench-end on the rear south choir stall. Those are the arms of the Reverend Henry Cave-Browne-Cave. Although he was not popular, he was given recognition here. We can see he came of an aristocratic family: he was descended from Sir Thomas Cave, a Royalist who fought in the English Civil War and was created a baron in 1641. The ancestral home is Stanford Hall, Northamptonshire.

The quartered arms are for the Caves the diagonal net-like mesh called 'fretty' (silver on blue, Foster tells us – it was born by a William Cave in Henry III's reign) and the chevron and three escallops that in the account of the 1887 restoration are said to signify Browne. Escallops again, and the impaled wife bears familiar arms locally, namely the Long family.

Now look up at the wall plaques on the north arcade. They are for Henry's predecessor, Samuel Littlewood, and his two wives: Mary died in 1831 and Ellen died in 1870. There is a shield-shaped metal plaque in the nave floor to Edward Lawrence Littlewood, born on 10 July 1834 and died on 29 November the same year. Samuel's other children gave the brass eagle lectern in 1880 in memory of his long ministry here. Of about the same date is the reproduction eighteenth-century candelabra here in the nave – a hazard to every novice crucifer and a distraction, once swinging, to the congregation.

A Scudamore organ built by Nelson Hill of Warminster was placed in the church in 1860 in 'the hope the congregation would join in the singing'. It was replaced by the present organ (by Henry Jones and Sons of South Kensington) in 1905; the Scudamore went to Tilshead church. The brass plate above the console of the present organ reveals that the cost was £500, of which £250 was given by Mr Andrew Carnegie of New York and the balance by the vicar, the Reverend George E. Long, parishioners and their friends.

Andrew Carnegie was born in Dunfermline in 1835 and went as a child to America. Steel made him his fortune, and by the 1890s it was said he was the second richest man to have lived – with a fortune, in 2007 terms, of $298 billion. He became a great philanthropist worldwide, mainly providing universities and libraries.

As we go round to St Giles altar, a bench end on the north choir stalls marks the Bishop of Salisbury, Bishop John Wordsworth, having preached here at the post-restoration reopening service on Wednesday 30 September 1891. Reading the *Wiltshire Times* account of the occasion, I found the following: 'After some prefatory remarks, the Bishop said when

William of Edington founded that church and when his predecessor, Robert Wyvil, consecrated it, neither of them could have foreseen the altered circumstances under which they met that day.' Clearly he thought that both bishops were here at the original dedication. Of William, Bishop Wordsworth said he knew little, yet 'he was sure he must have had a bold and adventurous heart, touched by the spirit of the age . . . and elevated by contact with the heroes with whom he was associated, stimulated to do something for God . . .' He went on to refer to contemporary events close to the building dates – in 1351 the First Statute of Proviso, in 1356 the battle of Poitiers and in 1362 the substitution of English for French:

> It was an age of transition. The completion of one great period of our national history, and the commencement of another, a time of new departures and of newer and freer forms of life, a passing away of what was old and worn out, the glorious beginning of some of the greatest movements that have influenced and moulded society in this country . . . England, under the third Edward first thoroughly became England, the England in which Norman and Saxon were permanently and completely blended into one nation, the England of Wyclif with its free discussion of all sorts of problems, moral, social and religious, the England of Chaucer, with its many coloured activity, its co-operation of various classes in a national life.

And now a closer look at the pulpit from which the bishop spoke. The tester sounding board is in the Ellen Littlewood sketch. This wonderful staircase typifies, I think, the genius of Charles Ponting. It is so right for the character of the place he wished to create. Opposite it on the column is a crucifix to focus the mind of the preacher. Sometimes I wish it had a clock beneath as well! I wonder how many have appeared to the preacher to be listening attentively while reading the 1852 benefaction board on the north wall.

My rambling silent soliloquy might be: 'Mr George Tayler formerly of Edington, late of Keevil, Gentleman by a codicil . . .

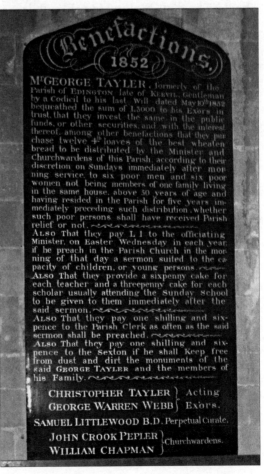

- 197 -

bequeathed the sum of £3000 . . .' That's a lot of money for 1852. How much does that next plaque say the restoration cost thirty-nine years later? £6535. Was George trying to win back church congregation that had been lost to the Methodists? It was 1846 when their Tinhead Society (formed in 1796) extended their 1828 Salisbury Hollow chapel to seat 300! 'Churchwardens – William Chapman and John Crook Pepler.' We have seen William Chapman before – a brass floor plaque in the sanctuary; his family gave the 1930s reredos. It can't be the same person, or can it? No. 'Pepler': Penelope Carew Hunt found that a 'John Peplar, the sonne of John Peplar' was baptized, according to a surviving parish register, on 31 August 1625. That's 173 years before the death of the James Pepler who was recorded with a floor slab in the south transept. It's quite a record that the family is still here at Ballards Farm, Tinhead. Were they in sheep? Was that why they christened one of their number Crook? The distribution of twelve 4lb loaves each Sunday: from the dole stone – or Mr Roots' shed if wet? Would an over-fifty year old eat one in a week? A pound sterling for a sermon 'suited to the capacity of children'. I wonder how this 'officiating minister' would fare getting down to that level.. 'Easter Wednesday'– were the children always on holiday then? A 6d cake for teacher and a 3d cake for each child after that sermon – perhaps they were back at school and marched two-by-two to church

on that day. Was Edington School built then? I wonder if the verger here still receives an index-linked 1s 6d for dusting the Tayler monuments. Tayler rather than Taylor? Oh yes, there are plenty of them remembered on this north wall. That huge memorial looks as though it mimics the children along the front of the Lewys monument. What about the four plaques on the nave west wall – are they Tayler? Better not look round!

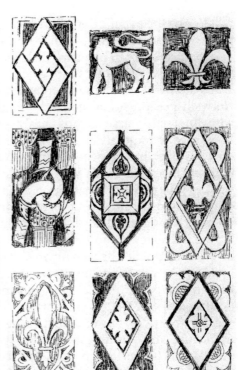

'If there was a village school here in 1852 surely it would have been a Church of England foundation, for there was no state provision then?' Well, apart from Sunday school I know of no church involvement at any stage. Just a moment, though: I have a note from among Penelope's effects, which shows that education for working-class children may have started here very early on. 'In 1808, 10 girls were educated and clothed at the expense of the Lord of the Manor and 30 more were paid for by their parents. By 1835 there were three infant schools in the parish providing education for both sexes at the parents' expense. In 1849, forty to fifty girls were being taught to read and sew, but not write, in a cottage room 16ft square, by a mistress of doubtful competence.' Forster's Education Act of 1870 required education to be made available for all at a small fee. Attendance was not compulsory until 1880. Edington and East Coulston were made a united district for this purpose, and the school board opened a school in East Couston in 1876. The school in Tinhead was built in 1877, and the other closed fairly soon afterwards.

Let's move on. See how the two windows behind the organ have no ancient glass. This confirms what is written of the 1887–91 restoration: all the best pieces were concentrated in the windows that were more visible, which probably indicates that the Scudamore organ must have been in the same place then as this one. An article in *The Antiquary* of 1882 indicates that an organ was in the south transept at that date. The window by the benefactions board has a female figure and a quarry with most of the word 'INRI', so they may come from a crucifixion window here or elsewhere in the north aisle windows.

Moving west to the next window. Writing of the north transept crucifixion window in the Friends' Report of 1961, Dennis G. King, the Norwich glass restorer, noted: 'A fragment of the Hungerford Arms, with interesting associations, has been leaded into this window.' We know it was removed in 1972 for future installation elsewhere. I can only assume that elsewhere turned out to be this north aisle window opposite the south door. Can you see it? Centre panel, bottom left border, right against the sill. This fragment has three garbs (wheat sheaves) two over one and centrally three sickles entwined. You have heard about Sir Thomas Hungerford moving to Farleigh Montfort from Heytesbury, having been steward to Bishop William and executor of his will. A year before William died he paid for an obit in this church. That was 1365, and I told you he went on to be steward to John of Gaunt and first Speaker of Parliament, dying in 1398. His arms included sickles.

His son, Sir Walter Hungerford, was born in 1378, was fifteenth speaker (1414–15), our diplomat at the Council of Constance, fought at Agincourt, and was an executor to Henry V's will. Having been made first Baron Hungerford in 1426, he succeeded John Stafford for six years as lord high treasurer under Henry VI. He died in 1449.

Sir Walter's first wife was Catherine Lady Peverell, and her arms were as those of the Earls of Chester: three garbs. Remember that the title was held from childhood by the Black Prince and inherited by Richard II. He having no male issue, the title died out. Boutell tells us: 'In token of feudal alliance, many Cheshire families bear one or more garbs.' Catherine's arms can still be seen in the chapel of St Anne in Farleigh Castle. Her father-in-law, Sir Thomas, had this built off the north side of the then village church, St Leonard's, as a burial place for himself and his wife Joan Hussey. Three entwined sickles appear in quarries in the St Anne's chapel, on the tower of Tellisford church and, perhaps from much earlier, on the remains of an altar slab from the Hungerford chapel in Heytesbury church.

It was Walter who named the castle Farleigh Hungerford and built the outer court enclosing the church and chapel in c. 1420–30. He almost certainly built the present village church, dedicated in 1443. He capitalized on the marriage with a sickle either side of one garb on his seal, and carved that in stone in many places. Nowhere, though, is the three garbs, three sickles design as in our pane. If it was to celebrate the marriage, then the pane could not have been made before say 1395.

Plenty of Hungerfords managed to get themselves executed, such that in 1462 the castle was granted to Richard, Duke of Gloucester, who on becoming king in 1483 granted it to John Howard, Duke of Norfolk. Norfolk died at Bosworth. A Walter Hungerford was knighted there, and allowed to recover Farleigh in 1486. His grandson was the Lord Hungerford of Heytesbury who was executed alongside Thomas Cromwell in 1540.

One last gruesome story. The latter Hungerford's father, Edward, died in 1522 and left all to his widow Agnes. She was hanged at Tyburn in 1523, found guilty of sending two men of Heytesbury to strangle her first husband John Cotell at Farleigh in 1518 so that she could marry Edward. She had arranged for the body to be burnt in the kitchen furnace. I do recommend a visit. Besides cremation they do a good line in lead coffins: there are six adults and two children in the crypt, on four of which are death masks – the finest collection of such sixteenth- and seventeenth-century coffins in the country. Of course, their commonest use was for bringing home the bodies of the dead, because they could be made airtight. That may explain those in our crypt – brought home from Jamaica.

Talking of preserved faces, do you see four that look as if they are looking through a narrow doorway in the border of this same north aisle window? They are most probably benefactors, but I like to think they might be the master mason, master carpenter, master glazier and clerk of works. It is amazing to have four portraits contemporary with the build of this church. Which do you think was the clerk of works? Yes, the sour profile!

GFL

Finally in the border glass of these shallow aisle windows, I would ask you to note the beautiful designs woven mainly around the fleurs-de-lis.

And so we come to the font, that most moved item in English churches. Originally it stood adjacent to the public entrance

into the church and was tub-shaped, to allow the person being baptized to stand in it and squat down to almost total immersion. The location then moved to near the high altar, and the design became shallower, commonly square in shape. Finally it moved to a specially prepared room, the baptistery, sometimes separate from the church or to the rear west end. Edington church was built at about the time of the latter move, when design started to favour an octagonal shape.

In the thirteenth century it became the practice to cover the font with a secure lockable lid. The water for baptism was blessed at Easter and not changed for a year! It was feared that the water would be stolen for the purposes of witchcraft. The hygiene implications were eventually realized, and the water was blessed at the time of each baptism. The lid became one of those things that benefactors could give, and more and more decorative versions appeared. Ours dates from 1626. The date is on it along with the initials of the churchwardens at the time: Edward Carpenter (he lived at Tinhead Court) and William Gunstone.

The *Wiltshire Times* account of the restoration tells us that 'The bowl of the old font was too far decayed to admit of any repair; it has therefore been copied in Devon marble and set up on the old shaft and surmounted by the old Jacobean cover. A new pavement of marble mosaic with a marble step have been provided for the baptistery, the design consisting of a ground work representing a net with fishes surrounding the font, and four medallions containing the subjects of "The baptism of Christ", "The passage through the Red Sea", "The entry into the Ark" and "Christ blessing little children".' Anchors add another nautical touch.

The article names the installer of the mosaics as Messrs Burke. This was Salviati, Burke and Company of Venice and Hammersmith, London. Antonio Salviati founded his Laboratory of Mosaic Art in Venice in 1859. They exhibited and won enormous fame, filling important architectural spaces in such places as St Paul's Cathedral, the Houses of Parliament, Westminster Abbey and St Mark's Church, North Audley Street.

When we were first at the Cheney monument a possible decimal counting aid graffiti was mentioned over in this corner. Here it is, shoulder height, beneath the middle of the left panel of the west window of the north aisle.

Let us go to the centre of the nave, noting the brown staining of the floor around where the Irene Cave-Browne-Cave floor tablet was placed. The stain is from a huge heating furnace that stood here. It is said to have been extinguished when heavy rain caused water to flood over the floor.

The backs to the nave pews have linen-fold panels, some of which may have come from the previous box-pews. The *Wiltshire Times* article says that 'The nave and aisles have (at the wish of the Parish Committee, and by funds raised by them) been seated with oak benches, into which the old parts preserved from the fifteenth-century seating have been incorporated.' While talking of woodwork, it tells us: 'The old door of the south entrance has been repaired, and new oak doors have been put to the double western portal (these are the gift of Mr Newman), to the original entrance from the monastery [north aisle] and the side doors of the chancel. The sound parts from the old oak doors have been made up into small doors for the turret staircase.' Presumably this staircase is one of those off the transepts. When we reach it, you will see that the parvis staircase door out of the porch looks as though it may be original.

This consecration cross above the west doors doesn't seem to have the additional holes for the cover plate, and earlier I said this area was all blocked up until the late nineteenth century. I think the explanation is that Ponting had to renew some or all of the stone into which the cross is set. But that reminds me: when I went to Ottery St Mary the other day, because its lovely church has double west doors, I learned two things. Firstly I could find no need when it was built in the 1340s for side-by side entry of dignatories. However, I was concerned to read in its current conservation plan that the church's twenty-one consecration crosses are 'the largest collection in the country. There are twenty in Salisbury Cathedral and seventeen at Cannington in Somerset. There would originally have been twenty-four.' It seemed that this was used to show how unaltered is the original build. We have surviving evidence of all twenty-four here ! The plan mentioned that fixings for a candle holder were visible on some external crosses, and stated that these were lit on the anniversary of the consecration. This led me to check ours, and I'm sorry I did not point out earlier the many holes inside and out that remain for pricket candle brackets, like those four in the chancel.

Right, now look up to the north arcade at clerestory level. There are six of the original thirty-six clerestory window saints: from the left, St William of York, St Paul, St Christopher, St Cuthbert, St Audon and St Leodegar (normally spelt Leger).

Someone nearly always asks me if there is a connection with the horserace, so I looked it up. The answer enables me to follow up on my jest in the chancel about lady masons. The founder of the race at Doncaster in 1776 was a Colonel Anthony St Leger, former Governor of St Lucia. Amusingly, the source stated him to be a cousin of the first lady freemason! She unwittingly witnessed an initiation ceremony presided over by her father, Lord Doneraile. He decided the only thing to do was admit her. In consequence she achieved great social acclaim. That aside, it is interesting to speculate why this very French saint should be included. He was Bishop of Autun, who surrendered himself to save the town from attack in about 675. This resulted in his eyes being drilled out and the sockets cauterized, together with his lips and tongue being cut off. He survived, only to be exiled to a monastery at Fécamp in Normandy, from which he was dragged into the forest near Sarcing on the Somme and martyred in 679. I can only think that our Bishop William was affected by the tale on a visit to Calais.

Of the others, St William of York took shelter at one stage with Henry de Blois at Winchester, hence perhaps Bishop William wanting his remembrance here. St Audon is known in France as St Ouen, Archbishop of Rouen in the seventh century. He had the abbey in Rouen renamed after him on his death. He is also remembered with a commune area in north Paris, and in Jersey as the name of one of the twelve parishes, the most northwesterly – the one containing the site of Grosnez Castle. St Ouen is special protector to the deaf and associated with a contemporary St Eloy, who may also have been up there. Both are among saints classified as 'myroblites', whose bodies were believed to emit a healing balm. With the Black Death so fresh in everyone's minds, their association with a miracle cure may have been relevant to selection. St Ouen claimed that when he draped the tomb of St Eloy in his cathedral in Lent to hide the jewels, the cloth became saturated with the balm. To cure any infirmity only required one drop of the fluid. St Eloy is the patron saint of stonemasons, jewellers, metalworkers and all workers with animals, including veterinary surgeons. Several churches in England bear their anglicized names of St Audon and St Loys.

There are two more graffiti in the church on the west wall in the south aisle. Under the right jamb of the window are a number of interlacing circles thought to be associated with the cinquefoil tracery of the window. They may have been for the glazier or to make templates for the stonework of the north aisle window, to match this one but with different mouldings. The second graffiti depicts a crude river craft – low down behind the kitchen unit. It has a square-rigged sail, which was used to go upstream when the wind suited; to come downstream, even with contrary wind, one went with the flow!

The *Wiltshire Times* article that told us who manufactured the mosaics named Mr N. Hitch of London as supplier of the wooden screenwork, Messrs Jones and Willis of Birmingham for the choir stalls and Harold Hems of Exeter for the carvings on them. These were all top quality providers of church furniture at the time. The article does not say who made the pews, nor the superb wood carvings that you might have missed if you didn't look upwards from the aisles. If I turn on the light at the south door you can see the standard of carving of this green man as an example of the many different designs of the knees that support the aisle roofs. Along there is one of musical instruments threaded with a scroll inscribed 'Praise Ye the Lord'. My drawing of it was used on the cover of the programme for the 1996 Edington Music Festival.

The festival, which I have mentioned several times, is a celebration of music within the liturgy. Singers from many of the great cathedral and collegiate choirs, Anglican and Roman Catholic, are invited by the director, not a village person, to come together to take part in daily services. There are no tickets, and financially it supports itself mainly through collections at the services, though participants pay a contribution towards their food during the week. There are three choirs. The offices of matins and compline are sung to plainsong by one choir, which additionally contributes to the principal services. These are led by a nave choir of men and boys and by a consort of mixed voices. Between services the church and parish hall are rehearsal venues, and many people are fascinated to witness how little practice there is for such superb performances.

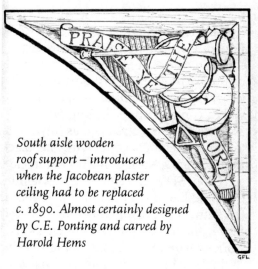

South aisle wooden roof support – introduced when the Jacobean plaster ceiling had to be replaced c. 1890. Almost certainly designed by C.E. Ponting and carved by Harold Hems

The Friends of Edington Priory hold their annual gathering on the Saturday and, after the AGM and tea, members and anyone else around enjoy a lecture or recital. I have been privileged to be asked to talk three times, and have covered virtually all that I had to say on those occasions in this tour. Leaflets on sale by the south door cover many other contributions by the society's lecturers over the years, and much that I have told you was gleaned from them.

There is also a music festival association, which has two purposes:

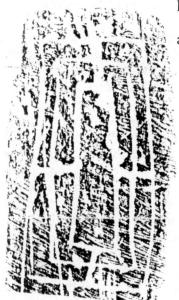

Nine Men's Morris graffiti on walls at Sparsholt (left) and Edington porch west wall (right)

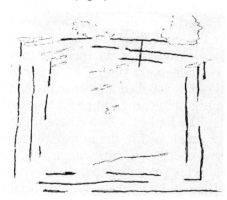

it aims to deepen and broaden awareness of the festival, both among the regulars and to encourage newcomers; and it maintains a financial reserve, which can balance the books in lean years or afford in others such things as the commissioning of new music. The festival has a fine library of sheet music, which has been found a home here.

The festival is always held the week before the August Bank Holiday: the seventy-odd singers have a day to recover after farewells here following lunch on the Sunday. It is a pretty exhausting week and not just because of the music: late nights in the pub, a cricket match and entertaining the choirboys, with excursions to Longleat, Stonehenge and so on, all contribute. Do sign up on the mailing list if you are interested.

The best graffiti have been saved to last. The removal of the porch notice-boards from the west wall means that we can see them. Left to right there is first a game of nine men's morris, which could only have been used for play when the stone was horizontal. There is one in a similar location at Sparsholt, Berkshire, where the same conclusion was reached. Next are a number of pelicans, one pecking its breast to produce blood for its brood. This is an allegorical symbol for the Resurrection and for the Eucharist. Then there are depictions of what is thought to be a Christ figure and finally a fine fourteenth-century ship just like the one on the gold noble of Edward III of 1344, struck to commemorate the battle of Sluys. Perhaps it was used to illustrate the Noah's Ark story; hence what might be a gangway. That fittingly brings us back to William of Edyndon: he may well have been the driving force behind the reform of the coinage, which included the minting of gold for the first time since the Norman Conquest. As usual, he was wily in 1351 when introducing groats worth 4d, with proportionately less silver than in the equivalent pennies!

It remains only to say thank you for visiting Edington Priory. I hope you now appreciate William's legacy as much as I do, and feel that down the centuries it has been stewarded well. I pray that two days revealing that history have been worthwhile, and will inspire continued effort to sustain this beautiful place.

William of Edington in his Winchester Cathedral chantry

Bibliography

There have been many sources of information, including those freely available on the internet, in the Victoria County Histories for Wiltshire and Hampshire, and the Journals of the Church Monument Society. The nineteenth- and twentieth-century transactions of the Wiltshire Archaeological and Natural History Society are referred to throughout the text, including the writings of (in appearance order) - Canon J.E. Jackson MA FSA, C.E. Ponting FSA, Sir Harold Brakspear KCVO FSA, E. Kite, F. Stevens OBE FSA. Likewise, use has been made of twentieth-century articles of the Society of the Friends of the Priory Church Edington – G.E. Chambers BA FSA, Dr J. Chandler, J. d'Arcy, Canon R.E.H. Dudley, Canon N. Heavisides, Dr J.R.L. Highfield, J.L. Kirby MA FSA, P. Plummer, K.H. Rogers, A.M. Rome FSA, D. Seth Smith, Prof D. Whitelock FSA.

Published books include:
Bedford W.K.R. *The Blazon of Episcopacy*.
Bell A. *English Bishops, Kings and later Saints*.
Bettey J.H. *Suppression of the Monasteries in the West Country*.
Bevan B. *Edward III*.
Boutell C. *Manual of Heraldry*.
Braun H. *Parish Churches – Their Architectural Development in England*.
Brown S. & O'Connor D. *Glass-Painters*.
Bryant A. *The Age of Chivalry*.
Carter G. *Outlines of English History*.
Coldstream N. *Medieval Craftsmen- Masons and Sculptors*.
Cunnington P. *How old is that church?*
Cutts E.L. *Scenes and Characters of the Middle Ages*.
Denny J. *Anne Boleyn*.
Foster J. *The Dictionary of Heraldry. Some Feudal Coats of Arms*.
Friends of St Andrews *Short History and Guide to Bere Ferrers Church*.
Hamilton Rogers W.H. *The Strife of the Roses and Days of the Tudors in the West*.
Harvey J.H. *The Medieval Architect. Medieval Craftsmen. The Perpendicular Style*.
Hockey S.F. *The Register of William Edington, Bishop of Winchester -   Hampshire Record Series*.
Kingsford H.S. *The Epigraphy of Medieval English Seals*.
Lloyd A. *The Hundred Years War*.
Macklin M.W. *Monumental Brasses of England and the Art of Brass Rubbing*.
Marshman M. *The Wiltshire Village Book*.
McKilliam A.E. *A Chronicle of the Archbishops of Canterbury*.
McKisack M. *The Fourteenth Century*.
NADFAS *Inside Churches*.

Papworth J.W. *Ordinary at Arms.*

Pevsner N., and Cherry B. (eds.), *Wiltshire;* 2nd ed, 1976 (Buildings of England series)

Prestwich M. *The Three Edwards – War and State in England 1272-1377.*

Ravensdale J.R. *History on your Doorstep.*

Rickman T. *An Attempt to Discriminate the Style of Architecture in England.*

Salzman L.F. *Building in England down to 1540.*

SPCK *The Study of Liturgy.*

Stevenson J.H. *The Edington Cartulary, Wiltshire Record Office.*

Tuchman B.W. *The Distant Mirror – The Calamitous Fourteenth Century.*

Ziegler P. *The Black Death.*

Index of Families and Persons

(omitting English Royalty and authors – see separate Index and Bibliography)

Abbess of Romsey 1, 9, 20, 21, 26, 49-51, 60, 131
Abbess of Shaftesbury 62
Aldrig, Ralph 173
Alexander, Revd. E.C. 70
Alexander V, Pope 115
Andrew & Dury, map 32
Anne, Duchess of Brittany 190
Arthur, mythical king 41
Arundell, Sir Thomas 129
Ashley, Edith 134
Asser, bishop 20
Aubrey, John 189
Aylesbury, John de (Ailsbury) 3, 8, 9, 79, 85, 91, 113, 174
Ayscough, William, Bishop of Salisbury 95, 99, 114

Babington, Thomas Macaulay, baron 105
Banks, Joseph 105
Basset family 25, 52
Basyng, Hugh de 80
Bath and Wells, bishops of 110, 111, 114
Bayly, Thomas 195
Baynham, Revd. Arthur 94
Baynton family 126-128, 130-132, 135, 136, 155, 161, 162, 168
Beauchamp family 12, 86, 137, 143-7, 154
Beaufort, Henry, Bishop of Winchester 63, 94, 116
Beautre, John de 81
Becket, Thomas a, Arch. of Canterbury 60, 61
Benham, Gilbert de 42
Berkeley, Lennox 87
Berners, William 128
Bessels, Sir Thomas 24
Beswick, Lavinia – see Fenton
Bird, Revd. Maurice 139
Bird, William 129
Blacking, Randolph 91
Blair, Dr. 169
Bloebury, John de (Blebury, Blubyri) 135, 163, 171

Boleyn family 124
Bradwardine, Thomas, Arch. of Canterbury 52
Brazier, James 168
Brekevyle, John, Prior of Mottisfont 115
Brienne, Margaret de 194
Briggs, Sir John 131
Brinton, Thomas, Bishop of Rochester 174
Broke – see Willoughby
Bruera, Gilbert de 35
Buckler, John 6, 44, 59, 87-89, 93, 161, 172
Bulkington family 135, 161, 162, 168
Burgess, James 94
Burnley, Professor J.D. 169, 170
Burton, William 162
Bush, Paul, bishop 128, 133, 134
Butler, Mark 139, 140
Byrd, professor 104

Cade, Jack 95, 96, 117, 125
Calvin, John 117
Cammays, Isabella, Abb. of Romsey 49
Canning, George, Prime Minister 105
Carew Hunt, Penelope 138, 139, 198, 199
Carnegie, Andrew 196
Carpenter family 155, 173, 202
Cave-Browne-Cave family 4, 14, 16, 94, 140, 195, 203
Caxton, William 117
Charles, Prince of Wales 182
Champernoune family 191, 193
Chantrey, Francis Legatt 105, 106
Chapman, William 85, 198
Charlemagne, Emperor 79, 194
Chaucer, Geoffrey 169, 197
Cheney family (Cheyne) 20, 23, 44, 49, 55-57, 61, 62, 66, 74, 85, 89, 93, 99, 115, 118,
122, 163, 164, 167, 181-194
Chichele, Henry, Arch. of Canterbury 115-117, 122 164
Churchill, Sir Winston 182
Clark, Ivor 101, 106
Clement VI, Pope 9, 51, 53

Clifford, Lady Anne 86
Colt-Hoare family 93
Comper, Sir Ninian 106
Condor, Thomas, map 31
Constable, John 105
Corfe, John de 163
Corniche, Thomas 164
Cotell, John 201
Count d'Eu 51
Courtenay, William, Arch. of Canterbury 114
Cranmer, Thomas, Arch. Of Canterbury 125, 128, 129, 134
Cromwell, Oliver 12, 146
Cromwell, Thomas 124, 126-130, 132
Culmer, Thomas 115
Culpepper family 130, 131
Cunnington, Miss 141

Dacre family 184
Danvers, Henry 85
Danvers, Jane 85
Danyell, John 115
Daubenay, Lord 190
De Blois, Henry, Bishop of Winchester 63, 107, 108, 204
Delme, Peter 148
Despenser, Hugh 166
Devenish, Nicholas 54
Doneraile, Lord 204

Edington, Amice 54, 55, 57
Edington, John 50, 54-56
Edington, Roger 54, 55
Edington, Thomas 55
Edington, William, Bishop of Winchester 3, 8, 9, 11, 18, 20, 21, 23-25, 27-30, 41-43, 46-49, 50-56, 58-66, 70, 72, 74, 77-83, 85, 102, 108-110, 114, 121, 130, 135, 148, 150, 159, 160, 162-65, 170-172, 182, 190, 196, 200, 204, 208
Edmund, 2nd Earl of Cornwall 79
Edmund of Woodstock 52
Edward of Woodstock, the Black Prince 8, 51, 52, 78, 79, 85, 112, 171, 194
Elphinstone, Mountstuart, baron 105
Enoc, Roger 61
Ephraim 47
Ergham, Ralph, Bishop of Salisbury 112, 113

Erheth, Robert 83
Erleigh family (Erles, Earley, Herleis) 182-187, 194
Eustace de Hache 24, 25, 86

Fenton, Lavinia 137, 138
Ferrers family (Ferriere) 191-193

Gandavo, Simon de, Bishop of Salisbury 62
Garrick, David 139
Gaunt, John of, Duke of Lancaster 112, 116, 200
Gervays, Joan, Abb. of Romsey 49
Glemsford, John de 42
Glenham, Sir Henry 145
Gloucester, Duke of 94, 95
Godwyn, William 170
Gooden, Elizabeth 103, 108
Green, Gilbert 38
Gregory, Pope 27
Greville family (Grevyle) 119, 191
Grey, Catherine 146
Guescelin, Bertrand de 194
Gunstone, William 202
Guthrum 18, 26-28

Haley, Alex 137
Hallam, Robert, Bishop of Salisbury 115
Harliston, Sir Richard 190
Healey, Denis 160
Heavisides, Revd. Neil 156
Hems, Harold 206
Henley, Joseph John 187
Hitch, N. 205
Hastings, Sir Henry 132
Herbert, George 85-90, 134, 147
Hogarth, William 138
Holbein, Hans 129
Holland family 51, 52, 113
Hortone, John 120, 174
Howard family 125, 130, 131, 135, 146, 20[...]
Hungerford family 112, 121, 124, 126, 128, 129-131135, 163, 174, 200, 201
Huss, Han 120
Hussey, Joan 200

Icthe, Joan, Abb. of Romsey 49
InnocentVI, Pope 81,
Innocent VII, Pope 115
Islip, Simon, Arch. of Canterbury 52

Jeremiah, Book of 47
Joan d'Arc 94, 95
Joan, the Fair Maid of Kent 46, 51, 52, 112, 113, 169
John II, King of France 78
Jones & Willis 205
Jones, Henry 196
Jones, William 126

Kaerwent, Nicholas 163
Kelveston, Richard 62
King, Dennis G. 200
King, Thomas York 173
Kirby, J.L. 150
Kitchin, map 31

Lakynton, Richard 119
Langham, Simon, Arch. of Canterbury 174
Langley, Sir Geoffery 70
Langton, , Bishop of Winchester 163
Lansdowne, Marquis of 8
Latimer family 192
Laud, William, Arch. of Canterbury 142, 143
Lavynton, Thomas 113, 115
Lawrence, Sir Thomas 105
Legh, Thomas 127
Leigh, Isobel 131
Leland, John 8, 9, 50, 70, 109, 135, 163, 188, 189
Leucas, Walter 30
Lewis, George 94
Lewys family (Lewis) 86, 87, 90, 136, 137, 145-147
Lincoln, bishops of 9, 116
Lisle, Bishop of Ely 78
Littlewood family 139, 149, 153, 173, 195, 197
Long, Revd. George E. 94, 158, 172
Long, Sir Henry 127, 130, 131
Long, Robert 30
Long, Rt.Hon. W.H. 94
Lott, John 180
Luce family 166
Luther, Martin 120

Mackay, Alexander 94
Malmesbury, Earl of 105
Manassah 47
Marmium, Miss 182
Marshman, Michael 21

Martin V, Pope 116
Mauduit family 122, 135
Maundrell, John 134
Mayne family 104, 147
Mills, Alexander 151
Middleton, Gilbert de 60-63, 163
Mitford, Richard, Bishop of Salisbury 114
Molineaux family (Molines) 3, 135
Mortimer, Roger 52, 62, 63, 78
Morton, John, Arch. Of Canterbury 123, 124
Munro, Sir Thomas 105

Nelson, Horatio 104
Nelson Hill 196
Neville, Robert, Bishop of Salisbury 113
Newman, William 113
Newton, William 170
Norholt, Inger 146, 147
Nubbeleye, John de 49
Nugent, Sir George, General 104

Odyham, Thomas 113, 115
Offord, John, nominated Arch. of Canterbury (Ufford) 52
Oldcastle, Sir John, 116
Orleton, Adam, Bishop of Winchester 54, 60, 62, 63, 174

Panter, Robert 113
Paulet family (Pawlett, Powlett) 90, 126, 128, 132, 133, 136-138, 148, 177
Paveley family 3, 52, 85, 181-183, 186-188, 192, 193
Pecock, Reginald, Bishop of Chichester 123
Pedro the Cruel, King of Castile 194
Pembrokes, Earls of 86
Penley, Sir Richard 135
Pepler family (Peplar) 139, 198.
Peverell family 24, 25, 50, 192, 200
Pinnegar family 140
Pitt, William, Prime Minister 105
Philip IV, King of France 28
Philip VI, King of France 46
Philip de Valois 28
Plummer, Pauline 172, 173
Poyntz family 126, 134
Price family 155.

Rachel, jewish matriach 47
Raeburn, Sir Henry 105

Ramsey, William de 41, 42, 48, 64, 65, 70, 72
Read, Lucy 142
Rede, John de 49
Rees family (ap Rice) 127
Reynolds, Sir Joshua 147.
Richard, 1st Earl of Cornwall 79
Rickman, Thomas 65
Risden, chronicler 191
Roches, Sir Jean des 190
Rolle, Richard 47, 123
Romsey, John 174
Romsey, John de 21
Romsey, William de 21, 62
Roots, Revd. William 137, 138, 198
Rous family (Roos, Rows, Rufus, Ruffus) 33, 35, 114, 122, 135, 168
Rowere, John 113
Ryve, John 126, 127

Sackville family 12, 86
St Andrew 191
St Audon (Ouen) 204, 205
St Christopher 204
St Cuthbert 27, 204
St Edward the Confessor 42, 60, 61, 102
St Eloy (Loys) 205
St Ethelfleda 50, 51
St George 41, 42, 58, 61, 160, 164, 172, 182, 194
St Giles 33, 36, 37, 160, 196,
St James the Apostle 9, 49, 50, 107
St Jerome 156
St John 47, 99, 100, 143, 151, 182
St John family 177, 182
St Katharine of Alexandria 9, 60, 85, 123, 160
St Leodeger (Leger) 204
St Lo, Sir John 182
St Lucia 204.
St Luke 76, 99, 124
St Margaret of Antioch 123
St Mark 99, 100, 203
St Mary, the Blessed Virgin 9, 41, 58, 60, 70, 85, 119, 122, 123, 143, 150, 151, 160, 165, 172
St Matthew 47, 99, 121
St Michael 37, 38
St Neot 27
St Paul 62, 64, 65150, 163, 203, 204
St Peter 150, 163.
St Stephen 61, 64, 65

St Swithin 54, 80, 174
St William of York 204.
Salisbury, bishops of 9, 11, 16, 24, 53, 62, 78, 81, 91, 94, 95, 99, 102, 112-115, 139, 150, 174, 196
Salisbury, Earls of 51, 52, 113
Salviati Burke & Co. 203
Scarlett, Walter 3, 9, 56, 80
Scollay family 187
Scott, John 133
Sevenhampton, Walter de 80, 91, 162, 163
Seymour family 86, 126, 128, 130-132, 135, 146, 183
Sharington, Sir William 130
Siddons 139
Simeon 76
Smith, Joshua 148, 149, 156
Smith, Richard 113
Sondes family (Sandys) 184
Sponlee, John 48, 164
Sprent, Revd. F.H. 160
Stanhope family 132
Stafford family 94, 96, 114-119, 122, 125, 168, 189, 190, 192
Stevens, Frank 175
Stratford, John, Arch. of Canterbury 51, 92
Stretche, Cecily 183, 189
Stretton, Robert de, Bishop of Lichfield 52
Strong, Lt. W.B. 158
Stumpe family 132, 133, 135

Tayler family 197, 199
Taylor family 103, 106, 108, 141, 147, 158, 199
Taylor, Stephen 113
Temmes, Joan. Abb. of Lacock 113
Thoresby, John, Arch. of York 78
Thynne, Sir John 136
Tinhead, Philip de (Tunhede) 21
Tregonwell, Sir John 128-130,
Tubb, William 18
Turner, J.M.W. 105
Tyler, John 94
Tyler, Rachel 168

Ufford family 52, 192

Verney family 191.

Wake, Blanche 78
Wakerley, John de 3
Waltham, John, Bishop of Salisbury 114,

115
Walton, William 87
Wamba, king 36
Warre family 94, 140, 159, 160
Washington, George 182
Watson Taylor family 4, 23, 88, 93, 94, 105, 106, 108, 137, 139, 141, 149, 150
Webb family 91
Wellington, Lord 105
Wey, William 107, 108, 117
Whittaker, Jeffery 31
Whittaker family 136
Wilkie 105
Williams family of Imber 38
Williams, Ralph Vaughan 87
Willoughby family 122, 131, 188-193
Winchester, bishops of 21, 41, 54, 60, 62, 63, 69, 70, 81, 85, 94, 107, 108, 112, 113, 116, 163.
Wolf, William 55
Wolsey, cardinal , Arch. of York 124
Worcester, bishops of 62, 114
Wordsworth, John, Bishop of Salisbury 196
Wormenhall, John 83
Wyclif, John 112, 113, 120
Wykeham, William , Bishop of Winchester 21, 41, 69, 70, 81, 85, 112, 113, 159, 171, 174
Wyvil, Robert, Bishop of Salisbury 9, 11, 53, 78, 81, 91, 102, 112, 150, 174, 196

York, Richard, Duke of 95, 96

Zwingli, Huldrych 120

Index of Kings and Queens of England

(Years of reign)

Alfred the Great (871-901) and Queen Ealhswith 18, 20, 26-28
Edgar the Peaceable (959-975) 20, 26, 51
Ethelred (978-1016) 37
Edward the Confessor, saint (1042-1066) 42, 60, 61, 102
William I (1066-1087) 21, 36, 162
William II (1087-1100) 36
Henry I (1100-1135) 80
John (1199-1216) 79
Henry III (1216-1272) 35, 41
Edward I (1272-1307) 52, 79
Edward II (1307-1327) and Queen Isabella 41, 63
Edward III (1327-1377) and Queen Philippa 3, 9, 24, 28, 29, 41, 42, 49, 51-54, 60, 61, 78, 79, 81, 112, 114, 116, 186, 191, 197, 208
Richard II (1377-1399) 52, 113, 114, 116, 169, 200
Henry IV (1399-1413) 113, 114, 116

Henry V (1413-1422) 114, 116, 200
Henry VI (1422-1461) and Queen Margaret 94-96, 114, 116, 122, 200
Edward IV (1461-1483) 197, 208
Richard III (1483-1485) 189
Henry VII (1485-1509) 165, 188
Henry VIII (1509-1547) 8, 41, 53, 86, 124, 125, 128-134
Edward VI (1547-1553) 57, 133, 143, 146
Jane Grey (1553) 146
Mary (1553-1558) 16, 125, 133, 134, 143, 146
Elizabeth I (1558-1603) 125, 128, 132-134, 143, 146
James I (1603-1625) 33, 86
Charles I (1625-1649) 16, 33, 46, 143, 146, 153
William III and Mary (1689-1702) 132
George III (1760-1820) 149
George IV (1820-1830) 105
William IV (1830-1837) 149
Victoria (1837-1901) 149

Index of Places Worth a Visit

(outside the parish)

Abb: abbey, Br: bridge, C: castle, Ch: church, Cath: cathedral, Hse: house. P: palace

Bampton, Oxon. [Ch] 106.
Beckington, Som. [Ch & Abb] 31, 161, 162, 172, 182, 184, 187, 194
Bemerton, Wilts. [Ch] 86, 134
Bere Ferrers, Devon [Ch] 191, 193
Berkhampsted, Herts. [C ruin] 79
Bishopstone, Wilts. [Ch] 64
Bishops Waltham, Hants. [P ruin] 55, 82
Blakenall, W.Midls. [Ch] 160
Bowood, Wilts. [Hse] 8
Bradford-on-Avon, Wilts. [Barn] 62, 130
Bratton, Wilts. [Ch & Fort] 20, 27, 31, 56, 64, 131
Bristol [Cath] 40, 48, 70, 96, 126, 128, 133, 134, 151, 162
Brixton Deverill, Wilts. [Ch] 38
Bromham, Wilts. [Ch] 126, 130, 135
Buckland, Oxon. [Ch] 24, 82, 131, 133, 148, 165
Cheriton, Hants. [Ch] 56, 63, 174
Coleshill, Bucks. [Ch] 91, 131, 133
Cottingham, Northants. [Ch] 62
Coulston, Wilts. [Ch] 20, 32, 148
Ely [Cath] 58, 77, 78
Farleigh Hungerford, Som. [C ruin] 96, 112, 129, 163, 200, 201
Gloucester [Cath] 41, 42, 43, 53, 64, 65, 70, 72, 74, 166
Grozney, Jersey [C ruin] 190, 205
Hailes, Glos. [Abb ruin] 79
Hatch Beauchamp, Som. [Ch] 25, 86.
Heytesbury, Wilts. [Ch] 128, 163, 168, 175, 200, 201
Holcombe Burnell, Devon [Ch] 106
Imber, Wilts. [Ch] 31, 32, 33, 35, 36, 37, 38, 131, 135, 168, 180
Iron Acton, Glos. [Hse] 126, 134
Keevil, Wilts. [Ch] 115, 131, 134, 136, 197.
Knole, Kent. [Hse] 12
Lacock, Wilts. [Ch & Abb] 127, 130, 175, 176
Lichfield [Cath] 41, 105
Longleat, Wilts. [Hse] 3, 123, 135, 136

Maiden Bradley, Wilts. [Ch] 131
Malmesbury, Wilts. [Abb] 93, 126, 132, 133
Middleton Cheney, Northants. [Ch] 61, 62, 66, 74, 163
Milton Abbey, Dorset [within school] 130
Montacute, Som. [Hse] 12
North Bradley, Wilts. [Ch & Hse ruin] 21, 24, 49, 92, 96, 118, 123, 128, 131, 153
Norton St Philip, Som. [Inn] 133
Old Wardour Castle, Wilts. [C ruin] 129
Ottery St Mary, Devon [Ch] 203
Redcliffe, Bristol. [Ch] 70
Romsey, Hants. [Ch] 20, 21, 25, 49, 50, 51, 63, 115, 172
St Cross, Hants. [Ch] 27, 55, 56, 63, 108, 124
Salisbury, Wilts. [Cath & Museum] 18, 28, 29, 31, 42, 55, 64, 82, 86, 95, 105, 110, 134, 149, 175, 176, 189, 203
Seend, Wilts. [Ch] 31, 193.
Sherborne, Dorset. [Abb] 120, 182
Southwark, London. [P ruin] 3, 21, 82, 130
Sparsholt, Oxon. [Ch] 207
Staverton, Wilts. [Br.] 28, 31
Steeple Ashton, Wilts. [Ch] 21, 27, 30, 31, 115, 188
Stourhead, Wilts. [Hse] 93
Tellisford, Som. [Ch] 200
Tewkesbury, Glos. [Abb] 131, 164, 166
Wells, Som. [Cath] 62, 67, 164, 179
Westbury, Wilts. [Ch] 20, 21, 32, 122, 131, 136, 140, 147, 184, 187, 190
Westminster Hall, London 65
Wilton, Wilts. [Hse] 86, 126
Winchester, Hants. [Cath, C & Hall] 6, 20, 22, 23, 24, 27, 41, 46, 49, 54, 55, 58, 63, 72, 74, 79, 82, 85, 107, 131, 150, 163, 164, 171, 172, 174, 178, 184, 188, 204
Windsor Castle. 41, 42, 43, 52, 64, 66, 70, 72, 74, 164, 182
Witham Friary, Som. [Abb ruin] 174
Yeovil, Som. [Ch] 47, 48, 110
York [Cath] 65, 67, 124

Lightning Source UK Ltd.
Milton Keynes UK
03 August 2010

157836UK00003B/2/P